ISAAC ON
JEWISH AND
CHRISTIAN ALTARS

FORDHAM SERIES IN MEDIEVAL STUDIES

Mary C. Erler and Richard F. Gyug, series editors

ISAAC ON JEWISH AND CHRISTIAN ALTARS

Polemic and Exegesis in Rashi and the Glossa Ordinaria

DEVORAH SCHOENFELD

FORDHAM UNIVERSITY PRESS

New York   2013

Fordham University Press has no responsibility for the
persistence or accuracy of URLs for external or third-
party Internet websites referred to in this publication
and does not guarantee that any content on such
websites is, or will remain, accurate or appropriate.

Fordham University Press also publishes its books in a
variety of electronic formats. Some content that appears
in print may not be available in electronic books.

Library of Congress Cataloging-in-Publication Data

Schoenfeld, Devorah.
    Isaac on Jewish and Christian altars : polemic
    and exegesis in Rashi and the Glossa ordinaria /
    Devorah Schoenfeld. — 1st ed.
        p. cm. — (Fordham series in medieval studies)
    Includes bibliographical references and index.
    ISBN 978-0-8232-4349-5 (cloth : alk. paper)
    1. Isaac (Biblical patriarch)—Sacrifice. 2. Bible.
    O.T. Genesis XXII, 1–19—Criticism, interpretation,
    etc. 3. Rashi, 1040–1105. Perush Rashi ʿal ha-Torah.
    4. Glossa ordinaria. 5. Judaism—Controversial
    literature—History and criticism. I. Title.

    BS1238.S24S36 2013
    222'.11092—dc23 2012003481

Printed in the United States of America

15 14 13   5 4 3 2 1

First edition

CONTENTS

ACKNOWLEDGMENTS

I am grateful to the many people whose help went into the making of this book. Foremost, I would like to thank Christopher Ocker for his guidance throughout my research. I continue to be grateful for his advice and mentorship. No less do I thank Daniel Boyarin and Arthur Holder for their contributions. At different stages, this project also benefited from the help and wise guidance of David Biale, Sergey Dolgopolski, Robert Harris, Franklin Harkins, Joshua Holo, Naomi Janowitz, Daniel Joslyn-Siemiatkoski, Deanna Klepper, Lesley Smith, and Mark Zier.

I am also grateful to Kristina Grob, Michele Johnson, Yonah Lavery-Yisraeli, and Garrett Smith for their editorial and translation help, and to Will Cerbone and Eric Newman at Fordham University Press for the work they did in preparing this book for publication.

Some of the manuscript research for this book was conducted at the Centre for Medieval and Renaissance Studies in Oxford and supported by a grant from St. Mary's College of Maryland. Manuscripts were consulted at the Bodleian Museum in Oxford, and microfilms were consulted at the Institute for Microfilmed Manuscripts at Hebrew University and at the Hill Museum and Manuscript Library, which supported me in residence as a Heckman Fellow.

My deepest thanks go to Michael Signer, who believed in this project but did not live to see it published. This book is dedicated to his memory.

NOTES ON FORMAT

For ease of identification, I have assigned each comment from Rashi and the Gloss a unique number. (This numbering system was suggested by Mark Zier in conversation.) I have numbered the comments as (verse number). (comment number). So, for example, Rashi's second comment on the first verse of Genesis 22 is comment 1.2. For Gloss comments, I have added an *i* for interlinear glosses and an *m* for marginal comments. Comment 3.2i would thus be the second interlinear gloss on verse three of Genesis 22. Because this study is on Genesis 22, I have often omitted the chapter number, so the full citation of comment 3.2i should be understood to be 22.3.2i. Here I have omitted the chapter number as unnecessary.

Gloss numberings follow Codex Admontensis 251 (manuscript A), to make it possible to find my references in the attached edition. This is even the case when A is nonrepresentative. For example, the comment by Alcuin that begins *caritatis admonitione* is identified throughout as 2.1i, even though it is marginal in almost all manuscripts aside from A.

For ease of identification, I have bolded all biblical verses.

INTRODUCTION

The *Glossa Ordinaria* and Rashi's commentary were two of the most influential Christian and Jewish Bible commentaries of the High Middle Ages. Both were standard texts for Bible study for at least two centuries after their composition, and Rashi's influence continues to the present day. The Gloss was the foundation of twelfth- and thirteenth-century monastic and cathedral education and the basis for supercommentaries (commentaries on the Gloss itself) through the end of the Middle Ages and into the modern period. Volumes of the Bible with the Gloss were more widely copied in the twelfth century than any other book,[1] and it remained in use through the Reformation. Rashi's commentary was the starting point for all subsequent European Jewish exegesis through the Enlightenment. It exists in more manuscripts than any other Jewish Bible commentary and was the first Hebrew book to be printed. The two commentaries are roughly contemporary: Rashi died in 1106, and Gilbert of Auxerre (who, according to the consensus of scholarship, was the primary compiler of the Gloss on the Pentateuch) died in 1135. Both commentaries continued to develop textually over the course of the early twelfth century.

Genesis 22, the story of the near-sacrifice of Isaac, (Heb. *Akedah*), was a central text for articulating both Jewish and Christian self-definition. Jews and Christians used their various re-tellings of this story to think through questions of chosenness, identity, sacrifice, history, and continuity. It was a key text for Jewish martyrs of the Crusade era and figured prominently in Christian anti-Jewish polemic.[2]

The twelfth century was a pivotal period in the medieval Jewish–Christian relationship. The tacit acceptance of Jews under the Augustinian accommodation began to break down, first with the massacres of Jews during the Crusades and then with the new impulse to convert or expel the Jews. At the same time, exegetical literature was developing and flourishing among both Jews and Christians. Examining Rashi and the Gloss together shows similarities in how Jews and Christians read not only the Bible but their own traditions of exegesis during the formative twelfth century.

In the late eleventh and early twelfth centuries, the story of the near-sacrifice of Isaac took on new significance for both Jewish and Christian self-understanding. This story took on new meaning for Jews during that period as a model for Jewish martyrdom during the Crusades. In the renewed Christian anti-Jewish polemical literature, the Christian allegorists read Isaac as one of the prefigurations of Christ that they described Jews as willfully unable to see. Rashi and the Gloss use similar or even identical techniques in their exegesis of this passage. Even polemic, as it appears in these commentaries, does not involve a conflict over techniques of interpretation but rather a struggle in which Jewish and Christian polemicists use similar techniques to interpret the Bible.

RASHI AND THE GLOSS

Rashi was the most influential Jewish Bible commentator of the Middle Ages, and his commentaries—still widely read—cover the entire Bible (with the exception of Chronicles, Ezra, and Nehemiah), as well as most of the Talmud. Rashi's commentary on the Bible shaped the subsequent history of twelfth-century Jewish biblical exegesis to the extent that for the rest of the Middle Ages almost all Ashkenazic biblical exegesis responded to Rashi's commentary.[3] He also strongly influenced Christian exegetes such as Herbert of Bosham,[4] Andrew of St. Victor,[5] and Nicholas of Lyra.[6] Rashi organizes his commentary in short comments on individual verses. Most of his comments quote or paraphrase midrashic or other late antique Jewish exegesis. Rashi is not merely a compiler, however; he adapts his sources to promote his own exegetical agenda.

Prior to Rashi, the major genre of Jewish exegesis in Europe was that of midrash, such as *Midrash Bereshit Rabbati* of Rabbi Moses the Darshan of Narbonne in the eleventh century.[7] This Bible commentary may have been one of Rashi's sources and will be discussed in more detail later on. Rashi renewed the genre, gave it new life, and effectively began the Jewish study of the Bible in northern France. The century following the commentaries' publications saw an explosion of Bible and Talmud study in northern France. As an example of the breadth of exegetical creativity, Avraham Grossman mentions ten commentaries written during this century on the book of Job alone.[8] Major Bible commentators from this subsequent period included Rashbam (Rabbi Samuel ben Meir), Shemaiah, Joseph Kara,

Eliezer of Beaugency, and Joseph ben Isaac Bekhor Shor. Of these, Joseph Kara,[9] Shemaiah,[10] and Rashi's grandson Rashbam[11] explicitly wrote their commentaries as a response to Rashi's, and the others were also strongly influenced by his exegesis.[12] Rashi's students and descendants and their school, then, were responsible for much of twelfth-century exegesis. Rashi stood at the beginning of the expansion and development of Jewish biblical scholarship in France.

Following convention, I have so far spoken of Rashi in the singular and will continue to do so. But Rashi was not the sole author of his commentary. As we will see, later scribes continued to supplement his exegesis through the twelfth century. Rashi's commentary, then, is of complex authorship, made up almost entirely of rabbinic quotations on the one hand, developed by his successors on the other. Nevertheless, Rashi himself doubtless had a pivotal role in creating and shaping it, and his commentary contains a great deal of his innovative thinking.

The *Glossa Ordinaria*, which came out of the school of Laon, was compiled by Anselm, Ralph of Laon, and Gilbert of Auxerre; Gilbert compiled the Gloss on the Pentateuch, which is the section of the Gloss I shall be considering.[13] The Gloss covers the entire Christian Bible, both Old and New Testaments. Like Rashi's commentary, the Gloss is constructed largely out of earlier exegesis. The Gloss is made up of two kinds of glosses: marginal and interlinear. In the Gloss on Genesis 22, all marginal glosses are direct quotations or paraphrases from patristic or Carolingian exegesis, as are many interlinear comments. But, like Rashi's commentary, the Gloss adapts and transforms the sources that it compiles. And like Rashi's commentary, as we shall see, the Gloss continued to develop textually over the course of the early twelfth century. It was the standard Bible commentary of the twelfth century, and in the generation after its composition exegetes such as Peter Lombard framed their exegesis as a continuation of the Gloss.[14]

The *Glossa Ordinaria* is a transitional text that shows characteristics of both monastic exegesis and the exegesis of the cathedral schools.[15] Its extensive quotation of earlier exegesis is typical of monastic commentaries, as is its verse-by-verse analysis, which was a technique used in eleven-century monastic schools. In the mid–eleventh century monastic reformers began to institute Bible-based education, in which monks would learn Latin language and rhetorical style from the Bible rather than from secular texts as had been the norm.[16] The secular texts that the reformers were replacing often contained interlinear glosses to help the student understand the author's syntax and vocabulary.[17] For the new Bible-based program of education to work, the reformers needed a similar commentary on the Bible, one that could lead students word-by-word and line-by-line through the biblical text and explain its language, syntax, and rhetorical techniques. The *Glossa Ordinaria* developed, Margaret Gibson suggests, in order to meet this need.

In other ways the Gloss was typical of the exegesis of the schools. Like later cathedral school exegesis, it is organized by chapter, and is relatively brief. The Gloss on Genesis 22, as is typical, approaches the biblical text from a number of different perspectives. It does not label or name these approaches, however, or even indicate that it considers them to be separate approaches.

Although Rashi lived in a Christian context and undoubtedly was aware of some basic Christian doctrines, there is no evidence that Rashi read Latin or read Christian biblical exegesis.[18] The compilers of the Gloss seem to have had no direct access to Jewish doctrines; they base their exegesis on the Latin Vulgate text and show no evidence of any knowledge of Hebrew. The only Jewish exegesis with which they are familiar is transmitted by their late antique sources, primarily Jerome. This study, therefore, will not argue for any direct influence or contact between Rashi and the Gloss. Rather, the similarities between them are based on their shared biblical (and late antique) heritage and their common presuppositions about how to interpret scripture. These similarities reflect shared Jewish and Christian trends in late-eleventh- and early-twelfth-century biblical exegesis.

RASHI, THE GLOSS, AND THE LITERAL SENSE OF SCRIPTURE

In the twelfth century, Jewish and Christian exegetes began to emphasize a sense of scripture that has been variously called literal, historical, or contextual.[19] Jewish exegetes such as Joseph Kara and Rashbam interpreted scripture in ways that they saw as more consistent with the words of the biblical text than rabbinic exegesis. These exegetes were attentive to questions of grammar and language. They sometimes even interpreted legal texts in ways that were at variance with established Jewish law by arguing that scripture could be interpreted on multiple levels.[20] Likewise,

Christian exegetes such as Hugh[21] and Andrew of St. Victor[22] and Herbert of Bosham[23] focused on grammatical and linguistic exposition in their commentaries, often at the expense of Christological interpretation. These writers too saw scripture as divided into multiple levels. To understand the literal interpretation, which they saw as the basis for the spiritual, they often returned to the Hebrew and, following Jerome, even consulted Jewish exegesis.

Rashi has been associated with this trend of literal exegesis since the Middle Ages. For the Christian thinkers Herbert of Bosham,[24] Andrew of St. Victor,[25] and Nicholas of Lyra,[26] Rashi was a source (and an authority) for the literal sense of scripture. The words of Beryl Smalley reflect the enduring quality of this medieval approach by describing Rashi's commentary as "scientific and rational."[27] Jewish opinion was less uniform. Rashbam's opinion on the literality of his grandfather's exegesis is more ambiguous: In his commentary on Genesis 37:2, Rashbam claims that Rashi had attempted to compose a *peshat* (literal or contextual) commentary but had not entirely succeeded. The late-eleventh- and early-twelfth-century Spanish Jewish exegete Abraham Ibn Ezra was even harsher, writing that Rashi had constructed a commentary based on midrash while claiming that it was a *peshat* commentary, while in reality Rashi gave a *peshat* interpretation less than one in a thousand times.[28]

Debates about the literality of Rashi's commentary continue in contemporary scholarship. In the investigation of Rashi's method, perhaps the most basic question is as follows: Did Rashi follow a *peshat* approach to the exegesis of scripture, or was his approach more based on midrash? And if *peshat* does describe his method, what does it mean?

The respected twentieth-century Israeli Bible commentator and teacher Nechama Leibowitz, who helped rekindle popular interest in the study of Rashi, presents Rashi as consistently following a *peshat* approach.[29] She describes Rashi as seeking "to explain difficulties and answer questions, and not to adorn, beautify, or supplement scripture."[30] Avraham Grossman follows this categorization in his study of literal Jewish exegesis in Northern France.[31] In his study of Rashi he quotes and adopts Leibowitz's definition of *peshat*, which he translates as the literal sense of scripture.[32] Sarah Kamin points out that Rashi does not in fact use the term *peshat*. The term that Rashi uses instead—*peshuto shel mikra*—although it can also be translated as "the literal sense of scripture," was different from what later commentators (such as Rashi's grandson Rashbam) understood as *peshat*. She suggests that Rashi's commentary was intended to integrate rabbinic expositions and narratives with the biblical text rather than analyzing biblical language, grammar and syntax, literary composition, and structure, as would be the case in a *peshat*-focused commentary like those of the later twelfth century.[33] Edward Greenstein and Jonathan Kearney build on Kamin's approach by showing how both *peshat* and *derash* (interpretations of midrashic origin) in Rashi's commentary respond to linguistic problems.[34]

Conversely, contemporary scholarship rarely raises the question of whether or not the Gloss was a literal commentary. Beryl Smalley comments that in the twelfth century the Victorines had to "start again from the beginning" in developing literal exegesis,[35] but does not explicitly describe the Gloss, which preceded them by a generation, as non-literal. G. R. Evans similarly does not directly address the question of literality, although she does note that the brevity of the interlinear glosses inhibited their ability to explore the language of scripture.[36] Although Margaret Gibson examines the use of the Gloss for teaching syntax and rhetoric, she also states that the Gloss was "as much the convenient record of patristic opinion."[37] Gilbert Dahan, in his discussion of literal techniques of analysis (such as systematic grammatical and linguistic analysis, rhetorical analysis, and the study of the style of each biblical book)[38] occasionally observes the Gloss practicing these techniques.[39] Lesley Smith describes the interlinear gloss as consistently emphasizing the moral and spiritual senses, leaving philological and historical analysis to the marginal gloss.[40]

The similarity between Rashi and the Gloss, and the difference in whether or not they have been understood as literal, raise questions about the possibility of applying the term "literal sense" as an objective category even in a historically limited twelfth-century context. In this study, then, I do not attempt to define the term "literal exegesis," nor do I take a stand on whether or not Rashi and the Gloss were literal commentaries. Rather, the difficulty in categorizing them is a commonality manifesting in how both manipulate and transform their late antique sources to make them appear to respond to grammatical and rhetorical problems in the biblical text. This is a technique of exegesis that can be called literal or "simple,"[41] but it does not need to be.

In differentiating between levels of scripture and techniques of exegesis I draw my inspiration from Frances Young, who demonstrates that patristic literal and allegorical exegetes used similar methods of interpretation, and therefore that the distinction between levels of scripture is not absolute.[42] She proposes a list of eight methods of interpretation used in the construction of allegory,[43] from "rhetorical allegory" in which allegory is used like metaphor as a figure of speech to "theological allegory" in which every text is really about Christ (or God). The distinction between levels of exegesis and methods of interpretation is essential for understanding the Gloss, which, unlike most twelfth-century exegetes, does not identify its exegesis unequivocally as *litteralis* or *spiritualis*. It also makes it possible to compare the Gloss with Rashi, even though the terms of Christian interpretation are foreign to Rashi's exegesis.[44] In applying Young's insight to the Middle Ages I follow Gilbert Dahan's conclusion that the literal and spiritual sense were both based on the same medieval assumptions about scripture: the unity of scripture and the multivocality of the divine word.[45]

JEWISH AND CHRISTIAN BIBLICAL INTERPRETATION: INFLUENCE, SIMILARITY, AND CONVERGENCE

As David Stern writes in his introduction to the anthology *Jewish Biblical Interpretation and Cultural Exchange*,[46] the histories of Jewish and Christian biblical interpretation have traditionally been studied separately. Even the recent magisterial anthology *Hebrew Bible/Old Testament* edited by Magne Sæbø treats Jewish and Christian biblical interpretation as parallel tracks. As Sæbø writes in his introduction, Jewish and Christian interpretation are a "long double story. . . . These two main roads [of Jewish and Christian exegesis], with several minor deviating paths, have mostly been kept apart by the ancient Synagogue and Church—who have moved forward in relatively great isolation from one another, with only a few signs of combining tracks."[47] As Stern asks, if the histories of Jewish and Christian interpretation are parallel lines that do not intersect then what is the point of studying them together?[48]

One classical answer has been to look for influence, either Jewish influence on Christian exegetes or Christian influence on Jewish exegetes. Scholars who emphasize Jewish influence on Christian exegesis have typically compared earlier Jewish commentators with later Christian commentators. Beryl Smalley has pointed out the Jewish influence on Andrew of St. Victor[49] and Rainer Berndt has emphasized, following Smalley, the relationship between Rashi and the Victorines.[50] He describes Christian exegetes (such as Andrew of St. Victor, Hugh of St. Cher, and Herbert of Bosham) as seeking clarifications from their Jewish neighbors about the literal (and only literal) sense of scripture.[51] Deborah Goodwin has also followed this approach in her study of Rashi's influence on Herbert of Bosham.[52] Deeana Klepper (following Herman Hailperin) has detailed Rashi's formative influence on Nicholas of Lyra.[53] These studies demonstrate the influence that Jewish exegesis had on the development of the Christian literal sense.

Recently, some Jewish studies scholars have taken the opposite approach. Israel Yuval has argued that given a minority Jewish society within a larger Christian society, in the absence of evidence to the contrary, the default assumption should be that the majority influenced the minority.[54] Ivan Marcus in his *Rituals of Childhood*[55] has demonstrated the presence of some Christian influence on Jewish Ashkenazic rituals. These are important revisions to the traditional understanding of medieval Jewish history, because they show that the Jewish–Christian relationship is not one-sided. Jews were active parties in the relationship who learned and changed just as the Christians did. Sarah Kamin has followed this model in her study of the influence of Victorine exegesis on Rashbam.[56] She suggests that the concept of the twofold meaning of the biblical text in the Rashbam's exegesis— the idea that the literal and midrashic can coexist simultaneously—was influenced by the Christian dichotomy between the literal and the allegorical senses. In her framework, this is the difference between the meanings of the literal sense in Rashbam (who lived in Northern France) and Ibn Ezra (who lived in Spain). Christian exegesis, she argues, shaped Rashbam's understanding of the literal sense, while Islamic exegesis influenced that of the Spanish exegete Ibn Ezra.[57] Still, though, this model of Jewish–Christian relations depends on influence and known contact.

As Kamin and Berndt show, when one reads a later Jewish interpreter along with an earlier Christian interpreter, or a later Christian interpreter along with an earlier Jewish interpreter, it is easy to find a one-directional influence. Gilbert Dahan has recently suggested an alternative approach by focusing on the similarities in the sources and in the contexts of Jewish and Christian medieval exegesis of scripture. He builds on the late antique Jewish–Christian polemical relationship, in which each defined its exegesis against the other's by dividing the shared Hellenistic tradition of mythic and allegorical exegesis.[58] Medieval Christian exegesis not only adopted the Hellenistic tradition of allegorical exegesis, including that of Jewish-Hellenistic exegetes such as Philo, but it also defined itself as different from Jewish exegesis by doing so.[59] In the eleventh and twelfth centuries, Jewish and Christian exegesis began to reconverge. The worsening of the Jewish–Christian relationship and the development of polemic paradoxically made it necessary to find a common language in which to debate about scripture. At the same time, the new importance of reason in scriptural exegesis and the development of literal exegesis made it possible for Jews and Christians to learn from each other. With this convergence, the need to mark the border between Jewish and Christian exegesis was renewed. But they were marking this border using the same tools: the biblical text and the inherited tradition of patristic and midrashic exegesis. Using the same tools and responding to the same need, it is not surprising that they arrived at similar results.

Rashi and the Gloss developed at the same time with no known contact between them. The similarities between them arise not from influence, mutual or otherwise, but because in twelfth-century France Jews and Christians shared a way of reading text that shaped their interpretations of the central religious narrative, as typified by their interpretations of the near-sacrifice of Isaac.

This similarity in approach is intertwined with a polemical emphasis that goes beyond that of their sources. Michael Signer has examined the question of anti-Jewish polemic in the Gloss in his study of the Gloss on Genesis 37 and has found that the Gloss goes beyond its sources in reading anti-Jewish polemic into the biblical text.[60] Avraham Grossman and Elazar Touitou see anti-Christian polemic as one of the main preoccupations of Rashi's commentary, and present his commentary as a weapon against the Christian majority that surrounds him.[61] In examining the polemic of Rashi and of the Gloss together, this study will show that Rashi and the Gloss used similar techniques of exegesis to read the same passage of scripture to argue for the primacy of their tradition over the other's.

THE STORY OF THE NEAR-SACRIFICE
OF ISAAC IN RASHI AND IN THE GLOSS

Before progressing to central themes in the exegesis of the near-sacrifice of Isaac in Rashi and in the Gloss, let us begin with a summary of the story in each as it might appear to the reader. Neither commentary is written as a single, seamless narrative. Rashi's comments are occasionally contradictory. In verses 1 and 6 for example, Rashi interprets a verse in two alternative ways. Later on, in his comments on verses 8 and 9, Rashi sets up a contradiction between Isaac going willingly to be sacrificed and Isaac being bound and placed on the altar, and (unlike his source *Midrash Tanchuma*[62]) Rashi never resolves this contradiction. Rashi does not summarize his own interpretation of the story and does not explicitly connect his comments on individual verses into a coherent narrative.[63]

The Gloss also contains complexities and contradictions. The *Glossa Ordinaria* is made up of two kinds of comments: marginal and interlinear glosses. These two kinds of glosses form one commentary, and one is never found without the other,[64] but they have distinct approaches to the biblical text. The interlinear gloss, made up of short, anonymous comments, inserts words into the Bible in order to tell its story.[65] These short comments weave together to tell a generally consistent story: A reader, on encountering the story of the near-sacrifice of Isaac through the Gloss, would be led immediately to the conclusion that Isaac represents Christ.[66] The marginal gloss, on the other hand, is made up of quotations and paraphrases from patristic and Carolingian authors, often filtered through Rabanus. The contradictions between these patristic and Carolingian authors generate unresolved tensions within the marginal gloss itself. The Jerome-based material in which the Jews are an exegetical authority coexists uneasily with the Isidore-based material in which the Jews see and understand nothing. The marginal and interlinear glosses also sometimes have slightly different emphases. While the interlinear gloss stresses Abraham's obedience, the marginal gloss mentions his love and faith as well.

Despite these disjunctions, it is possible for a reader to construct a narrative out of the materials that Rashi and the Gloss each present.[67] A reader of Rashi might tell the story as follows: The near-sacrifice of Isaac was necessary in order to show the greatness of both Abraham and Isaac to an audience made up of Ishmael, Satan, the nations of the world, and various hostile and undefined "others" (comment 1.1). In order to make this demonstration, God told Abraham to go to the place of the future Temple (1.3) and offer his son as a sacrifice. Abraham and Isaac both went willingly (8.1). Ishmael and Eliezer went with them, but were left at the bottom of the mountain with the donkey (3.3). Once Abraham had proved his willingness to sacrifice Isaac, God declared that Abraham's greatness and worthiness of God's love had been demonstrated to Satan and the nations of the world (12.2), and then Abraham sacrificed a ram in a way that foreshadowed both the Temple sacrifices and post-Temple Jewish prayer (14.1, 14.2).

Like the story in Rashi, the story in the Gloss can also be told simply: The Gloss, like Rashi, emphasizes that the near-sacrifice of Isaac was a performance, a demonstration of Abraham's greatness rather than a test of it (1.1i, 12.1i, 1.1m). This performance had two intended audiences: Abraham, who understood its full meaning (1.1i, 2.3i, 2.5i, 12.1i, 15.1i, 1.1m, 14.2m) and the Jews (represented by the donkey), who did not (5.1i, 3.1m, 5.1m, 5.2m). This near-sacrifice, which took place at the location of the future Temple (2.3m, 4.1m), symbolized both the sacrifice of Christ (2.4i, 3.3i, 4.1i, 6.1i, 7.1i, 9.2i, 4.2m, 8.1m, 9.1m) and its re-enactment through the Eucharist (9.1i). Abraham learned from this test that he was truly willing to obey God, but more importantly he also learned about the future redemption to come (2.5i, 11.1i). The Jews, whose presence as unseeing witnesses is centrally important to the narrative in the Gloss, will only understand at the end of days (19.1i, 19.2i).

This paraphrase serves to highlight important similarities in how Rashi and the Gloss read the near-sacrifice of Isaac. Both read the events as a performance and polemic for the benefit of a hostile, non-chosen "other." Abraham's test proves not only the absolute greatness of Abraham, but that Abraham is greater than someone else. This greatness is rewarded not only by God's love for Abraham, but by a future sacrifice (at the same location: the Temple) that will be re-enacted in a future liturgy for Abraham's descendants.

This brief comparison, though, already highlights an important difference. The Gloss clearly and repeatedly identifies the Jews as the non-chosen "other." Rashi's "others" are vague and unclear. Although Rashi does not name Christians explicitly, his commentary consistently interprets the near-sacrifice of Isaac as a refutation of claims of chosenness by other peoples and a justification for the Divine election of Israel. For Rashi, the narrative of the *Akedah* was primarily a way of refuting non-Jewish doubts about the greatness of Abraham and Isaac and, by extension, the Jewish people.

However, both Rashi and the Gloss used a similar technique of manipulating late antique exegesis to create the impression that they arise directly from the biblical text. They change their sources as they manipulate them, and create an implied dialogue over the meaning of the story that is more directly polemical than the sources on which they base their exegesis. Their interpretations reflect their shared twelfth-century context and the intensification of Jewish–Christian polemic.

In this study, the first chapter provides an overview of the relevant twelfth-century context for understanding the development of the Gloss and Rashi's commentary, along with and their relationship. It situates these texts in the context of the deteriorating Jewish/Christian relationship, the First Crusade and the ideology of martyrdom attached to it, and the growth and development of biblical exegesis in Northern Europe. The second chapter shows that Rashi's commentary draws selectively on a range of prior commentaries (most particularly *Genesis Rabbah* and *Midrash Tanchuma*) to transform earlier exegesis for his purposes. Using a variety of strategies, he adapts them to represent his exegesis as arising directly from the biblical text. Furthermore, analysis of the manuscript tradition shows that while some scribes of later recensions emphasize Rashi's commentary as a way of compiling and teaching midrash, others focus in their additions on the ways in which Rashi answers textual questions. These two alternative readings of (and scribal interventions in) Rashi's commentary are similar to the two approaches to exegesis and textual authority found in the marginal and interlinear glosses of the *Glossa Ordinaria*. The chapter concludes by showing that the most important themes in Rashi's commentary are closer to those in the *Glossa Ordinaria* than to those of his midrashic sources.

The third chapter explores the textual history of the Gloss, from its sources through the twelfth- and thirteenth-century manuscript tradition. The early glossators derived the marginal gloss from the commentary of Rabanus and, over the course of the twelfth century, generations of scribes gradually transformed it into a series of paraphrases rather than quotations from patristic literature. This chapter will demonstrate the difference in exegetical method between marginal and interlinear glosses by suggesting that the marginal and interlinear glosses are two alternative strategies for generating meaning and locating authority. While the marginal glosses appear as a record of patristic opinion and locate authority in Church tradition, interlinear glosses appear as an outgrowth of the biblical text and locate authority in the autonomous reader. In reading these two kinds of comments together a medieval reader could easily be brought to conclude that tradition and autonomous reading lead to the same inevitable interpretation. In conclusion, this chapter will suggest similarities and differences in how Rashi and the Gloss adapt their respective sources. The fourth chapter shows the thematic similarities between Rashi and the Gloss in their exegesis of the near-sacrifice of Isaac. In particular I will argue that both interpret the near-sacrifice of Isaac polemically in a way that makes the "other" a crucial figure in the story. The two texts converge precisely where Jewish and Christian medieval exegeses have been thought to diverge: in their shared typological reading, or in reading the near-sacrifice of Isaac as a foreshadowing of a future redemption.

The structure of this book is thus a four-way comparison. The comparisons between Rashi's commentary (in many of its manuscript versions) and its midrashic sources, and the Gloss (in its most prominent manuscript versions) and its patristic sources, show the ways in which each have manipulated their sources to arrive at an original commentary. The comparison of Rashi and the Gloss to each other illustrate the similarities between Rashi and the Gloss that derive not merely from their shared late antique heritage, but also from their common twelfth-century context, and the Jewish–Christian polemic in which they both, implicitly or explicitly, take part.

CHAPTER ONE

THE DEVELOPING

JEWISH–CHRISTIAN POLEMIC

Rashi and the glosses of the *Glossa Ordinaria* on Genesis 22 are similar in both method and content. Such similarity develops out of their shared historical context. These two commentaries developed at a time of scholarly ferment and intensification of the Jewish–Christian polemic. The authors of these commentaries (or their schools) were part of both these developments. This chapter will survey developments in Jewish–Christian polemic during the eleventh and twelfth centuries and situate Rashi and the Gloss in the context of these developments.

The polemical themes in Rashi and in the Gloss on Genesis 22 relate to polemical themes that appear elsewhere in Rashi's writings and in other writings from the school of Laon, notably in the *Dialogus inter Christianum et Judaeum de fide Catholica* [Dialogue between a Christian and a Jew about the Catholic faith], a polemical work composed in the school of Laon during the time of the early development of the Gloss. Rashi did not write any explicitly polemical works, but implied polemic runs through Rashi's biblical commentaries. Finally, this chapter will survey the various ways of thinking about the near-sacrifice of Isaac that were common in Jewish and Christian exegesis in eleventh- and early-twelfth-century Europe.

CHRISTIAN ANTI-JEWISH POLEMIC IN THE TWELFTH CENTURY

At least four major anti-Jewish polemical works were composed in the early twelfth century: Guibert of Nogent's *Tractatus de incarnatione contra Iudeos* [Treatise on the incarnation directed against the Jews],[1] Peter Abelard's *Dialogus inter philosophum, Iudeum et Christianum* [Dialogue between a philosopher, a Jew and a Christian],[2] Rupert of Deutz's *Annulus sive dialogus inter christianum et iudeum* [The ring, or a dialogue between a Christian and a Jew],[3] Odo of Tournai's *Disputatio contra Judeum Leonem nomine de adventu Christi filii dei* [Argument against a Jew by the name of Leon about the advent of Christ the son of God],[4] and the *Dialogus inter Christianum et Iudeum de fide Catholica*[5] ascribed to William of Champaux but in fact by an anonymous author from the school of Laon. One may also include Herman the Former Jew's narrative of his own conversion, *Hermanus quondam Iudeus: opusculum de conversione sua* [Herman once a Jew: a little book about his conversion],[6] and Anna Sapir Abulafia has argued that Gilbert Crispin's *Disputatio Christiani cum gentili de fide Christi* [Argument with a pagan about the faith of Christ][7] was also a veiled anti-Jewish polemic.[8]

With the expansion of polemical literature in the early twelfth century came new emphases in Christian anti-Jewish polemic. Amos Funkenstein[9] and Anna Sapir Abulafia[10] have identified in these texts a new model of rational argumentation, proving Christianity on the basis of reason rather than scriptural prooftexts. This new, more rational argumentation—based on Aristotelian philosophy—had the capacity to lead to increased toleration, as in the *Dialogue* of Peter Abelard. More frequently it led to the conclusion that Jews were incapable of being rational and were therefore not fully human. To Abulafia, rational argumentation for Christianity (beginning with Anselm) is what led to the worsening of the Jewish–Christian relationship in the twelfth century. In accepting Aristotle, she suggests, Christian philosophy tended to reject the Jews.

Overt Jewish anti-Christian polemic did not begin until the late twelfth century. In the 1170s European Jews began to develop works of anti-Christian argumentation, such as *Sefer milchemot Hashem* [Book of the Wars of the Lord] and Joseph Kimchi's *Sefer habrit* [Book of the Covenant]. Prior to this, works of overt anti-Christian polemic were typically written in the Islamic world.[11] However, in the two generations after Rashi, some Jewish Bible commentators (in particular Rashbam and Bekhor Shor) wrote anti-Christian polemic into their exegesis,[12] and as we shall see Rashi seems to have done so himself. Biblical interpretation (along with crusade narrative, to be considered shortly) seems to have been the genre of choice for early-twelfth-century Jewish scholars in responding to Christian attacks.

The study of Jewish exegesis at the school of St. Victor shows that some intellectual contact between Jewish and Christian exegetes persisted even in the later twelfth century.[13] In the tenth and eleventh centuries Jerome was a main source of Rabbinic exegesis in Christian Bible commentaries.[14] Also influential was a commentary on Samuel, Kings and Chronicles written by a Carolingian (ninth century) converted Jew, which quickly became ascribed to Jerome.[15] In the twelfth century, scholars such as Hugh of St. Victor, Andrew of St. Victor, and Herbert of Bosham learned Jewish interpretations from the Parisian Jews of their time, and even learned Hebrew from them.[16] These exegetes occasionally quoted Jewish interpretations in order to refute them,[17] but more often they presented these interpretations as useful and authoritative, particularly for determining the literal sense of scripture.[18]

The commentaries of Rashi and the Gloss, then, were written at a time when Jewish–Christian relations and polemic against the "other" made up a central intellectual concern for both Jews and Christians. These themes are at the center of both these commentaries on the near-sacrifice of Isaac.

RASHI AND THE HEBREW CRUSADE NARRATIVES

The Hebrew First Crusade narratives, written between 1096 and the mid-twelfth century, developed during the period of the composition or redaction of Rashi's commentary, and they share themes with Rashi's interpretation of the story of the near-sacrifice of Isaac.

There are three primary crusade narratives: the Mainz Anonymous, the Eliezer bar Nathan Chronicle, and the Solomon bar Samson Chronicle.[19] The precise dating and relationship between them has been the subject of much recent discussion. Abulafia considers the Mainz Anonymous to have been written first, possibly at the time of the events. She dates the Eliezer bar Nathan Chronicle to before 1146. The Solomon bar Samson Chronicle is probably latest, sometime after 1140.[20] Robert Chazan agrees that the Mainz Anonymous is probably the oldest, written between 1097 and 1106, shortly after the events of 1096.[21] The Eliezer bar Nathan Chronicle was written in the mid-1100s after the Second Crusade.[22] Chazan describes the Solomon bar Samson Chronicle as a compilation of four separate documents, together with an editorial prologue and epilogue,[23] and dates its redaction to between 1140 and 1149, toward the beginning of the Second Crusade.[24] Eva Haverkamp uses linguistic evidence to show that the Chronicle of Solomon bar Samson and the Eliezer bar Nathan Chronicle were not dependent on each other but instead used an earlier source, and otherwise found Abulafia's dating to be consistent with philological examination of the manuscripts.[25] She is skeptical of some arguments for a very early date of the Mainz Anonymous Chronicle but still considers it to have been written earliest, definitely before 1140.[26] The consensus seems to be that all were written between 1096 and the mid–twelfth century.[27] This sets them within the time period when Rashi's commentary was developing and becoming influential.

Historians have debated the impact of the First Crusade on contemporary French Jews.[28] The Hebrew crusade narrative ascribed to Solomon bar Samson describes vividly and horrifically the massacres of the Jews during the First Crusade, and describes the Jewish martyrs of the time as outshining those before and after. Following these chroniclers, some contemporary historians have argued that the First Crusade was the turning point in which the previously tranquil relations between Jews and Christians in France and the German principalities began to deteriorate.[29] Robert Chazan,[30] following Salo Baron,[31] points out that despite the violence and the vivid historical memory of the events, European Jewry rapidly recovered from the traumas of the First Crusade. His main evidence is demographic, that the Jewish population of Europe grew during the years after the First Crusade in a way that shows immigration. The early years of the twelfth century show the Jewish communities of Europe growing intellectually and economically as well as demographically. Therefore, Chazan argues, Jews still felt relatively comfortable and safe in Europe even after the First Crusade. The legal, cultural, and social state of Jews in Northern Europe only began to deteriorate in the mid–twelfth century, long after the First Crusade was over.[32]

Chazan also argues that the effects of the Crusades in France must be distinguished from their effects in the Rhineland. Although Pope Urban II called for crusade from the French city Clermont and some French bishops were involved in the First Crusade, France seems to have been spared some of the random Crusade-associated violence. The Jewish crusade narratives that so graphically describe Jewish suffering in the Rhineland have little to say about France, and would hardly have refrained from describing (or been unaware of) massacres of French Jews had they occurred.[33] These crusade narratives are redacted into a composite Spires chronicle[34] that describes the murder of thirty Jews in Blois in 1171, but contains nothing on tragedies in France during the First Crusade.

Although there is no Jewish chronicle of massacres of French Jews during the First Crusade, Guibert of Nogent describes such a massacre as context for the conversion of a Jew who became a monk during these persecutions. In his account, the crusaders rounded up all the Jews of Rouen
and killed those who would not convert to Christianity.[35] Because there is
no other record of this massacre, and because Guibert's account gives few
details and no date, some scholars have suspected that this massacre never
took place.[36] Although there may be less record of French crusaders killing
Jews in France, it is not in dispute that French crusaders took a key role in
the massacres of Rhineland Jews.[37]

Even though they were not direct targets of Crusade-related violence,
French Jews were still aware and afraid of it. The Hebrew crusade narratives describe French Jews as afraid of being killed by Crusaders, even if
(in these narratives) they were in fact left alive. The Mainz Anonymous
Chronicle tells of French Jews declaring days of fasting and prayers to be
saved from the Crusaders.[38] Solomon bar Samson tells of bribes given by
French Jews to Crusaders and even letters these Jews gave to the Crusaders
with instructions to other Jews to give provisions to French Crusaders as a
bribe to leave them alone.[39]

This French Jewish fear of Crusaders may be a later projection.
While Robert Chazan has consistently defended the historicity of these
narratives[40]—Chazan argues that these three narratives represent both
the spiritual world of the late eleventh century martyrs and that of mid-
twelfth-century chroniclers[41]—recently, some scholars have suggested that
the three crusade narratives might be fictitious and may not reflect historical reality, such that they can teach us only about the spirituality of
the mid–twelfth century, and nothing about the time of the Crusades itself.[42] Steven Schwartzfuchs suggests that the idea of the First Crusade as a
turning point in Jewish–Christian relations developed later in the twelfth
century, when the situation of Jews in Europe did severely deteriorate.[43]
Jeremy Cohen,[44] following Ivan Marcus,[45] has argued that the crusade narratives ought to be investigated from a literary perspective rather than as
factual recountings of the events of 1096.

Can we see the Jewish response to the Crusades as an influence on
Rashi? If Chazan is correct,[46] the earliest eyewitness accounts of the Crusades (1096), which were the major source for the crusade narratives,
would have been written in Rashi's lifetime (1040–1106). However, it seems

unlikely even in this case that they could have reached Rashi's hands early enough to directly influence his thinking. Nevertheless, Rashi's commentary continued to develop in the half-century after his death, so the possibility of some direct influence cannot be ruled out. Even according to the latest dater, Cohen, the narratives had developed by 1150. If, however, Chazan is correct about the dating of the Mainz Anonymous chronicle to before 1106, then French fear of the Crusaders is attested even during the lifetime of Rashi. It is therefore plausible that Rashi's commentary would respond to the anxieties and polemics of the First Crusade.

Whether or not the Crusades were a turning point for Jewish–Christian relations from the perspective of social history, they certainly were a turning point from the perspective of literary history. Whether written in response to the First or the Second Crusade, Jewish crusade narratives were among the first genres of Jewish polemical writings to be produced in Christian Europe.

The effect of the Crusades on Rashi's thought must be conjectured, since clear and unambiguous references to it in his writings are rare.[47] One of his *responsa*[48] requires a Jewish legal divorce for a Jewish couple who got married while living as Christians following their forced conversions during the First Crusade. When he bewails the troubles of the Jews in his commentaries he never specifically mentions the crusades.[49]

Some scholars have found subtle references to the First Crusade in Rashi's commentary.[50] He begins his Bible commentary with the statement that the land of Israel belongs to the Jewish people.[51] His descriptions of persecutions include events that could plausibly have taken place during the First Crusade: Jews who refuse conversion are killed or buried in donkey skins or dog's intestines.[52] Rashi possessed consciousness of anti-Jewish violence, if not willingness to mention the crusade directly.

Despite the absence of explicit mentions in Rashi's commentary, then, the First Crusade and its aftermath is likely to have impacted Rashi's commentary. Although the First Crusade largely spared French Jewry, even the earliest sources record their awareness and fear of such violence. Since Rashi does not explicitly discuss the violence of the First Crusade, the impact of the Crusade and its aftermath is most clear from the thematic similarities between Rashi's commentary on the near-sacrifice of Isaac and the polemical use of this theme in the crusade narratives.

The Near-Sacrifice of Isaac in the Hebrew Crusade Narratives: Polemic and Counternarrative

Jeremy Cohen, Ivan Marcus, and Israel Yuval have examined the Hebrew crusade narratives as a Jewish response to Christian polemics. As Cohen describes it, "the Hebrew chronicle claimed for the Jewish martyrs of 1096 the zeal of the crusader, the selfless altruism of the monk, and the salvific effectiveness of Christ on the cross."[53] In particular, they have shown that the Jewish crusade narratives adapt and re-write Crusading ideology and popularized Christian theology in a counternarrative showing Jewish moral and religious superiority. One major trope in these narratives is that pious Jews in killing their children to save them from baptism re-enact the near-sacrifice of Isaac, or the *akedah*. In the Hebrew crusade chronicles the term *akedah*, referring to the Binding of Isaac, becomes for the first time commonly used as a general term for all forms of martyrdom.[54] The Eliezer bar Nathan Chronicle calls the suicides of the Jews of Xanten their *akedot*, or bindings, using a term clearly meant to evoke the story of Abraham and Isaac.[55] The Solomon bar Samson Chronicle describes the martyrdom of the Jews of Mainz as greater even than the *akedah*:

האם היו אלף ומאה עקידות ביום אחד כולם כעקידת יצחק בן אברהם. על אחד הרעיש העולם, אשר נעקדה בהר המוריה, שנאמר . . . ו [רעשו] שמים [שמש וירח] קדרו [וכוכבים אספו נגהם]. מה עשו, למה השמים לא קדרו והכוכבים לא אספו נגהם . . .

Were there ever 1,100 Aqedot on one day—all of them like the Aqedah of Isaac, son of Abraham? The earth rumbled over just one Aqedah that was bound on Mount Moriah, as it is said, **"And the heavens [trembled, the sun and moon] grew dark, [and the stars gathered in their brightness]"** (Joel 2:10). What did they do now? Why did the heavens not grow dark and the stars not hold back their splendor?[56]

In this text, the *akedah* is the only possible precedent for the martyrdoms of Xanten. Like the *akedah,* these martyrdoms demand a divine response. The idea that the heavens darkened during the *akedah* seems also to be an innovation of the Hebrew crusade chronicles, and in particular of the Solomon bar Samson Chronicle.[57]

Another *akedah* parallel is in the story of Mistress Rachel of Mainz, who is described as killing her children in a way parallel to the *akedah* in both the Mainz Anonymous Chronicle and the Solomon bar Samson Chronicle. Her son and her father are both named Isaac, and she is described, in language intentionally evocative of Genesis 22:10, as taking the knife [ותקח את המאכלת] to slaughter her son.[58]

In the story of Isaac the *Parnas* [synagogue official] (as told by Solomon bar Samson), the children state their willingness to be sacrificed: "And the pious one asked his children, 'Do you want me to sacrifice you to our God?' They said to him, 'Do with us as you wish.'"[59] The children's willingness to be killed is similar to how Isaac consents to his own sacrifice in Rashi's interpretation of the *akedah*, as well as in Rashi's midrashic sources, as shown in chapter two. The children in these chronicles go willingly like Isaac, just as the magnitude of their father's sacrifice makes him like Abraham.

Further, the narratives connect the killing of Jewish children in the Crusades to the Temple sacrifices. Solomon bar Samson calls the Rabbi who leads the Jews of Xanten in their suicide a *kohen l'el elyon*, a priest of the God most high.[60] This motif is explicit in Solomon bar Samson's telling of the story of Rabbi Isaac the *Parnas*. Before killing his mother, he says to her "I have decided to sacrifice a sin-offering to the God of heaven, so that I can find atonement in it."[61] After killing his children and sprinkling their blood before the ark, he declares, "May this blood cleanse me of all my sins."[62] Jeremy Cohen suggests an intentional irony here, that to reject Christianity this Isaac accepts the Christian doctrine of atonement through sacrifice.[63] As we will see, Rashi's interpretation of the Binding of Isaac describes it as an atoning sacrifice and connects it to the Temple sacrifices in line with these narratives.

These stories provide a powerful argument for the power of Jewish martyrdom. The redemptive power of Crusade-era martyrdom looks back to another, even more redemptive sacrifice. These narratives, then, developed in narrative form a theology of redemption through suffering which makes reference both to Christian symbols and to the near-sacrifice of Isaac. The Jews, not Christ, are both High Priest and sacrifice taking the place of the atoning sacrifices of the Temple. The martyred Jews are the chosen of God, just as Isaac was God's chosen sacrifice. These themes closely parallel those that Rashi chooses to emphasize in his interpretation of the near-sacrifice of Isaac.

POLEMIC IN RASHI AND FROM THE SCHOOL OF LAON

Rashi on Christians and Christianity

As we have seen, Rashi wrote in the context of developing Jewish–Christian polemic, a worsening Jewish–Christian relationship, and the aftermath of the Crusades. This context was reflected in Rashi's attitude toward Christians in his legal and exegetical writings. In his Talmudic commentaries, Rashi is clear that he considers Christians to be idolaters. The closest that Rashi gets to suggesting that his Christian contemporaries might be different from the idol-worshippers of the Bible and rabbinic literature is to say that "Gentiles in our time are not experts in idolatry."[64] In his commentary on the Babylonian Talmud, he permits business with Gentiles of his time not because they are not idolaters but because "we dwell among them and our sustenance is from them."[65]

In addition to idolaters, Rashi also describes Christians as מינים [*minim*], sectarians. In his commentary on BT Sotah 49b, he says that in his generation:

המלכות השולטת על רוב העולם תהא למינות נמשכים אחרי טעותו של ישו ותלמידיו הנקראים מינים.

The kingship that rules over most of the world has become sectarianism [*minut*], following after the error of Jesus and his followers who are called sectarians [*minim*].[66]

Christians, therefore, are both idolaters and sectarians in Rashi's writings, and Rashi never explains how it is possible for them to be both. He does not seem to have a consistent ideology about Christians, and even occasionally describes them positively.[67] He uses a variety of terms for them: sectarians, "nations"[68] or idolaters, although given the degree to which Rashi's manuscripts evolved over the course of the twelfth century it is possible that some of these terms may have been added or changed by later copyists.

An early study of Rashi's commentary on the Pentateuch which describes it as a polemical work is that of Y. Baer, who argued in 1950 that Rashi's main intent in many of his comments (particularly on Psalms and Isaiah) was to refute Christianity and Christian exegesis.[69] Baer argued that Rashi intentionally diverged from rabbinic exegesis of these books in order to give interpretations that refute Christian exegesis.[70] Based on these passages, Baer concluded that "the events of the period [i.e., the Crusades and Christian anti-Jewish polemic] really determined the purpose which should be attributed to Rashi's commentaries in general, and not only to those places where 'to respond to the heretics' is specifically stated."[71] In other words, Baer argued that a key purpose of Rashi's commentary was to respond to Christianity.

Baer's argument was revolutionary on two fronts. First, it attributed the growth of Jewish exegetical literature in Northern France, in which Rashi was key, to anti-Christian polemical motivations. Second, it situated some of Rashi's commentaries on the Tanakh as among the first works of Jewish anti-Christian polemic to be written in Christian Europe.

In 1958, Y. Rosenthal tested Baer's argument by collecting fourteen apparent references to Christianity in Rashi's commentary on Proverbs[72] as well as twenty-five from elsewhere in the Bible. He argued that this collection of references shows the importance of polemic in Rashi's commentary, although he does not agree with Baer that polemic was among Rashi's main motivations.[73] Almost all Rosenthal's references are in Rashi's commentaries on Prophets and Writings, with only three references to comments from Rashi's commentary on the Pentateuch: two from Genesis (1.26 and 49.10) and one from Leviticus (11.2).[74]

Some of the comments that Rosenthal identified are not clearly references to Christianity. The comment on Leviticus, for example, states that Israel is distinguished from the other nations by its observance of the commandments and does not give any other information about which nations are under discussion.[75] The polemical nature of Rashi's comment on Genesis 49.10 is also subject to debate (discussed below).

Elazar Touitou developed Baer's argument by identifying references to Christian theology in Rashi's commentary on Genesis 1–6.[76] In response to the Crusades and the Christian yearning to conquer the land of Israel, Rashi writes on Genesis 1.1 that the Torah begins with the creation of the world by God:

משום **כח מעשיו הגיד לעמו לתת להם נחלת גוים** שאם יאמרו אומות העולם לישראל לסטים אתם שכבשתם ארצות שבעה גוים, הם אומרים להם כל הארץ של הקב"ה הוא בראה ונתנה לאשר ישר בעיניו, ברצונו נתנה להם, ברצונו נטלה מהם ונתנה לנו.

So as **to tell the strength of his deeds to his people, to give them the inheritance of nations** (Psalms 111:6), that if the nations of the world should say to Israel, "You are robbers because you conquered the lands the Seven Nations," they can say to them, "All the land belongs to God, He created it and gave it to whom He sees fit. It was His will to give it to them, and by His will he took it from them and gave to us.[77]

Rashi here explains that the entire purpose of the creation story was to establish Jewish ownership over the land of Israel.[78] Touitou, following D. Louys,[79] argues that this comment was Rashi's response to the theological challenge of the Christian conquest of Israel during the Crusades. Rashi here makes the point that the right of the Jews to the land of Israel is implicit in the beginning of creation and not dependent on historical events.[80]

Similarly, in his comment on Genesis 1.2 Rashi explains that the phrase "the spirit of God moved over the waters" means that "the royal throne stands in the air and is moved over the face of the waters by God's breath and His word, like a dove hovering over its nest." Rashi's source for this comment, according to Touitou, is *Midrash Socher Tov* on Psalms 93:3.[81] This is a relatively obscure source on an altogether different part of the Tanakh. There are many alternative explanations that Rashi could have chosen for this verse from sources that he draws on more often, for example *Genesis Rabbah* 8:1, which explains the spirit of God as the soul of Adam and *Genesis Rabbah* 2:4, which identifies it as the soul of the messiah.[82] The explanation that Rashi chose, however, has the advantage that it cannot be used to support a christological or trinitarian reading.[83] Touitou offers similar explanations for many of Rashi's comments on the first six verses of Genesis, and concludes that a large part of Rashi's intent in his exegesis of Genesis 1–6 was to respond to Christian exegesis and to present "a Jewish position in the Jewish–Christian debate."[84]

Shaye Cohen rejects the interpretations of Baer, Rosenthal, Touitou and others,[85] and instead claims that Rashi does not respond to Christianity in his commentary on the Pentateuch. He points out that Rashi explicitly mentions *minim* in his commentary on Psalms but not in his commentary on the Torah.[86] In his commentary on Psalms, Rashi occasionally mentions that the purpose of one of his interpretations is "to refute the sectarians (*minim*)." There are also references to "Esau," "Edom" and "Rome" in Psalms and Isaiah. In his comments on Ps. 2.1 and 21.2, he interprets "the annointed one [*mashiach*/messiah]" and "the king" as references to David rather than the messiah "to refute the sectarians," although he admits that the latter is rabbinic tradition.[87] There are no similar comments on the Pentateuch that necessarily refer to the Christians surrounding Rashi rather than to the various nations and sectarian groups that the rabbis of the Talmud and Midrash polemicized against.

Cohen suggests that all the comments that Touitou identifies as responses to Christianity are in fact simply Rashi reproducing midrashic arguments and living in "Talmudic time"[88]—as opposed to Rashbam and Bekhor Shor, who polemicize explicitly against Christianity with innovative and original argumentation.[89] Cohen's key example is their respective exegesis of Genesis 49.10: "The scepter shall not depart from Judah nor the staff from between his feet until Shiloh comes." Rashi interprets the scepter as a reference to the exilarchs of Babylonia and Shiloh as the messiah:

לא יסור שבט מיהודה. מדוד ואילך, אלו ראשי גלויות שבבבל שרודים את העם בשבט
שממנים על פי המלכות . . .

עד כי יבוא שילה. מלך המשיח שהמלכות שלו.

The scepter shall not depart from Judah. From David onwards. These are the exilarchs in Babylonia who rule the people with a scepter, because they are appointed by the kingdom . . .

Until Shiloh comes. This refers to the Messiah as King, when the kingship is his.[90]

Rosenthal argues that Rashi here is refuting the Christian anti-Jewish polemic that Jewish kingship ceased with the coming of Christ.[91] Cohen disputes this reference and points out that Rashi refers to the exilarchs, who were powerful in Talmudic times but not since. Rashi makes no effort to update this idea by referring to current or future Jewish rule.[92] Cohen points out that the comments of Rashbam and Bekhor Shor demonstrate a more overt polemical agenda. To Rashbam, the scepter is simply the Davidic kingship and Shiloh is nothing but the name of a city. Rashbam states that this interpretation is specifically intended to refute heretics and Christians. Bechor Shor similarly understands this verse as a reference to the historical house of David. Of these explanations, Rashi's is the only one based on rabbinic exegesis. Cohen concludes that because Rashi (unlike Rashbam) does not explicitly attack Christianity, and because his explanation is set in rabbinic time, Rashi must be reproducing rabbinic exegesis rather than creating anti-Christian polemic.[93]

Cohen's rejection of the scholarly consensus regarding Rashi's commentary on Genesis raises compelling points. Although Touitou draws thematic connections between Rashi's commentary on Genesis and the world of his time, Touitou does not examine Rashi's sources. Because Touitou does not show any difference between Rashi and his sources, he does not prove that Rashi's polemical agenda developed specifically out of the eleventh and twelfth centuries rather than the historical context of Rashi's rabbinic sources.

The comparison between Rashi's commentary and the Glossa Ordinaria supplies new evidence not only for Touitou's argument that Rashi polemicizes against Christianity, but even for Baer's more extreme statement that polemical considerations are central to Rashi's thought. As Chapter 4 will show, a comparison of Rashi's commentary on Genesis 22 both to rabbinic exegesis of Genesis 22 and to the Glossa Ordinaria on Genesis 22 shows that Rashi reads the near-sacrifice of Isaac as a polemic against the "other" in a way that is not based on his sources and is parallel to the interpretation in the Gloss. Without specifically referring to Christianity, Rashi makes polemic against Christians one of the crucial points of this central biblical narrative. This polemic is Rashi's and not Talmudic or rabbinic. It is not part of a rabbinic polemic against all non-Jews but original to Rashi's commentary and developed in the context of Jewish–Christian polemic of the eleventh and twelfth centuries.

Polemic from the School of Laon: Pseudo-William's Dialogue and the Central Role of Genesis 22

Just as Rashi, coming out of the historical context of the late eleventh and early twelfth centuries, is more polemical than his sources, so too is the Gloss (also the product of a more polemtical context) more polemical than its sources. The Dialogus inter Christianum et Iudaeum de fide Catholica (ascribed to William of Champeaux) is an anti-Jewish polemic by an anonymous author from the school of Laon.[94] Although there is no evidence to connect it to Gilbert of Auxerre, the probable author of the Gloss on Genesis,[95] it was written during his time period, or close to it, by a monk of his school, and it reflects the Laon concerns with biblical exegesis as the center of Christian learning. This work was written between 1123 and 1148, after the composition of the first versions of the Gloss and during its early development. Therefore, not only was the Gloss on Genesis composed in the context of developing Jewish–Christian polemic, but the school that produced it also produced explicit anti-Jewish polemic.

The *Dialogus* is divided in half. The second half—which takes place after the Jew has accepted the arguments of the Christian, and is so not immediately relevant to our study—is a discourse on the subjects of free will, incarnation, and the fall. In the first half, however, the Christian viciously attacks Jewish belief and justifies Christian doctrine. Most of the attacks center on the Jew's inability to properly understand the Bible.

The dialogue opens with a long discussion of how to interpret scripture, both legal and narrative texts. Following a well-known metaphor from Gregory the Great,[96] the Christian compares scripture to a nut: One who eats it whole chokes, and one must crack the shell to consume the meat.[97] The biblical text, similarly, requires exegesis in order to make sense. For an example, the Christian teaches the Jew how to interpret Deuteronomy 18:15, which the Jew understands to be speaking of Joshua[98]:

> Si Moysi verba diligenter attenderes, procul dubio ista non diceres, tanquam me, inquis **prophetam vobis Dominus suscitabit**[99]; Josue legislator tanquam Moyses non fuit, sed tantummodo populum Dei in terram promissionis induxit; Christus autem novae legislator tanquam Moyses veteris exstitit, quia lex per Moysem data est, gratia autem et veritas per Jesum facta est, ipse audiendus et credendus est; et omnis eum non audiens de populo Dei exterminandus est: idcirco vos estis exclusi et remoti a Dei plebe, quia talem prophetam non vultis audire: vos inaniter Christum exspectatis venturum, et carnales ceremonias observatis, sed timendum est dum ipsum venisse non creditis et alium exspectatis, ut non ipsum sed alium suscipiatis.[100]

If you would diligently pay attention to the words of Moses, you certainly would not talk like that when you are with me. You cite "**The Lord will raise a prophet for you**," but Joshua was not a lawmaker like Moses, and only led the people of God into the promised land. Christ was the legislator of a new law, just as Moses was for the old. Since the law was given through Moses, but truth and grace were made through Jesus, he is the one who must be listened to and believed; and those of the people of God who don't listen to him must be destroyed. Therefore you are a people excluded and distant from God, because you are not willing to listen to such a prophet: you are foolishly expecting that the Messiah will come, and you observe physical ceremonies. But while you do not believe that the Messiah has come and await another, it must be feared that not you may receive not him, but another.

Pseudo-William here explains that Deuteronomy 18:15 could not possibly be referring to Joshua, because Joshua was not a lawgiver like Moses. The verse from Deuteronomy needs to be connected with a different part of the Bible—in this case, Christ as a new lawmaker—in order to make any sense at all. The application of reason to the biblical text inevitably demands a Christ-centered reading. The Jew who is unable to see this must be "not willing to listen," and therefore "distant from God," on which account he "must be destroyed."

This emphasis on reason, as Anna Sapir Abulafia has shown, is an innovation of twelfth-century polemicists, who responded to the challenges of newly recovered classical thought by positing that reason and Christian revelation inevitably led to the same conclusions.[101] This was intended to be inclusive of even pagan philosophers: all humans have reason and reason leads to the same conclusions as Christianity, therefore all humans can be Christian, even those to whom the revelations of Christ were not available. But it also led to the development of a new form of anti-Jewish argumentation that led to worse consequences than earlier Bible-based polemic. If Jews refuse to accept the truth of the revelation of Christ, it must be that they are willfully blind. If Jews are incapable of reason then they are not fully human. The *Dialogus*, Abulafia argues, provides evidence for the influence of the new style of argumentation even on polemicists still using the traditional biblical and patristic prooftexts.[102]

The *Dialogus* continues with other rational and biblical proofs for the truth of Christianity. For example, the Christian goes on to demonstrate that the internal and external must logically be connected in rituals such as baptism. The physical sign of baptism is necessary because the physical cannot be divided from the spiritual.[103] These proofs reach their culmination with the discussion between the Jew and the Christian regarding the near-sacrifice of Isaac in Genesis 22 and the subsequent promise to Abraham. Was Isaac the promised seed, or was Christ? The Jew asks:

Quid ergo allegorizas de Christo, quod non de ipso sed de Isaac et Salo-mone dici apertissime vides? . . . scripturas subripiendo pervertis, quon-iam tua fides verborum tuorum volubilitate circum circa rotatur.[104]

So what you allegorize about Christ—you must clearly see that it is not about him but about Isaac and Solomon. . . . You pervert scripture by stealing because your faith is turned by the whirling of your words around in a circle.

The Christian responds:

porro seminis Abrahae benedictio non in Isaac sed in Christo completa est, quoniam non per Isaac sed per Christum in omnes gentes larga Dei benedictio effusa est.[105]

Again, the blessing of the seed of Abraham was not completed in Isaac but in Christ, since not through Isaac but through Christ the great bless-ing of God was extended to all nations.

The blessing to Abraham, the Christian argues, makes no sense if it refers to Isaac. God blesses Abraham that **all nations** (Gen. 22:18) will be blessed through Abraham's seed. Isaac does not personally extend God's blessing to all nations. Therefore, someone else must be intended, and that someone is Christ.[106]

It is this exchange that wins the argument. Once the Christian can prove that he does not pervert scripture by stealing it (*nec etiam Scripturas sub-ripiendo perverto*)[107] but rather that his exegesis has the weight of logical inevitability behind it, the Jew is defeated and has nothing to do but ask to be instructed in doctrine.

Pseudo-William's arguments may hint at the reason that the Gloss on Genesis 22 does not distinguish between the different senses of scripture. For Pseudo-William, Christ-centered exegesis can be arrived at by reason. It does not require faith. It is simply the only possible way to read scripture. Therefore, there is no reason to separate it out into a distinct sense.

The new vehemence of this argumentation may also suggest some of the reason for the polemical emphasis of the Gloss.[108] We will see in the Gloss on Genesis 22 frequent reiteration of the theme of Jewish willful blindness. Pseudo-William's discussion of the irrationality of Jews shows some of the importance of this theme.

CONCLUSIONS

A number of important transitions took place in the late eleventh and early twelfth centuries. These years saw the growth of Jewish biblical exegesis in Northern Europe, in which Rashi was a pivotal figure. Christian biblical scholarship underwent a transition at the same time, from the more morally didactic approach of the monastic exegetes to the organized and systematic approach of the exegetes from the cathedral schools. Both Jewish and Christian exegetes developed a new interest in what came to be called literal interpretation of scripture. At the same time, the Jewish–Christian relationship was beginning to deteriorate. The legal evidence of papal protections and the narrative evidence of the Hebrew crusade chronicles all show Jews increasingly frightened of Christian violence. Christian anti-Jewish polemical literature also increased in volume during this time period, and began to include new genres such as the blood libel. The *Glossa Ordinaria* and the commentary of Rashi on Genesis 22 are transitional texts that can shed light on these shifts.

Given the deterioration of Jewish–Christian relations that took place during the time period of Rashi and of the Gloss, given the importance of the story of the near-sacrifice of Isaac in the Hebrew crusade narratives, and given school of Laon's own authorship of polemical literature, one would expect to find polemic in both commentaries on Genesis 22. Chapter four will show that these two commentaries do in fact interpret near-sacrifice of Isaac polemically and that they do so in similar ways. Chapter four will also show similarities in their approach to reading scripture that reflect their transitional position in the history of exegesis in Northern Europe.

The shared method of Rashi and of the Gloss, as we shall see, seems paradoxical: almost all their exegesis is based on earlier sources, and much of it is made up of direct quotations or (more often) close paraphrases of patristic, Carolingian, or midrashic sources. At the same time, their commentaries respond to contemporary developments in the Jewish–Christian relationship. The next two chapters will show how Rashi and the Gloss adapt and transform their source material to build out of pre-existing materials a commentary that responds to their own exegetical needs.

CHAPTER TWO

RASHI AND HIS SOURCES

R ashi and the Gloss both build on their rabbinic and patristic
traditions. This chapter, on Rashi, and the next chapter, on the
Gloss, will show that they both draw selectively on a range of
different sources and adapt them using a variety of strategies
to present their exegesis as arising directly from the biblical text. These
strategies of adaptation and change allow them to present themselves as in
continuity with their respective exegetical traditions.

At the same time, as these chapters will show, both commentaries represent themselves as reading the Bible as a self-glossing text: Difficult passages in one part of the Bible can be explained by reference to other parts of
the Bible, and no sources outside the Bible are necessary to understand it.
Paradoxically, the exegeses presented in Rashi and in the Gloss can be read
as an original and rational response to the biblical corpus as a whole and
also as an authoritative record of rabbinic or patristic opinion.

Rashi and the Gloss both build on their rabbinic and patristic traditions,
and these clear continuities have affected how contemporary scholars have
interpreted the central themes of these commentaries. Shaye Cohen, in his
attempt to prove that there is no anti-Christian polemic in Rashi's commentary on the Pentateuch, interprets Rashi's heavy reliance on midrash
as evidence that any polemic is that of the midrash, not Rashi.[1] Elazar
Touitou, who identifies a great deal of anti-Christian polemic in Rashi's
exegesis of the first six chapters of Genesis, describes Rashi as deriving this
polemic, as well as many of his other ideas, directly from rabbinic sources.[2]
Similarly, scholarship on the Gloss by Beryl Smalley,[3] Margaret Gibson,[4]
and Gillian Evans[5] has tended to emphasize its continuity with patristic
literature rather than its originality. However, the dichotomy between
originality and continuity is a false one for both Rashi and for the Gloss in
their commentaries on Genesis 22. Both draw on their respective sources,
and both arrange and adapt these sources in a way that responds to their
twelfth-century context.

Scholars of Rashi have had a consistent interest in his motives and method.[6] This chapter builds on their work and explores an alternative theoretical model that explains how originality and quotation function together in Rashi's commentary.

THE SOURCES OF RASHI ON GENESIS 22

Each of Rashi's comments on Genesis 22 has at least a partial parallel in an earlier, midrashic source. This is true whether he describes his comment as contextual/literal (פשוט) or midrashic. Rashi draws on diverse sources that were composed over nearly a thousand years. Rashi's main sources for his commentary on Genesis 22 are *Genesis Rabbah* and *Midrash Tanchuma*, but he does not follow the narrative of either of these sources and frequently quotes from them out of context. Rashi also uses the Babylonian Talmud as a source for alternative variants when he has a reason to prefer them, and takes isolated points from *Pirkei de Rabbi Eliezer*, the *Targum of Jonathan*, and *Midrash Bereshit Rabbati*. The *Targum of Onqelos* is his main source for translations, and is the only source he consistently cites by name in this chapter.

Genesis Rabbah, a midrashic collection edited in early fifth century Palestine,[7] is Rashi's most important source for his exegesis of Genesis 22. Rashi draws on *Genesis Rabbah* in 24 out of his 34 comments on the binding of Isaac.[8] Because of the extent of Rashi's reliance on *Genesis Rabbah*, the similarities and differences between his commentary and *Genesis Rabbah* can illustrate both the innovations and the continuities in Rashi's technique.

Genesis Rabbah expounds on the story of the binding of Isaac in chapters 55 and 56. Its exegesis of Genesis 22 is significantly longer than Rashi's commentary. In accordance with his method of using only midrash that "sets the words of the text in order" Rashi only cites a small part of it, but he follows the order of comments in *Genesis Rabbah* closely. But *Genesis Rabbah*'s preoccupations are different from those of Rashi. While *Genesis Rabbah* frequently focuses on a general principle which it derives by comparing Abraham's behavior to another's behavior, Rashi is only interested in the story at hand. Further, while *Genesis Rabbah* has Abraham confront God and even calls God's justice into question, Rashi does not. Instead, Rashi reads Abraham and Isaac as most intent on proving their own greatness, not to God, but to another being—human or angelic—who calls their virtue into question. So while Rashi takes much of his content from *Genesis Rabbah* he uses it for a very different purpose than *Genesis Rabbah* does.

Rashi's second most frequently used source, *Midrash Tanchuma*, is a homiletic midrash on the Pentateuch that was compiled in Palestine in the ninth century CE.[9] While exegetical midrash like *Genesis Rabbah* gives relatively short explanations of words and sentences, homiletic midrash is organized into homilies that use the biblical passage as a starting point for a wide-ranging and often lengthy discussion of themes and issues that may be only tangentially related to the passage in question. The *Midrash Tanchuma* organizes its comments on the binding of Isaac narrative into six homilies of various lengths in the standard recension.[10] Because Rashi's structure is so different from that of *Midrash Tanchuma*, he cites only small fragments of the larger homilies. Out of Rashi's thirty-four comments on Genesis 22, nineteen have a source in *Midrash Tanchuma*. Rashi does not make use of all of the homilies, though, but only of the first, fifth, and sixth of the six homilies on the binding of Isaac in *Midrash Tanchuma* Vayera 18–23.[11] In addition, six out of his nineteen *Tanchuma*-based comments quote from *Midrash Tanchuma* elsewhere. (A seventh has parallels both in this section and in another.) Most of Rashi's sources in *Midrash Tanchuma* also have parallels in *Genesis Rabbah*. Only five comments of Rashi's (1.2, 3.1, 9.1, 12.3, 13.1) are based exclusively on *Midrash Tanchuma*. Because *Genesis Rabbah* is exegetical while *Midrash Tanchuma* is homiletical, Rashi's truncations of *Midrash Tanchuma* take the specific points of exegesis out of the context of the larger homilies and rearrange them in a new context.

Rashi uses the Babylonian Talmud as a source of alternate versions of midrashic texts. All of Rashi's seven comments in Genesis 22 that have parallels in the Babylonian Talmud also have some parallels in *Genesis Rabbah* or *Midrash Tanchuma*. Of his seven comments that quote from the Babylonian Talmud, most are from the Tractate Sanhedrin: three (1.1, 2.1, 2.2) quote from b. Sanhedrin 89b and one (3.2) is from b. Sanhedrin 105b. Of the remaining two comments that have parallels in Babylonian Talmud, 2.3 has a parallel in b. Ta'anit 16a, 9.1 has parallels in b. Shabbat 54a and b. Tamid 31b,[12] and 14.3 has a partial parallel in b. Berachot 62b.[13]

Another source that Rashi uses much less frequently is *Pirkei de Rabbi Eliezer*. This late midrashic collection was written in the eighth or ninth centuries and includes references to Islam and Arab rule.[14] While many of Rashi's comments on Genesis 22 have parallels in *Pirkei de Rabbi Eliezer*, most of them appear in his main sources *Genesis Rabbah* or *Midrash Tanchuma* as well. There are only two of Rashi's comments on Genesis 22 that seem to be primarily sourced from *Pirkei de Rabbi Eliezer*. First, in 3.3, Rashi derives that Ishmael and Eliezer were the two lads/slaves to accompany Abraham and Isaac.[15] Second, in 13.4, Rashi derives that Satan was involved in entangling the ram in the thicket.[16] In both these cases Rashi relies on *Pirkei de Rabbi Eliezer* exclusively to introduce characters to the story which are not in the biblical text. While these three characters (Ishmael, Eliezer, and Satan) do appear in *Genesis Rabbah* and *Midrash Tanchuma*, Rashi uses the material from *Pirkei de Rabbi Eliezer* to expand their roles. As we will see, the expansion of the roles of these outsider characters is of central importance in Rashi's reading of the binding of Isaac narrative.

The Targum of Onqelos, Rashi's main source for linguistic information, is a continuous, complete translation of the Pentateuch into Aramaic. It was edited in Babylonia before the end of the fourth century CE and is based on an earlier version composed before 135 CE in Palestine.[17] Rashi quotes the Targum of Onqelos six times in his commentary on the Binding of Isaac, and it is the only source he cites explicitly, as Onqelos (2.3) or as *targum* [translation] (3.4, 13.2, 14.1).[18] In four of the six times Onqelos is mentioned, the material does not appear in any of Rashi's other sources. Rashi uses the Targum of Onqelos to define a difficult word in all six instances.

As is reflected in his commentary on Genesis 22, Onqelos is one of Rashi's most frequently quoted sources in his Pentateuch commentary.[19] Rashi gave his translation great weight, calling it in his Talmud commentary תרגום מסיני [a translation from Sinai],[20] by which he seems to mean that it accurately reflects the Oral Torah that was revealed at Sinai.[21] One of the reasons for its importance to Rashi was the practice of studying it alongside the Hebrew original, as was common in France and Germany. Copies of Onqelos were so readily available that many times Rashi simply directs the reader to him without quotation.[22]

Rashi quotes from medieval sources as well, including sources that predated him by less than a century. In comment 8.1, Rashi relies on the Targum of Jonathan ben Uziel, which was a late (eighth century or later)[23] Palestinian translation of the Pentateuch into Aramaic, to translate יראה

[will see] as יבחר [will choose]. He works this translation seamlessly into a comment with parallels in Genesis Rabbah 56.4 and Midrash Tanchuma 23. Rashi's most recent source in his commentary on Genesis 22 is Midrash Rabbati, which was written by Rabbi Moshe ha-Darshan [Rabbi Moses the Darshan, or expositor],[24] written in Narbonne in the first half of the eleventh century. Although Rashi does not mention him by name in this section, Rashi mentions him in his commentary on Numbers 15.41 and elsewhere.[25] Comment 9.1, which connects עקדה [akedah/binding] here with עקודים [akudim/striped] in Genesis 30.39, is based on the eleventh-century *Midrash Rabbati*.

We see, therefore, that Rashi used a wide range of midrashic sources that were composed over nearly a millennium. These sources all come from different historical contexts and approach the biblical text in different ways, and they all have different ways of understanding the story of the near-sacrifice of Isaac. The rest of this chapter will explore how Rashi refashioned these sources to fit his own approach to interpreting the near-sacrifice of Isaac the context of the twelfth century.

RASHI, MIDRASH, AND THE BIBLICAL TEXT

In her classic formulation of Rashi's method, Nechama Leibowitz argues that Rashi only quotes from midrash in order to answer questions that arise from the biblical text.[26] She bases this argument primarily on Rashi's methodological statements, for example, his comment on Genesis 3:8 states:

> יש מדרשי אגדה רבים וכבר סדרום רבותינו על מכונם בבראשית רבה ושאר מדרשים
> ואני לא באתי אלא לפשוטו של מקרא ולאגדה המישבת דברי המקרא ושמועו דבור
> על עפניו.[27]

There are many aggadic statements, which our Rabbis have already organized in *Genesis Rabbah* (and other places)[28] but I am only here for the literal meaning of the text [*peshuto shel miqra*] and for aggadah that explains the meaning of the words of the [biblical] text.

Based on this text, Leibowitz understands Rashi's method as carefully selecting midrashic comments that explain the literal meaning—that is, comments that answer questions that would arise naturally for any reader. Sarah

Kamin's alternative reading of the meaning of the roots פשט [*pst*] and דרש [*drs*] in rabbinic literature and in Rashi leads her to conclude that *peshuto shel miqra*, even in this passage, refers to the contextual meaning rather than the literal meaning.[29] *Aggadah hameyashevet divrei hamiqra* [*aggadah* that explains the meaning of the words of the [biblical] text], according to Kamin, does not mean midrash that makes sense of the words of the biblical text, but rather midrash that is consistent with the order of the words of the text.[30] She describes Rashi's method as compiling midrashic expositions that are consistent with (as in, not opposed to) the context and the order of the biblical verses. Rashi quotes from midrash when it is consistent with *either* the words *or* the order of the biblical text. The language of the biblical text drives Rashi's choice of which midrashic exegesis to incorporate, but Rashi does not quote midrashic texts in order to solve exegetical problems.

As we will see, the evidence of Rashi's use of midrashic sources in his commentary on Genesis 22 tends to support Kamin's critique of Leibowitz. Rashi often chooses between midrashic versions, each of which could equally answer questions about the biblical verse. However, the purely technical considerations of matching midrashic interpretations with the order of the words of the text also do not adequately explain Rashi's use of sources. Kamin's technical categories of *peshuto shel miqra* and *aggadah hameyashevet* are useful in most cases, but here they raise questions about specific comments (such as the second part of 3.3) that seem more interested in making a moral (or perhaps polemical) point than in connecting to the words or the order of words in the biblical text.

Unlike Kamin and Leibowitz, Yosefa Rachaman explains Rashi's selections of midrash at least occasionally on theological rather than technical or linguistic grounds, although she does still argue that Rashi's main principle for selecting midrashic material is "linguistic connectivity," or the closeness of the midrash to the language of the biblical text. Still, she allows for three non-linguistic principles that Rashi might use. Rashi, she argues, tends to prefer midrashic materials that connect different biblical narratives, that give a literary or psychological interpretation, or that solve a theological problem.[31] These non-linguistic reasons might better explain some of Rashi's exegetical choices in Genesis 22. Still, even Rachaman's list of reasons, encompassing all of Rashi's commentary on the Pentateuch, are too vague to provide a strong explanation of Rashi's reasons for including or excluding any particular midrashic quotation. While all of the midrashic quotations that Rashi incorporates in his commentary on Genesis 22 do fit into Rachaman's categories, much of the midrashic material from *Genesis Rabbah* and *Midrash Tanchuma* that Rashi omits could also fit into one of her categories. For example, Rashi regularly omits midrashic material that focuses on the connection between biblical narratives.

Kamin and Rachaman suggest that Rashi's methodological statements do not guide his choice of midrashic quotations, but his explications are not purposeless. The long list of methodological statements quoted by Leibowitz and Kamin would seem to suggest that Rashi had some interest in presenting his commentary as more closely connected to the words of the biblical text than that of his rabbinic sources. Rashi does not answer these questions or restrict his comments to exegesis of the literal or contextual meaning, but the claim that he does do these things is rhetorically effective: It adds the authority of the words of the biblical text to his moral, theological and polemical statements.

Leibowitz, Kamin, and Rachaman thus provide three alternative approaches to Rashi's relationship to his sources. Leibowitz argues that Rashi only quotes from midrash in order to answer questions that arise from the biblical text.[32] Kamin, conversely, describes Rashi's method not as answering questions but as collecting midrashic explanations that are consistent with the biblical verses. The language of the biblical text drives Rashi's choice of which midrashic exegesis to incorporate, but Rashi does not quote midrashic texts in order to solve exegetical problems. Rather, he is using a line-by-line commentary on the Bible as a mechanism by which to teach midrash.[33] Rachaman goes even further in suggesting that Rashi, at least at times, simply uses midrashic comments as source materials from which to construct his own theologically based exegesis. Rachaman's Rashi is teaching neither Bible nor midrash, but theology.

Does Rashi's commentary, then, teach Bible, midrash, or theology? Is it intended to lead the readers to seek answers about questions arising from the biblical text before them, or to delve into the richness of rabbinic tradition? Or, perhaps, to follow Rashi's lead in finding solutions to theological problems? What kind of reader is Rashi's commentary constructing? Rashi's ideal reader reads the layered commentary of recombined midrash worked into the language of the biblical text in terms of two possibly contradictory medieval assumptions about the biblical text: that the Bible is self-glossing, and that the Bible requires a layer of authoritative, inspired exegesis in order to be understood. Rashi's multilayered commentary, I will thus suggest in the next chapter, creates the same effect on the reader as the dual commentary of the marginal and interlinear gloss.

RASHI MANUSCRIPTS AND RASHI'S METHOD

Both Rashi's method and Rashi's conclusions shift over the course of the manuscript tradition, which makes it essential to consider the history of Rashi manuscript variants in thinking through the question of Rashi's theology. The early scribal interventions, I will suggest, give evidence for different early approaches to the question of Rashi's method in adapting midrash. The scribes' additions and subtractions show how they understand Rashi's pedagogical agenda, but these interventions transform that agenda by emphasizing certain questions, and certain answers to these questions, at the expense of others. The different manuscripts of Rashi's commentary therefore leave us with different approaches both to the relationship between the literal and midrashic sense and to theological issues such as the question of divine justice in the Abraham story.

The earliest definitively dated manuscript of Rashi's commentary on the Pentateuch is from 1233, nearly one hundred and twenty years after his death.[34] Nearly all other early Rashi manuscripts are from the fourteenth and fifteenth centuries and in the intervening time Rashi's commentary most likely underwent many changes. Students copying Rashi's comments added to the same page of text their own commentary, which could consist of relevant excerpts from the midrash or of their own original insights.[35] Sometimes these additional comments had some sort of notation to indicate that they were not from Rashi, but sometimes those symbols were omitted or lost over time.[36]

Some manuscript changes were introduced very early on by R. Shemaya, Rashi's student and scribe. Others seem to have been made by Rashi himself.[37] Rashi's grandson Rabbenu Tam (ca. 1100) wrote a lengthy discussion of permitted and forbidden corrections to address reported incidents in which students erased a text they deemed inaccurate and replaced them with their own.[38] A decree that was made in the eleventh century had tried to stop this practice by forbidding the correction of manuscripts[39] but clearly was only partly successful.

One way to bypass the problem of the nearly 120-year gap between Rashi and the first manuscript of his commentary is to look at manuscripts of Tosafistic commentaries. The Tosafot were students and descendants of Rashi who lived in Northern France in the twelfth and thirteenth centuries. Their exegetical works are all based on Rashi's, and they quote Rashi extensively as part of their commentaries. Their method is based on solving difficulties in Rashi, so unlike other copyists of Rashi manuscripts they would be disinclined to eliminate or alter difficult passages.[40] Manuscripts of Tosafistic commentaries are ideal for this project because of the textual discrepancies in the Tosafistic commentaries themselves. Once the text of Rashi's commentary shifted, the citations of Rashi in the Tosafistic commentaries reflect the later, corrupt version of Rashi with which a given copyist was familiar. Later in this chapter I will show how a Tosafistic commentary can give evidence of a variant reading.

For this study, I have examined thirty-one manuscripts of Rashi's commentary on Genesis 22.[41] Three examples of variant readings found in these manuscripts of Rashi's commentary on Genesis 22 illustrate scribal interventions. Some interventions overemphasize the continuity between Rashi and his midrashic sources. These interventions add midrashic stories that emphasize themes that are important to his main midrashic sources—*Genesis Rabbah* and *Midrash Tanchuma*—but are not otherwise reflected in Rashi's commentary on this chapter. Other interventions remove or change material that is taken from Rashi's midrashic sources but is not relevant to the biblical text under discussion. These add analyses intended to teach the reader how to ask questions of that particular verse.

One kind of manuscript diversity is shown by variation, not of the content but of the layout. Scribes had two kinds of layout for the text of Rashi's commentary. The most common is a simple manuscript of Rashi's commentary, without any other text attached. In the second layout, which appears in twelve manuscripts,[42] scribes arranged Rashi's commentary around a biblical text. Sometimes the scribes placed the commentary so that the comments fall near the biblical verses to which they refer. This arrangement would be logical if the reader is intended to refer back and forth between the commentary and the Bible and to use the commentary as a resource for answering questions that naturally arise when reading the biblical verse. In two manuscripts,[43] though, the scribe begins copying Rashi's commentary in the margins of a Bible, starting at the beginning and continuing on to the end without any attempt to connect the verse to the commentary—Rashi's commentary on Genesis 22 appears in these manuscripts alongside biblical passages in Numbers and Deuteronomy. The scribe here still sees a relationship between Rashi's commentary and the Bible, since he is copying Rashi's commentary into a Bible manuscript and not a manuscript of *Genesis Rabbah* or any other text, but the relationship is not verse-by-verse or even chapter-by-chapter. This layout prepares the reader to read Rashi's commentary not as a verse-by-verse commentary intended to answer questions but as an excursus on the Bible as a whole.

A second kind of manuscript variant is an addition that makes clear that the scribe understood Rashi's commentary to be guide to the Bible as a self-contained, self-interpreting text. An example of this kind of variant can be seen in the following comment, which appears in three manuscripts:

ר' יוסף ברבי שמעון פרש **אחר נאחז בסבך** שנקל לקחתו משם שאם נאמר וירא והנה איל ולא בסבך בקרניו היה נראה שצריך לחזר אחריו. וכך נהגי כל הכתובים על כל מילה שעתידין הבריות לחלק הוא מייתר הלשון ומיישר הדרך לפניהם.

Rabbi Yosef son of Rabbi Shimon explains: The verse says "**After [the ram] was caught in a thicket**" to show that it was easy to take. For if it had been written, "He saw, and there was a ram," without explicitly saying "caught by its thorns in a thicket," it would read as though he had to go back after it. This is the way of all Biblical texts: to prevent people from disputation in the future, it adds words and straightens the way before them.

This is the version from Oxford Bodeleian 190. It also appears in Oxford Bodleian 26 can. or. 62. In Oxford Bodeleian 195 (Opp. Add. 4 to 77) it is ascribed to R. Shimon, not to R. Yosef. "Yosef b. Shimon" most likely refers to R. Yosef ben Shimon Kara, or Joseph Kara, who lived from 1065 to 1135 and was a student of Rashi's. Still, it is integrated into Rashi's text rather than added in a supercommentary. This quotation does not have, as far as I was able to find, a midrashic source, which makes it the only comment in any version of Rashi's commentary on Genesis 22 to have no basis in midrashic literature. Rather, it is directed to guiding the reader in asking questions about the text. It tells the reader to look for extra words, and to identify possibilities for misunderstandings that these extra words might be there to eliminate.

Variants in Rashi manuscripts can suggest that Rashi's early readers, who participated with Rashi in the construction of his commentary, understood Rashi's own techniques of reading in different ways. Was Rashi condensing and adapting midrashic exegesis? Or, conversely, was Rashi pointing out questions that the midrash might answer? Was Rashi intending to teach midrashic theology (and theodicy) or to create his own theology using some midrashic materials? The different kinds of additions and interventions suggest opposite answers to these questions.

The diversity of Rashi manuscript variants also suggests the richness of the Rashi manuscript tradition, and the possibilities that open up when Rashi variants are viewed not as accretions to be stripped away but as part of the Rashi tradition. Rather than only one interpretation of the purpose behind the near-sacrifice of Isaac, the manuscript tradition gives us three. Rather than rejecting the questioning of God's justice, the manuscript tradition wavers on it. With its variant methods and even contradictory conclusions, the manuscript tradition can give us access to centuries of dialogue between the constructed and constructing readers of Rashi's commentary.

RASHI'S THEODICY, RABBINIC THEODICY

The story of the near-sacrifice of Isaac is a key location for rabbinic exegetes to examine the question of why God causes the righteous to suffer. Rashi's commentary constructs out of his sources a new answer to this question: It is not God but hostile others—human and satanic—who cause suffering, and God allows suffering as a way to prove the greatness of the righteous to these hostile others.

Yosefa Rachaman has already shown that Rashi makes substantive shifts in his citation of midrashic sources. She suggests that he changes his midrashic sources in accordance with his sense of realism (primarily about human motivations and emotions[44]), his moral concerns (Rachaman's examples point to Rashi's tendency to teach moral lessons through the actions of righteous people[45]), and his theology.

Rachaman's criteria cover all of Rashi's commentary on the Pentateuch in a very general way. But in Genesis 22 there are three specific theologically motivated thematic shifts. First, Rashi describes the purpose of the binding of Isaac as the proof of Abraham's righteousness to the world, and to a hostile "other" in particular, rather than to God or to the angels. Second, Rashi emphasizes the role of Satan as an accuser rather than as a tempter. Third, Rashi minimizes discussion of the question of theodicy by omitting all the midrashic comments that question God's morality in this chapter. These three shifts come together to create a coherent approach to the question of the suffering of the righteous, in which it is a hostile "other" and not God who is responsible for this suffering.

More Beloved than the Other Nations
Rashi describes the purpose of the binding of Isaac as a performance and polemic for a hostile audience. In addition to Satan, the audience includes "the nations of the world" or simply "the others." The role of the audience is one of Rashi's most important emphases in his commentary. He constructs this role by juxtaposing and building on quotations from *Genesis Rabbah* and *Midrash Tanchuma*, even though this theme is not explicit in either commentary. *Genesis Rabbah* 55.1 suggests the possibility that the purpose of the trial was to exalt Abraham, but omits an "other" for God to exalt Abraham (or Isaac) over. Similarly, "others" or "nations" are entirely absent as an audience in *Midrash Tanchuma*. *Genesis Rabbah* 55.4 and *Midrash Tanchuma* Vayera 18 mention the conversation between Isaac and Ishmael in which they argue about who is greater, but only as one possible motivation for the test among many. In both of these texts Ishmael is absent after this conversation. In *Pirkei de Rabbi Eliezer*, Rashi finds a source for Ishmael's presence as a silent witness, the son who is not chosen.

Rashi's source texts express hostility in different ways toward various non-Jewish communities. *Genesis Rabbah*, which was written in a Christianized Palestine in the fourth or fifth centuries,[46] has a polemic against the non-Jewish "other," but it is different from Rashi's. In *Genesis Rabbah* 56.5 God smites the angels of the idolaters above while the binding of Isaac is going on below. Comment 55.2 defines Mount Moriah as "the place where God teaches the nations and sends them to hell."[47] Although this is perhaps harsher toward the "other nations" than anything Rashi quotes, it is not one of the main themes in *Genesis Rabbah*'s exegesis of Genesis 22. Also, Rashi is not interested in seeing Gentiles sent to hell, or even in the possibility of their repentance. He is interested in their participation as witnesses to the binding of Isaac. The polemic here is about the superiority of Abraham, not about the evil of anyone else.

Pirkei de Rabbi Eliezer's commentary on Genesis 22 portrays Ishmael as an ambiguous character, but makes clear that he is not chosen by God.[48] One example of this is a conversation in which, though it makes clear that Abraham loves Ishmael, God explicitly clarifies to Abraham *not* to sacrifice Ishmael (describing him as "the son born before circumcision").[49] In his commentary on Genesis 22, Rashi derives only two details from *Pirkei de Rabbi Eliezer* that are not in *Genesis Rabbah* or *Midrash Tanchuma*. First, in 3.3, Rashi states that Ishmael and Eliezer were the two lads (or, depending on the translation, slaves) to accompany Abraham and Isaac.[50] Second, in 13.4, Rashi derives the idea that Satan was involved in entangling the ram in the thicket.[51] In both these cases Rashi relies on *Pirkei de Rabbi Eliezer* solely to introduce characters to the story that are not in the biblical text. While these three characters (Ishmael, Eliezer, and Satan) do appear in *Genesis Rabbah* and *Midrash Tanchuma*, Rashi uses the material from *Pirkei de Rabbi Eliezer* to expand their role. As we will see, the expanded role of these outsider characters is of central importance in Rashi's reading of the binding of Isaac narrative.

Rashi only uses *Pirkei de Rabbi Eliezer* in these few instances, and there are many fascinating stories in it that Rashi does not cite. *Pirkei de Rabbi Eliezer's* exegesis of Genesis 22 includes a story about Abraham's miraculously created donkey[52] and an argument between Ishmael and Eliezer about which one of them would be Abraham's heir after Isaac's death.[53] Out of these comments, Rashi only selects those relating to his point about the hostile "other" as witness.

By taking these two details from *Pirkei de Rabbi Eliezer* and interweaving them with *Genesis Rabbah* passages from Christian Palestine, Rashi blends texts in which Ishmael may have functioned as a stand-in for Islam with passages in which Ishmael may have functioned as a stand-in for Christianity. Writing in Christian Europe, Rashi quotes exegetical polemics against Islam to apply them to Christianity.

Rashi's commentary weaves together pieces from earlier commentaries that all have different polemical agendas. *Midrash Tanchuma* on Genesis 22 de-emphasizes the role of the "other." *Genesis Rabbah* is only occasionally and unsystematically polemical, and the polemic that is present is about destroying the other rather than (as in Rashi) turning the foreign nation into a witness. *Pirkei de Rabbi Eliezer* specifically affirms Isaac's chosen status over Ishmael and has no interest in any outside figure. Rashi brings this diverse material together into a reading of the Binding of Isaac as a polemical act that turns Satan, undefined nations and "others" into unwilling witnesses to Abraham's righteousness.

The Shifting Role of Satan and the Angels

The most hostile "other" is Satan, and Rashi transforms Satan into both an accusing figure and a witness. In *Genesis Rabbah, Midrash Tanchuma,* and *Bereshit Rabbati,* Satan is a tempter rather than an accuser. Satan is absent from the beginning of the story and from God's decision to test. In these midrashic collections, Satan first appears as a tempter during Abraham's three-day journey. He tempts Abraham to turn back, he tempts Isaac to resist his father, and (in *Midrash Tanchuma* Vayera 23) he kills Sarah by bringing her the news that Abraham is planning to sacrifice Isaac. In Rashi, Satan's role is as instigator and witness to the test. In Rashi's first comment on Genesis 22:1 Satan demands that God test Abraham, and in Rashi's third comment on Genesis 22:12—the climax of the story—God declares the success of the test an answer to Satan's doubt and an affirmation of Abraham's worth. Satan thus functions both as the instigator and the intended audience for the test.

Satan takes in Rashi's commentary the role which the more positively viewed "ministering angels" perform in *Genesis Rabbah, Midrash Tanchuma,* and *Bereshit Rabbati.* In *Genesis Rabbah* the angels wonder why Abraham did not sacrifice to God, just as Satan wonders in Rashi's version. But the ministering angels, as *Genesis Rabbah* describes them, are God's court who act together with God and not, as in Rashi, an opponent to whom God must prove a point. The angels appear again at the climax of the story, in *Genesis Rabbah*'s exegesis of verses 10–12. In 56.9 they appear as witnesses to the binding of Isaac and weep as Abraham takes the knife to kill his son. In Rashi's commentary, Satan appears at the beginning of the story and in his comment on verse 12, the same place where *Genesis Rabbah* describes the conversation between God and the ministering angels. But while the angels are sympathetic witnesses and intervene only to help Abraham, Satan is a hostile, accusing witness whose false denunciation of Abraham sets the test in motion.

Midrash Tanchuma Vayera 18, God uses the test of Abraham as a reason that it is good for humans to have been created. *Midrash Tanchuma* imagines a conversation in which, prior to creation, the angels ask why

God would create humanity, seeing how they are going to be sinful, and God answers that humans are worthy of being created because of the future righteousness of Abraham. Here the angels, like Satan in Rashi's commentary, have an accusing and adversarial role, but against all of humanity rather than specifically against Abraham or the Jews.

Rashi seems to derive Satan's role as an accusing rather than tempting figure from b. Sanhedrin 89b, where, as in Rashi, it is Satan who accuses Abraham. Because he chose the Babylonian Talmud version of this story, he includes Satan in his third comment on Genesis 22.12 to show that Abraham fulfilled the purpose of the trial by proving his greatness to Satan. Rashi's source for this reading—that "God knowing" means "God making known"—is *Midrash Tanchuma* Shlach 14, but this midrash does not give any information about the one to whom God is making things known. Satan is not present in this section of *Midrash Tanchuma* at all.

Although Rashi's depiction of Satan's role differs from that of most of his sources, the idea that Satan instigated the binding of Isaac is ancient. Its first appearance is in the book of Jubilees which is probably the earliest commentary on the binding of Isaac story, written in the second century BCE. In this story, a certain Prince Mastemah challenges God by saying:

Behold, Abraham loves Isaac his son, and he delights in him above all things. Bid him offer him as a burnt-offering on the altar, and you will see if he will do this command, and you will know if he is faithful in everything in which you try him. (Jubilees 18.16)

The same Prince Mastemah appears in the Qumran fragment 4Q225, also as the instigator of the test of Abraham. Although Rashi would not have encountered either of these texts, it is possible that he, Jubilees, and the Qumran fragment independently understood the test of Abraham in the context of the test of Job. As God tested Job to demonstrate his greatness to Satan, so too Satan (or Mastemah) must have instigated the test of Abraham. But while Job might serve as Rashi's textual support, for Rashi the theme of the binding of Isaac as a demonstration to a hostile "other" is central to his story. Satan was necessary to fulfill the role of the "other" who can be hostile even to God.

But the manuscript tradition shows that Satan appears in only one variant. Here is an alternative:

ש מרבותינו אומרים אחר שקטרגה מידת הדין ואמרה ...

Some of our rabbis say, after the attribute of justice accused him, saying . . .

In six Rashi manuscripts, the attribute of justice takes the place of Satan.[54] This seems to be a later shift since it is not attested in quotations from Rashi in any of the Tosafistic commentaries that quote this passage. This variant appears in manuscripts from the thirteenth through the fifteenth centuries—in other words, through the history of the Rashi manuscript tradition. It disappears, though, from the early printed editions, so it is lost after the fifteenth century. In this version, Rashi beginning his story with a conflict between God's attributes rather than with a hostile other to whom God has to prove Abraham's superiority.

If Rashi's commentary is intended to answer the question that arises from this verse alone—the question of what the "things" are that the story takes place after—the "attribute of justice" variant does this more effectively while introducing fewer additional characters. It is less effective at teaching midrash, however, since it introduces a concept—the divine attribute of justice—that is not present in any of *Genesis Rabbah*'s exegesis of the stories about Abraham. The "Satan" variant, on the other hand, teaches the reader to draw connections between different parts of the Bible, and to draw analogies between the test of Abraham and the test of Job. If the test of Job involves Satan, it is only logical that the test of Abraham would as well. In addition, it teaches the reader to read rabbinic literature synthetically, in a way that allows for a unified narrative to develop between *Genesis Rabbah* and the Babylonian Talmud.

The "attribute of justice" variant and the "Satan" variant therefore represent two alternative reading strategies which result in two completely different versions of the purpose behind Abraham's test. In the "Satan" version, the test of Abraham, like the test of Job, is intended to prove Abraham's greatness to a hostile, accusing other. In the "attribute of justice" version, it is God himself who is the audience. The Satan version works together with the named and unnamed others so central to Rashi's exegesis to make clear that, for Rashi, the impetus for this test is from a hostile source other than God.

Theodicy and the Testing God

The importance of the hostile "other" in Rashi's commentary replaces and obscures the midrashic importance of the theme of theodicy: that is, justifying God's seemingly unjust actions. *Genesis Rabbah* is consumed with the injustice of the binding of Isaac. The first four sections all respond to the same question: how does God justify testing and tormenting Abraham? The rabbis of *Genesis Rabbah* are severe in their criticism of God's actions. For example, *Genesis Rabbah* 55.3 accuses God of hypocrisy:

אמר ר' אבין לרב שמצוה לתלמידו וא' לא תלוה ברבית והוא מלוה ברבית

Rabbi Avin said, it is like a teacher who commands his student, saying, "Do not lend at interest," and he lends at interest.[55]

As this teacher tells his student not to lend at interest and lends at interest, so God commands "do not test God" (Deuteronomy 6:16) but still tests Abraham.

Genesis Rabbah gives other, alternative answers to the question of why God tests the righteous. For example, in 55.4 Abraham doubts himself and God tests Abraham in response to Abraham's own doubts. The implication is that God could justify testing and tormenting both Abraham and Isaac because they both asked to be tested. In 56.11 there is a story in which Abraham demands that God swear never to test him or Isaac again. It explains this oath with a disturbing parable: a king has ten children with his wife, and divorces her after each child. In time the ten children go together to the king and force him to swear not to divorce their mother again. The ten children of the parable represent the ten tests that God forced Abraham to undergo. This rabbinic depiction of God as a perverse, fickle husband shows how troubled the authors of *Genesis Rabbah* were by God's behavior towards Abraham.

Midrash Tanchuma also begins its interpretation of the story of the near-sacrifice of Isaac with a lengthy discussion of tests and testing, focused on the question of why God tests the righteous. This discussion occupies four of its six sermons on the chapter.

Despite the importance of the theme of theodicy in the rabbinic literature on this chapter, this theme does not appear in Rashi at all. Nowhere does it seem that Rashi is concerned about Abraham's suffering or angry with God for imposing it. Aharon Mondstein, noticing this discrepancy, has suggested that Rashi understood the binding of Isaac as justified punishment for Abraham's sin of not offering thanksgiving sacrifices to God.[56] Mondstein bases his reading on Rashi's first comment, which begins with a reference to Abraham's alleged guilt in not bringing offerings after Isaac's birth. Rashi's polemical emphasis, however, suggests another possibility. For Rashi, the question of why God tested Abraham has a very simple answer: to show his greatness to an "other," whether it is human or Satanic. God does not instigate the test, the "other" does. God's behavior is justified and the "other" is morally responsible. For Rashi, theodicy is not a question that applies to the near-sacrifice of Isaac because it is this "other," not God, who is responsible for the suffering of the righteous.

Rashi's theodicy developed over the course of the manuscript tradition. Here is an alternative interpretation that appears in two Rashi manuscripts (Ox-B 21 opp. add. 4to 47 early 13th cent and Oxford Corpus Christi 165) and is quoted in two manuscripts of Tosafistic commentaries (Ox-B 4154 and 269 Can Or. 23):

והאלוהים נסה את אברהם. יי צדיק יבחן.

And God tested Abraham. God will test the righteous.

Rashi's comment here is in its entirety a quotation from Psalms 11:5. In three of the four versions it continues with a close paraphrase of *Genesis Rabbah* 55.2 on Genesis 22.1, which explains that God tested Abraham like a flax-maker beats flax in order to strengthen it. In this interpretation the test isn't at all directed at a hostile other. Rather, it is intended to perfect Abraham's character. God tests Abraham because God tests the righteous to perfect them.

Conversely, a late a manuscript variant that appears in five manuscripts[57] and in the Rome printed edition presents this debate between Abraham and God:

אמר אברהם אני אשפך לפניך את שיחתי אתמול אמרת לי **כי ביצחק יקרא לך זרע** חזרת ואמרת **קח נא את בנך** עכשיו אתה אמר **אל תשלך ידך אל הנער** אמר הקב"ה **לא אחלל בריתי ומוצא שפתי לא אשנה** לא אמרתי שחתיהו אלא העליהו. איסיקיתיה אחתיה.

Abraham said, "Let me speak before you. Yesterday you said to me, '**For in Isaac will your descendants be called**.' Then you changed your mind and said, '**Take your son**.' Now you say, '**Do not send forth your hand** against the lad.'" The Holy One said, "**I will not profane my covenant nor will I change what I have already said.** I did not say 'kill him,' only 'bring him up.' You brought him up, bring him down."

In this variant we see a theme which is important in Rashi's two main sources—*Bereshit Rabbah* and *Midrash Tanchuma*—but is otherwise entirely absent in Rashi's commentary: the use of the story of the near-sacrifice of Isaac as a way to interrogate the question of God's justice and goodness.[58] The alternative, more common version of Rashi's commentary simply omits this conversation and therefore does not have Abraham challenge the justice of God's command.

In the Rashi manuscripts, therefore, we see three possible approaches to the question of the intended audience for Abraham's test: Satan, God's attribute of justice, and Abraham himself. The last is most consistent with *Genesis Rabbah*. The first is least consistent with *Genesis Rabbah*, and encourages the reader the most to draw connections between biblical verses. The first—the variant that includes Satan—is the only variant that persisted through to the printed editions.

In these variants, then, we see that even the early scribes had differing approaches to the purpose of Rashi's commentary. If Rashi's commentary is drawing on midrash to answer questions in the biblical text, it is appropriate for Rashi to come up with his own solution to the question of theodicy in the story of the near-sacrifice of Isaac. If, conversely, the purpose of Rashi's commentary is to fit midrash to the order of the biblical text, then Rashi should not have omitted the midrashic challenge to God's justice. The later manuscript variants, which reintroduce midrashic texts omitted by Rashi, show the struggle between Rashi's scribes and readers over the substantial difference between Rashi's theodicy and that of his sources. These variants attempt to retain in Rashi's commentary the rabbinic struggle with the justice of God's test and alternative explanations for it. These manuscript variants show all the more clearly Rashi's innovation in reading the near-sacrifice of Isaac as predominantly in response to, and caused by, a hostile, non-chosen other.

FROM MIDRASH TO COMMENTARY: RASHI AND THE MIDRASHIC STYLE

Rashi truncates his source materials and combines them with other midrashic texts to bring new themes to light and to deemphasize others. By truncating and recombining, Rashi eliminates two of the defining characteristics of the midrashic style: the drawing of connections between one biblical story and another and the attribution of each idea to a particular rabbi (or chain of rabbis). Each of these shifts, while they might seem technical, impacts the meaning of Rashi's commentary in ways that bear on our understanding of what Rashi meant by *peshuto shel miqra*, a literal or contextual approach to scripture.

Midrash, as James Kugel states, is exegesis of verses rather than books or stories.[59] The proper midrashic context for interpreting any verse is all of scripture, rather than merely the story, chapter or book that contains the verse. Rashi, as a commentator building on the midrashic tradition, interprets the binding of Isaac as its own narrative and adapts midrash in a way that disconnects it from other stories. *Genesis Rabbah, Midrash Tanchuma*, and the Babylonian Talmud, in their exegeses of Genesis 22, are as interested in other stories as they are in this one, as long as they can connect these other stories to the verse in question. By excluding exegesis of passages other than the binding of Isaac, Rashi shows that he considers each story to be a discrete unit that he can consider and cite separately.

Frequently, a given passage in *Genesis Rabbah* focuses on a general principle which it demonstrates by comparing Abraham's behavior to another's behavior. This principle is *Genesis Rabbah's* primary concern, while verses from Genesis 22 (as well as from elsewhere in scripture) serve as proof for the principle. In quoting these comments from *Genesis Rabbah*, Rashi generally quotes only what is relevant to the verse at hand. For example, in 3.2, Rashi comments that Abraham saddled his donkey himself because אהבה מקלקלת את השורה [love breaks down the normal order of doing things]. *Genesis Rabbah* 55:8 is a comparison of Abraham and Balaam, who both saddled their own donkeys. It explains this similarity by the principle that both love and hate disturb the שורה [normal order of things]. Rashi does not mention Balaam or hate, but only points out the strangeness in Abraham's behavior and explains that love makes people act strangely.

Rashi's third comment on Genesis 22:3 is another instance in which his commentary ignores broader midrashic discussions to focus on the biblical story at hand. *Genesis Rabbah*, Rashi's main source in this passage, compares the actions of Abraham and Saul, explaining that Abraham behaved properly did here just as Saul did when he took two men with him on his visit to the woman of Ein-dor (*Genesis Rabbah* 55.8). Rashi restricts his discussion to Abraham. *Genesis Rabbah* 55.5 compares Abraham to Mesha, king of Moab who also sacrificed his son and Rashi does not make this connection anywhere in his commentary on Genesis 22.

The homiletical technique of *Midrash Tanchuma* brings many biblical texts together to make a point. Like *Genesis Rabbah* it contains many references to other stories omitted by Rashi. Rashi's selection from *Midrash Tanchuma* also reflects his interest or lack of interest in specific homiletical points. Homilies 19–21 compare Abraham with other figures to explore the idea of the testing of the righteous. Rashi has his own approach to this topic, and does not draw on these homilies at all.

However, Rashi draws on *Midrash Tanchuma's* exegesis of biblical passages outside of Genesis. For example, in comment 12.3, Rashi writes:

כי עתה ידעתי. מעתה יש לי מה להשיב לשטן ולאומות העולם התמהים מה היא חיבתי
אצלך, יש לי פתחון פה עכשיו שרואים **כי יראה אלהים אתה.**

Now I know. Now I have something to answer Satan and the nations of the world who wonder about my love for you. I have something to say, now that they know **that you fear God.**

The source for this comment is *Midrash Tanchuma* Shlach 14 on Numbers 15.1, where it is part of a very involved interpretation of the words **Go and eat your bread because God is already pleased with your deeds** from Ecclesiastes 9:7.

The passage from *Midrash Tanchuma* is as follows:

לפיכך פתח רבי חנינא, **לך אכול בשמחה לחמך וגו'** (קהל' ט ז). מהו כי **כבר רצה
אלהים את מעשיך** (שם). כיצד הפסוק מדבר. כנגד אברהם. בשעה שאמר הקדוש ברוך
הוא לאברהם, **קח נא את בנך את יחידך** (בראשי' כב ב), השכים אברהם, נטלו בזריזות
והוליכו והעלהו להר המוריה. אמר לו הקדוש ברוך הוא, **אל תשלך ידך אל הנער.** אמר
אברהם לפני הקדוש ברוך הוא, רבונו של עולם, לחנם אמרת לי, **קח את בנך.** אמר לו,
לאו, אלא להודיע טבעך בעולם, שנאמר: **כי ידעתיו וגו'.**

Therefore, Rabbi Haninah said, **Go and eat your bread etc.** (Ecclesiastes 9:7). What does it mean? **For God is already pleased with your deeds** (ibid.). What is the verse discussing? Abraham, at the time that God said to Abraham **take your son, your only son** Abraham rose early, took him eagerly and let him and brought him up to Mount Moriah. God said to him **do not send forth your hand against the boy.** Abraham said before God, "Master of the World, was it for nothing that you said to me, **take your son**?" He [God] said, "No. Rather, it was to let your nature be known in the world, as it is said: **for I have known you**" (Gen. 18.19).

Rashi derives from this passage the idea that "to know" means, "to show," in this case God showing to the world. He removes the context of Ecclesiastes and strips out the conversation between Abraham and God.

Rashi adds his own ideas to his quotation from *Midrash Tanchuma*. First, he introduces the idea of God's love for Abraham, ("my love for you" in comment 12.3) which, as Michael Signer points out, is one of Rashi's most important themes in his exegesis of the story of the near-sacrifice of Isaac.[60] But here, as elsewhere this theme appears, it is in conjunction with proving Abraham's greatness to someone else: Satan and the nations of the world. Rashi adds both Satan and the theme of God's love to the passage from *Midrash Tanchuma*.

Comment 12.3, therefore, illustrates Rashi's technique in adapting *Midrash Tanchuma*. He takes specific excerpts from larger homilies and weaves them together with his own ideas to make a different point than that of the original homily. By doing so he obscures the influence of *Midrash Tanchuma* and emphasizes his own role as an autonomous reader of the Bible.

Orality and Diversity

As Talya Fishman has shown, in the eleventh and twelfth centuries European Jewry was undergoing a process of "textualization," a shift from an oral culture to a written one.[61] Rashi himself consciously presented the written Talmud as primarily a record of its original, preferable oral form. As he writes in his Talmud commentary, "Mishnah and Gemara are finer [i.e. more desirable] than [the Bible] because they are dependent on oral recitation and are susceptible to being forgotten. For in their days, the Gemara was not in writing, nor was it permissible to write it."[62] At the same time, as Fishman demonstrates, Rashi's commentary on the Talmud both resulted from and contributed to this shift from oral to written culture by making it possible for a solitary reader to encounter the Talmud unaided.[63] Indeed, his commentary removes many markers of orality from its midrashic sources.

The transition from oral to written culture can also be seen in Rashi's midrashic sources themselves. Midrash represents itself as the written form of an oral literature. All of Rashi's midrashic sources attribute each statement to a specific rabbi, often to a specific rabbi quoting another rabbi, using the formula "Rabbi X said in the name of Rabbi Y." Midrash also appears in a question-and-answer structure (in e.g. *Genesis Rabbah*) reminiscent of an oral formulation, though Rashi removes this feature of midrash from his paraphrase.[64] For example, in comment 6.1 Rashi draws on *Genesis Rabbah* 56.3: "Rabbi Hanina said, 'Why is a knife called מאכלת [*maʾachelet*][65]? Because it prepares food.'" Rashi omits the question and paraphrases the answer as "[the knife] prepares meat for eating." The question-and-answer format creates the illusion of conversation, and when Rashi eliminates the question he removes a marker of orality. Rashi, in his truncation of midrashic comments, excludes most of the signs with which these midrashic sources mark themselves as the written record of an oral tradition. Martin Jaffee has argued that the representation of orality is an ideological construct in rabbinic literature, which the rabbis developed in the third and fourth centuries CE in order to establish their authority in the face of Christian and Greco-Roman challenges.[66] The removal of these markers from Rashi's commentary is consistent with the shift from oral to textual culture.

Another marker of orality that Rashi removes is the implied dialogue between different rabbinic opinions presented in late antique rabbinic texts. Rashi often combines different midrashic ideas in one comment, but does not call attention to the contradiction, nor does he place his sources in dialogue. Some sets of divergent opinions come entirely from *Genesis Rabbah*, but Rashi also freely melds ideas or language from multiple rabbinic texts. Sometimes he calls attention to his use of multiple interpretations through the use of דבר אחר [another explanation], or simply through the conjunction ו [and]. While דבר אחר calls attention to the possibility that the multiple interpretations might not be consistent, ו does not. For example, Rashi's two interpretations of the word מאכלת are based on *Genesis Rabbah* 56.6. One of these interpretations is brought in the name of R. Hanina and the other in the name of the Rabbis, which indicates that *Genesis Rabbah* saw them as inconsistent and in debate. Rashi joins these two options with a דבר אחר. In his second comment on Genesis 22.2, though, Rashi cites *Genesis Rabbah* along with b. Sanhedrin 89b, and joins the two comments using ו. Rashi on Genesis 22.2 explains the repetition of Abraham's name was necessary so that "[Abraham] would not go insane, and in order to make the command beloved to him." The first part of the explanation is from the b. Sanhedrin 89b, the second is from *Genesis Rabbah* 39.9 and 55.7.

As Jack Lightstone has shown, one function of the attributional formulae in the Babylonian Talmud is to highlight the multivocality of the text.[67] The Talmud will quote multiple opinions in the name of different Rabbis, and then create an imaginary dialogue in which the Rabbis defend their positions. This discussion is as important as any conclusion which might be reached. Rashi juxtaposes interpretations without any sources attached: neither names of Rabbis nor names of midrashic texts.[68] This invites the reader to read these comments as a single, unified text, not as orally stated opinions for scholars to debate. By merging passages from multiple midrashic sources without naming any of them, Rashi encourages the reader to see all of rabbinic literature on Genesis 22 as a unified whole.

BIBLICAL VERSES AND THE BIBLE AS A SELF-GLOSSING TEXT

Rashi quotes nine biblical verses from other chapters in his commentary on the binding of Isaac. These are (in the order that Rashi quotes them): 2 Chronicles 3:1 (the building of the Temple on Mount Moriah), Genesis 12.1 (God's command to Abraham to leave his land), Jonah 2.3 (from Jonah's prayer), 2 Samuel 19.18 (about crossing—or splitting—the Jordan), Genesis 15.5 (God's promise to Abraham that his descendants would be like the stars), Deuteronomy 32.42 (a line about a sword consuming flesh), Genesis 30.39 (on the striped markings on Laban's sheep), Genesis 21.12 (God's promise that Abraham's descendants will be through Isaac), and Psalms 89.35 (God's promise not to lie). Three of these nine quotes are from elsewhere in the Abraham story and have obvious relevance, but some others have a much murkier connection to the binding of Isaac. Rashi generally bases himself on his midrashic sources in making connections between the near-sacrifice of Isaac and verses found elsewhere in the Bible, but not always: In his fourth comment on verse three Rashi makes a connection between Abraham splitting logs and David crossing (or splitting) the Jordan without a midrashic source.

Rashi is clear and explicit about his quotations from other biblical books, and indeed he bases his commentary more on the juxtaposition of biblical verses than on midrash. He quotes biblical texts word for word and expects the reader to know his references, a very different treatment from his loose, unsourced paraphrases of rabbinic texts. By quoting so extensively and so clearly from biblical verses, Rashi substantiates his claim to be writing *peshuto shel miqra*, the literal or contextual sense of scripture. He justifies his exegesis, not through its midrashic sources, but by its close connection to the biblical text as a whole. His extensive juxtaposition and citation of biblical verses allows the reader of his commentary to imagine the Bible as a self-glossing text, even in the presence of constant quotations from rabbinic exegesis.

CONCLUSIONS: RASHI'S METHODS OF ADAPTING MIDRASH

Rashi's commentary blends together a wide range of prior commentaries, each written in a different time and context, and he uses each of his sources selectively. No source is quoted in full. Even most of *Genesis Rabbah*, the source he quotes most frequently, is omitted. There is no consistent pattern to his choices between interpretations from different sources. Within one comment or explanation, he incorporates material from multiple midrashic sources, and these details are selected based on thematic considerations rather than the authority of one midrashic collection over another.

The differing authority of different rabbinic texts is, however, seen in Rashi's citation practices. A reader of Rashi might imagine the Targum of Onqelos to be Rashi's main source, since it is the only one he names consistently. A reader familiar with rabbinic literature would also notice the absence of named rabbis, so important in midrashic literature, and could conclude that Rashi's commentary is less a compilation of a once-oral rabbinic tradition than original exegesis of the biblical text.

The corpus of rabbinic literature, for Rashi, is one unified (or unifiable) canon. Rashi juxtaposes quotes from diverse sources to create an original idea or emphasis. This creative juxtaposition of material allows Rashi to tell the story of the binding of Isaac in a way that is different from that of any of his sources. While *Genesis Rabbah* and *Midrash Tanchuma* question God's justice in testing Abraham, Rashi understands Abraham's test as polemical against an outside witness. Rashi, unlike his midrashic sources, interprets this story absolutely and does not quote midrashic material that connects this story to other stories (except in the case of the Temple sacrifices, which will be discussed in the fourth chapter). Rashi eliminates markers of orality and debate, as well as markers of tradition, and instead presents scripture as a self-glossing text, with rabbinic exegesis being no more than a tool for answering questions.

CHART OF RASHI'S MAIN SOURCES

	GEN. RAB.	TANCHUMA	PIRKEI DE RABI ELIEZER	TALMUD BAVLI	ONQELOS[69]	BIBLE VERSES	OTHER[70]
1.1 אחר הדברים	55.4 (varies significanly in one version.)	18 (varies significantly, R follows others)		Sanh. 89b			
1.2 הנני		22					
2.1 קח נא	55.6	22		Sanh. 89b			
2.2 את בנך	39.9 55.7	22	31	Sanh. 89b			
2.3 ארץ המריה	55.7			Taanit 16a	X	2 Chr. 3.1	
2.4 והעלהו	56.8						
2.5 אחר ההרים	55.7 39.9					Gen. 12.1 Jonah 3.2	
3.1 וישכם		22		[71]			

					Sanh. 105b			Yonatan ben Uziel
3.2 ויחבש	55.8							
3.3 את שער ראשו	55.8	Emor 2 Balak 8	31					
3.4 הרקיע					X		2 Sam. 19.18	
4.1 ביום השלישי	55.6	22						
4.2 וירא את המקום	56.1	23	31					
5.1 עד כה	56.2	23					Gen. 15.5	
5.2 ונשתחוה	56.2	23						
6.1 הנאבקה	56.3	23			X			
6.2 וילכו שניהם יחדיו	Interpretation of sources below. Much of the comment is original to Rashi.							
8.1 ותאר לו אשה	56.4	23						

CHART OF RASHI'S MAIN SOURCES (CONTINUED)

	GEN. RAB.	TANCHUMA	PIRKEI DE RABI ELIEZER	TALMUD BAVLI	ONQELOS[69]	BIBLE VERSES	OTHER[70]
9.1 ויעקב		23		Shabbat 54a Tamid 31b (closer parallel than Tanchuma)		Gen. 30.39	Bereshit Rabbati p.141
11.1 אברהם אברהם	56.7	43					Tosefta Berachot c. 1 Torat Kohanim Vayikra c.1 (earlier, but add nothing to other sources)
12.1 אל תשלח	56.7						
12.2 כי עתה ידעתי	56.8 (manuscript has variants like Rashi)	23				Gen. 21.12 Gen. 22.2 Psalms 89.35	

12.3 כי שתה ישעתי		Shlach 14				
13.1 הנה אל		Shlach 14 23				
13.2 אתה				X		
13.3 כסבך				X		
13.4 בקרבי	56.9		31			
13.5 החת כבו	56.9	Shlach 14				
14.1 ה יצאו				X		
14.2 אשר יאמר הים	The idea that 'This Day' refers to the future (also in 14.3) is original to Rashi.					
14.3 היום	56.10	23		Berachot 62b		
17.1 בדבר אבקנו	56.11					
17.2 הההבת אתה	56.11					

CHART OF RASHI'S MAIN SOURCES (*CONTINUED*)

	GEN. RAB.	TANCHUMA	PIRKEI DE RABI ELIEZER	TALMUD BAVLI	ONQELOS[69]	BIBLE VERSES	OTHER[70]
19.1 וראה שתי אדרים בצאן ישראל	54.6					21.34	
total: 34 comments	24 (7)	19 (5)	4	9	6		

CHAPTER THREE

THE SOURCES AND

MANUSCRIPT EVOLUTION

OF THE *GLOSSA ORDINARIA*

ON GENESIS 22

The *Glossa Ordinaria*, like Rashi's commentary, is a carefully constructed commentary in which every nearly comment has an earlier source. The *Glossa Ordinaria* on Genesis 22, like Rashi's commentary, truncates, paraphrases, and rearranges it sources to give the impression of unified authorship. Both Rashi and the *Glossa Ordinaria* blur the lines between continuity and change, and between tradition and originality.

The nature of the source material and the unevenness of the resources available necessitate a different treatment of Rashi and the Gloss. Because many early and late manuscripts of the Gloss have been preserved it is possible to trace its development and to compare early and late versions. The two recensions of the Gloss and the differences between them allow us to see the results of half a century of scribal intervention.

This composite nature of the Gloss has always made its authorship difficult to locate. The dramatic changes in the *Glossa Ordinaria* on Genesis 22 from manuscript to manuscript further complicate the question of authorship. Gibson writes that "Jerome, Bede, and Rabanus [Maurus] wrote it—but inadvertently"[1] because of the importance of both their commentaries and Jerome's Vulgate translation to the Gloss. E. Ann Matter writes of the authorship of the Gloss that "one could say that Jerome, Bede, or Hrabanus are the 'authors,' even though the text came together centuries after their deaths."[2] Rabanus deserves special emphasis as one of the inadvertent authors of the Gloss on Genesis 22, since the earliest version of the marginal gloss seems to have been taken nearly word-for-word from his commentary. Gilbert of Auxerre most likely also had a formative role in the construction of the earliest recension of the Gloss,[3] though he shared authorship of the final version with the many scribes who were involved in its transformation over the course of its manuscript history. Therefore, this chapter will examine the construction of the Gloss on Genesis 22 through the patristic and Carolingian authors, through Rabanus' redaction of them, and through the first and second twelfth-century recensions of the Gloss.

For the Gloss, tradition and continuity were as important as creativity and originality. As Lesley Smith writes:

> Beryl Smalley has shown that novelty—something that our own age prizes extraordinarily highly—was looked upon with suspicion, and instead tradition and continuity were enormously valued. And yet there was change; the intellectual life of the twelfth and thirteenth centuries thrived on it. The question, as at all times, was rather how change was to be negotiated and presented, and what it was thought or claimed to be based on.[4]

The importance of tradition did not at all mean that originality and change were impossible. Rather, change was thought to be additive rather than transformative, building upon tradition rather than overhauling it. As Matter describes it, the Gloss is "a particularly good example of medieval intertextuality, the conscious borrowing and re-articulating of old material in a new form."[5] The Gloss draws on patristic and Carolingian tradition while rearranging and adapting it to create something new.

The *Glossa Ordinaria* is made of two glosses, the marginal and the interlinear. The marginal gloss consists of lengthy quotations from patristic or Carolingian authors, and these are sometimes attributed. The interlinear glosses are much shorter—occasionally only one or two words—and while they often are influenced by patristic tradition they never cite a source. The very layout of the marginal and interlinear glosses suggests two alternative sources of meaning and authority: The marginal glosses record tradition and see it as authoritative, while interlinear glosses seem to come directly out of the biblical text. Even the layout of the gloss shows tradition and autonomous reading of scripture leading to the same conclusion.

The earliest version of the marginal Gloss on Genesis 22 seems to have been taken from the ninth-century commentary of Rabanus.[6] This text was used as a basis for further comments. Before the mid–twelfth century, marginal gloss manuscripts always left room for additional comments. Later manuscripts of the Gloss on Genesis 22 added fragments of Alcuin's commentary on Genesis to the marginal gloss. They also edited and re-organized the existing commentary to the point that in its latest form (as represented by the Rusch edition) the influence of Rabanus is not recognizable. The editors of even the tradition-steeped marginal gloss were interested in more than simply preserving and canonizing earlier exegesis. Rather, the Gloss was, at least in its early stages, a dynamic document that could be adapted for different needs.

The interlinear glosses do not cite sources and are not quotations from any earlier text (with the single exception of quotations from the Bible). Many of the ideas in them are taken from patristic or Carolingian authors, but they have been adapted and rearranged by the glossators. Interlinear glosses, like marginal glosses, sometimes date from later manuscripts. The interlinear gloss, like the marginal gloss, balances between continuity and change.

To show the evolution of the Gloss, this chapter will refer to two representative manuscripts. Manuscript A, the base manuscript of the critical edition in the appendix, represents the Gloss in its most influential mid-twelfth-century recension. Manuscript G, which is most likely the earliest manuscript represented in the critical edition, represents a less common but earlier recension.[7] Other manuscripts will be mentioned as needed.

ON READING THE MARGINAL AND INTERLINEAR GLOSS

The *Glossa Ordinaria* is in some ways a double commentary. The marginal and interlinear glosses have different methods of adapting sources and tend to have different emphases. Marginal glosses tend to be relatively close paraphrases or even quotations from patristic or Carolingian texts and sometimes cite their sources, but interlinear glosses are either not based on earlier sources or are very loose paraphrases of sources that they do not cite. Similarly, the marginal and interlinear glosses on the same passage can approach the passage in very different ways. The interlinear gloss tends to be Christological and philological, while historical discussions tend to be confined to the marginal gloss.[8] Michael Signer has shown that in the *Glossa Ordinaria* on the story of Joseph, the interlinear gloss consistently has a more anti-Jewish slant than the marginal gloss.[9] Although both glosses describe Joseph as a figure of Christ, and his brothers as the Jews who killed him, the interlinear gloss consistently repeats this identification and ascribes the Jews' motivation in killing Jesus to simple cruelty.[10]

On the other hand, as far as we can tell the marginal and interlinear glosses were intended to be read together. As Beryl Smalley has shown, no *Glossa Ordinaria* manuscript has ever been found that does not have both the marginal and interlinear glosses.[11] Although earlier tradition had attributed the marginal gloss to Strabo and the interlinear gloss to Anselm of Laon, following Migne, current scholarship has generally treated them as one commentary.[12]

The reader of the *Glossa Ordinaria* encounters the interlinear gloss at the same moment as the biblical text. The glosses are present in the center column, and while they are distinguishable from the words of the Bible through their slightly smaller script size,[13] they read as a continuation of it. The interlinear gloss will often use case endings that make the comment read as a continuation of the Vulgate text rather than as a commentary on it. For example, the third interlinear comment on Genesis 22:12 reads *obedientam meam* [my obedience], which can be only understood as a substitution of those words for the Vulgate's *propter me* [for me].[14] These strategies allow the reader to experience the interlinear gloss as a continuation of the biblical text.

The experience of reading the marginal gloss is that of reading a text surrounded by authoritative, integrated, ancient commentary. The irregular citation of names gives the impression that most of the sources are patristic, and that Jerome is the main source. In fact Isidore is the most quoted source, at least in the final recension, and the marginal gloss is shaped by the influence of Rabanus, but this is obscured by the consistent citation of Jerome, the infrequent citation of Isidore, and the total absence of citations of Rabanus. Reading the marginal gloss together with the interlinear gloss the reader is thus struck by the way in which ancient, authoritative interpretation blends seamlessly with exegesis that arises directly from between the biblical lines.

SOURCES OF THE INTERLINEAR GLOSS

The interlinear gloss on Genesis 22 consists entirely of anonymous comments. Some are loose paraphrases of earlier authors, but they are never attributed to a particular source, and are never direct quotations.[15] In the very few cases in which there is an attribution in an interlinear gloss it is because it has moved from the marginal gloss.[16] The interlinear gloss does quote directly from elsewhere in the Bible, in particular from the New Testament. These New Testament quotations often support Christological readings, which are more common in the interlinear than in the marginal gloss.[17]

Interlinear glosses frequently paraphrase or adapt material that is in earlier sources in a way that makes it difficult to identify precisely the source for each comment, especially since some comments have vague parallels in multiple sources. Sometimes the interlinear gloss paraphrases loosely and adapts the same material that the marginal gloss quotes directly or paraphrases closely.[18] For example, in explaining the meaning of Abraham's test, the first marginal gloss on Genesis 22 paraphrases Augustine:

> Aug. Jacobus dicit quod **neminem tentat deus** sed usualiter tentare pro eo quod est probare dicimus. Jacobus autem dicit de ea tentatione qua quisque peccato implicatur. Unde ne **forte tentaverit vos is que tentat.** Alibi enim scriptum est: **Tentat vos deus vester, ut sciat si diligantis eum,** id est, vos scire faciat. Vires enim dilectionis suae homo ignorat nisi experimento cognoscat.

> Augustine. James says that **God does not test anyone** (James 1:12) but usually we say "to test" when what we mean is "to prove." James, however, speaks only about a test in which someone is implicated in a sin. Whence: **Lest by chance he who tests should test you** (1 Thess. 3:5). Elsewhere it is written: **Your God may test you, that he may know if you love him.** (Deut. 13:3) That is, that he may cause you to know. A man is unaware of the strength of his love for him, unless he should know it through experience.

In the earliest recension (manuscripts G, B, and L) the first interlinear comment on Genesis 22 paraphrases only the conclusion:

> [Tentavit] ut notificaret ei eius perfectionem quam ipse ignorabat.

> [He Tested] in order to make known to him [Abraham] his perfection, of which he himself was unaware.

Most manuscripts in the later recension[19] add the word *non,* so that the last phrase becomes *quam ipse non ignorabat,* of which he himself was not unaware. This addition changes the antecedent of *ipse* from Abraham to God. Rather than saying that God tested Abraham because Abraham was unaware of his own righteousness, it now emphasizes that God tested Abraham even though God was aware of Abraham's righteousness. The first interlinear gloss in these manuscripts has become less a paraphrase of Augustine and more of a new idea.

In the previous case the marginal gloss on the same verse makes it likely that Augustine was the inspiration for the interlinear comment, but in most cases the relationship between an interlinear comment and its possible source is much looser. For example, the fourth interlinear comment on Genesis 22:2 describes the sacrifice of Isaac as *signum holocausti veri* [a sign of the true sacrifice]. One could, perhaps, connect this to the lengthy description of the parallels between the binding of Isaac and the crucifixion, as described in detail in the marginal gloss based on Isidore. But if so this comment is very far removed from the source.

Of the fifty-nine interlinear comments that appear exclusively in the interlinear gloss, eight[20] are related to earlier commentaries that are quoted or paraphrased in marginal glosses. Of those eight comments, one is related to Augustine (paraphrased in 1.1i and 14.1i) and the rest seem inspired by Isidore. Only 1.1i based on Augustine and 6.1i based on Isidore seem close enough to assume any relationship between them, and even in those cases the interlinear glosses are not direct quotations.

The interlinear gloss, therefore, adapts rather than quotes its sources. Even when the idea in an interlinear comment can be traced to an earlier source, the language of the interlinear gloss tends to be original. Often, however, interlinear glosses have no traceable source at all.

Biblical Quotes in the Interlinear Gloss
The interlinear gloss on Genesis 22 does not directly quote its sources, but it does quote verses from elsewhere in the Bible. In the interlinear gloss, biblical verses tend to appear either on their own as an entire gloss or else with a very short introduction. (The marginal gloss, as opposed to this, tends not to quote biblical verses on their own but only as part of quotations from patristic or Carolingian authors.) A total of thirteen biblical quotations from elsewhere in the Bible appear in the marginal gloss on the story of the binding of Isaac: four from the Old Testament[21] and nine from the New Testament.[22]

One typical example of the way the interlinear gloss might use a New Testament quote is in its first comment on Genesis 22.2, in which the interlinear gloss quotes John 3:16:

> sic deus dilexit mundum ut filium suum unigentium daret.
>
> God so loved the world that he should give his only-begotten son.

In manuscripts W, V, D, M, J, I, and Q, the interlinear gloss introduces this quotation with the word *mistice*, but without an attribution. Other manuscripts give this quotation without any further explanation. The purpose of this quotation is to draw the connection between Abraham in this story and God as the Father described in John's gospel. The interlinear gloss, by using the word *mistice*, highlights the purpose for which the interlinear gloss is using the quote. In another example, comment 3.2i paraphrases Romans 8:32 (*qui etiam Filio suo non pepercit sed pro nobis omnibus tradidit* [who therefore did not spare his own son but gave him up for us all]) as *pater proprio filio non pepercit* [the father did not spare his own son], again with no further explanation. The purpose of this verse is clear, to draw the parallel between Abraham's near-sacrifice of Isaac and God's sacrifice of his own son. Comment 3.2i does not give any attribution or explanation for this verse but simply refers to it.

Although the marginal gloss on Genesis 22 often gives attributions of patristic or Carolingian authors, neither the marginal nor the interlinear gloss gives attributions for biblical verses. As Lesley Smith has shown, this is typical for the Gloss.[23] It is clear that this is a deliberate choice, since the glossators remove attributions of biblical verses from the sources that they are quoting. Even when glossators do not identify the source of a quotation, they do identify its type: literal, historical, moral or mystical.[24] This happens particularly in the Pentateuch, but also in Kings, Chronicles, Ezra-Nehemiah, Job, Prophets, and the Gospels.[25] The interlinear gloss is therefore more likely to state the purpose for which it is using a verse than its source.

SOURCES OF THE MARGINAL GLOSS:
THE FORMATIVE INFLUENCE OF RABANUS

In its earlier recension (as represented by Manuscript G), the marginal gloss on Genesis 22 is a nearly word-for-word copy of the commentary of

Rabanus's commentary *Commentariorum in genesim libri quatuor* [Four Books of Commentary on Genesis] (ca. 819) on Genesis 22 as it appears in the *Patrologia Latina*.[26] His commentary consists entirely of a compilation of patristic exegesis, as is typical in Carolingian commentaries.[27] The comments of Rabanus Maurus on Genesis 22 consist completely of quotations from Jerome, Augustine, and Isidore. His commentary interweaves paraphrased material from Augustine's *Quaestionum in Heptateuchem Libri Septem* [Seven Books of Questions about the Heptateuch] with paraphrased material from Jerome's *Hebraice Quaestiones in Libro Geneseos* [Investigations about the Hebrew Book of Genesis]. A lengthy quotation from Isidore's *Quaestiones in Vetus Testamentum* [Investigations about the Old Testament] is all in one block of text at the end separate from the other commentaries. All quotations are exact or close to exact. The names of the authors quoted are not given.

The final form marginal gloss on Genesis 22 quotes from four sources: Jerome, Augustine, Alcuin, and Isidore. These four names can give the deceptive impression that the glossators worked from a library that contained works by each of these authors, if not more, but they seem to have been largely working from Rabanus. The *Glossa Ordinaria* is not consistent in its use of sources from book to book. Jerome and Augustine, when they appear in the earliest version of the marginal gloss on Genesis 22, seem to have been indirectly quoted through Rabanus.

Both recensions of the Gloss, like Rabanus, quote only one commentary by each author: Augustine's *Quaestionum in Heptateuchem Libri Septem*,[28] Jerome's *Hebraice Quaestiones in Libro Geneseos*[29] and Isidore's *Quaestiones in Vetus Testamentum*.[30] The later recension also adds Alcuin's *Interrogationes et Responsiones in Genesin* [Questions and Responses about Genesis].[31] The Gloss on Genesis 22 never names the books, only the authors. As Lesley Smith has shown, some books are full of attributions while others have few or none.[32] Genesis has an unusually large number of citations for the *Glossa Ordinaria*, with nearly half its sources cited by name in both the manuscripts and in the Rusch edition.[33]

Rabanus was a formative influence on many books of the Gloss. In some books, for example Chronicles and Proverbs, the glossators largely restricted their work to breaking Rabanus's commentary down into shorter pieces and organizing it into shorter comments tied to particular biblical verses or phrases.[34] Even in books in which this is not the case, when a commentary of Rabanus exists on a book it is likely to be a major source for the Gloss. This is difficult to prove, however, in the absence of a modern critical study of Rabanus.[35] Even when Rabanus is the main or only source, the Gloss does not usually attribute its comments to Rabanus but rather to Rabanus' sources, such as Jerome and Augustine.

In the Gloss on Genesis 22, there are only two minor differences between the marginal gloss in manuscript G and the commentary of Rabanus. One is that manuscript G places a comment on Genesis 22:4 which usually appears as interlinear in the marginal gloss, thereby adding a comment to the marginal gloss which is not directly taken from Rabanus. The second is that, in its single source attribution, it cites Augustine as the source for its first comment. Conversely, in its final, printed form (the Rusch edition), Rabanus is unrecognizable as the source of the marginal gloss. Almost all the changes that differentiate the marginal gloss from the commentary of Rabanus were made during the process of manuscript transmission.

The later recension (manuscript A) of the marginal gloss is substantially different from Rabanus and manuscript G. It paraphrases rather than quotes its sources, stripping the commentaries of Augustine and Isidore of their rhetorical structures, including all rhetorical questions and other techniques that call attention to textual problems. It breaks down the lengthy quotation from Isidore, paraphrases it, and interweaves it with the other commentaries. Manuscript A also adds comments from Alcuin, and begins to add in the names of its sources.[36]

There were therefore three stages of development between the patristic authors and the final form of the marginal gloss. The first was Rabanus' redaction of Jerome and Augustine into one continuous commentary with the block of Isidore's commentary added at the end. The second stage was the incorporation of the commentary of Rabanus into the first recension of the *Glossa Ordinaria*, as represented by manuscript G. In this phase, the names of sources who are not named in Rabanus began to be added, suggesting that some of the later glossators had some access to the original patristic texts and were not simply copying them from Rabanus.[37] The third stage was the truncation and revision of quotations from patristic authors in Rabanus and manuscript G (and B and L that follow it). At the same time, Isidore's commentaries were interwoven with those of Augustine and Jerome, and comments by Alcuin were added. This third step of redaction is represented by manuscript A and the rest of the manuscript tradition (including the Rusch edition).

Patristic and Carolingian Sources in Rabanus and the Marginal Gloss

As we have seen, the commentary of Rabanus on Genesis 22 consists of anonymous quotations from Augustine, Jerome, and Isidore. The first recension of the Gloss on Genesis 22 copies Rabanus precisely. The second recension of the marginal gloss makes some alterations to these patristic and Carolingian quotes, and adds quotes or paraphrases from Alcuin as well. Rabanus and then the two Gloss recensions (as exemplified by manuscripts G and A) transformed these patristic and Carolingian sources by truncating them and placing them in new contexts.

In constructing exegesis by juxtaposing patristic sources, Rabanus followed typical practice among Carolingian exegetes.[38] Even the particular sources found in Rabanus are common in Carolingian exegesis. Wigbod on Genesis quotes Jerome (completely, by name) and then Isidore (completely, not by name, flagged as *Explicatio spiritalis* [an explication of the spiritual sense]).[39] Alcuin quotes most of Augustine's interpretations later used by the Gloss as well as some of Jerome's. Pseudo-Bede paraphrases some of Jerome's commentary and some of Isidore's.[40] None of these authors name their sources or make any distinction between earlier comments and their own. In contrast with Pseudo-Bede, Rabanus used only one work by each of his patristic sources.[41] His particular combination is unique enough to establish that he is clearly the source of the marginal gloss, but his sources were commonly used by his contemporaries.[42]

The textual development of the Gloss obscures the influence of Rabanus on Genesis 22 to the point of rendering it nearly invisible. No manuscript, early or late, cites Rabanus as a source, even though it seems likely that glossators copied many of the patristic sources from Rabanus and not from manuscripts of the patristic commentaries. Further, the addition of Alcuin's commentary and the truncations and rearrangements that take place between the earlier and later recension make relationship between Rabanus and the Gloss difficult to notice, even for those familiar with both commentaries. The marginal gloss, then, constructs its exegesis through a recontextualization of the commentary of Rabanus, which in turn is a recombination of patristic exegesis.

Continuity and (Hebrew) Authority: Jerome in the Gloss

Jerome dominates the Gloss on Genesis 22. His commentary, in effect, appears in two places in the Gloss. His translation of the Bible is the central text around which all the exegesis is arranged. He is also the most frequently cited source in the marginal gloss, appearing in glosses 2.3m, 4.1m, 13.2m, and 14.1m.

The Gloss' use of Jerome's commentary in Genesis 22 is different from its use of other sources in two ways. The first is that the Jerome-based glosses are unusually stable and do not move from the marginal to the interlinear gloss from manuscript to manuscript. The second is that they are almost always attributed to him by name. Second, Jerome-based glosses are distinctive in content. All the information about the Hebrew language and biblical geography that appears in the Gloss is based on Jerome's commentary, and all the comments based on Jerome refer to geography or language in some way. Of the four Jerome-based glosses, 2.3m and 4.1m give geographical information about Mount Moriah and Abraham's journey, and 13.2m and 14.1m explain difficult Hebrew words. Further, only when quoting Jerome does the Gloss describe Jews in positive terms. In comments 2.3m and 14.1m, for example, the Gloss quotes Jerome citing *hebraeos* as a source. The unusual stability of Jerome's commentary and the consistency with which he is named show the importance of a named patristic authority to act as a credible source for Hebrew or Jewish-based exegesis to the copyists of the Gloss.

Jerome's commentary, *Hebraice Quaestiones in Libro Geneseos* (HQ), treats mostly linguistic and technical questions that derive from his translation and textual work. While in Palestine he encountered rabbis, and he cites Hebrew interpretations often in his exegesis. Jerome's use of Rabbinic sources in Genesis 22 is evident. In this chapter, the two interpretations Jerome gives as those of *hebrei* are both found in *Genesis Rabbah*.[43] *Genesis Rabbah* was composed in Palestine in the fifth or early sixth centuries, possibly late enough that Jerome may not have had access to it in its redacted form. The correspondence between Jerome and *Genesis Rabbah* in this chapter suggests that Jerome had some access to some of the traditions that were collected therein. Since, as was shown, *Genesis Rabbah* is one of Rashi's main sources, and since Jerome is one of the main sources of the Gloss, this creates a strange continuity in which a dialogue between fifth-century scholars is reflected in two heavily revised twelfth-century texts.

Because Rabanus alters Jerome's language, it is possible to show that the Gloss is quoting the material from Jerome exclusively from Rabanus and not directly from Jerome. Further, the glossators only use the material from Jerome that is quoted in Rabanus. For example, Jerome's first comment on Genesis 22 begins with the following phrase:

> Difficile est idioma linguae Hebraeae in Latinum sermonem vertere. Ubi nunc dicitur, vade in terram excelsam, in Hebraeo habet, MORIA מוריה quod Aquila transtulit τὴν καταφανῆ, hoc est, lucidam: Symmachus, τῆς ὀπτασίας, hoc est, visionis.[44]

> It is difficult to convert this idiom of the Hebrew language into Latin speech. Where now it is said, go to the high land, in Hebrew it has Moria, which Aquila translates as *ten kataphane*, which means "bright." Symmachus: *Tes optasias* means "concerning vision."

This line is absent in Rabanus and in all the Gloss manuscripts. In a more minor variation, Jerome's second comment on Genesis 22 uses the word *sentiunt* which is changed in Rabanus to *putant*, and all Gloss manuscripts have *putant*. Rabanus significantly edits Jerome's third comment on Genesis 22 and changes much of the language. Here also all Gloss manuscripts follow Rabanus. Although we are handicapped by the absence of a critical edition of Rabanus, we do have a critical edition of Jerome in the *Corpus Christianorum* series, which shows that none of the variants that appear in Rabanus and in the early marginal gloss appear in any of the Jerome manuscripts.[45] It is possible that manuscripts of Jerome's commentary simply did not circulate widely in France, since the *Corpus Christianorum* edition, in its comprehensive survey of Jerome manuscripts, includes four twelfth century manuscripts but none from France.[46]

The glosses based on Jerome are unusually stable and always appear in the marginal gloss. This is not true of any other patristic or Carolingian author quoted in the Gloss on Genesis 22.[47] All manuscripts except G mention his name,[48] making him the author whose name is most consistently cited in the marginal gloss on Genesis 22.[49] The consistent citation of Jerome's name is parallel to Rashi's use of the Targum of Onqelos. The Targum of Onqelos is the only source that Rashi constantly cites by name, as תרגום [Targum /Translation]. Onqelos is Rashi's primary linguistic source, just as Jerome is the only source the Gloss has for establishing the meanings of words. Both these commentaries, then, tend to ascribe translations (more than other kinds of exegesis) to a named earlier source. This suggests that for translations in particular the authority of a named source was more important than the appearance of originality or continuous commentary.

The Lasting Influence of Jerome's Hebraism
In two places Rashi and the Gloss have similar interpretations that seem to come from an exegetical encounter between Jerome and *Genesis Rabbah*. These two comments show the lasting influence of exegetical collaboration between Christians and Jews in late antiquity, and suggest that the histories of Jewish and Christian exegesis of Genesis 22 did not fully diverge even in the high middle ages. The third marginal gloss on Genesis 22.2 quotes Jerome quoting an interpretation of the *hebrei* as follows:

> Jer. Vade in terram .u. etc. Aiunt hebrei hunc montem esse in quo postea templum conditum est in area orne iebusei. Unde in Paralipomenon: Ceperunt aedificare templum mense secundo, secunda die mensis, in monte moria, qui idcirco illuminans interpretatur, et lucens, quia ibi est dabir, hoc est oraculum dei, et lex, et spiritus qui docet homines veritatem et inspirat prophetas.

> Jerome. **Go to the land etc.** The Hebrews say that this mountain is the one on which the Temple was later built, in the land of Orna the Jebusite, whence in Chronicles: They began to build the Temple in the second month, on the second day of the month, on the mountain of Moriah (2 Chronicles 3:1–2), which for this reason is interpreted to mean "illuminating" and "lightening," because there was the *dabir*, which is the word of God, and both the law and the spirit which teaches people the truth and inspires the prophets.

This comment is a very close paraphrase of Jerome's HQ on Genesis 22:2. The only variant that has an impact on the meaning is that Jerome has *spiritus sanctus* rather than *spiritus*.[50]

Rashi has a similar interpretation of Genesis 22:3. In his third comment on that verse he writes:

ארץ המוריה. ירושלים. וכן בדברי הימים: **לבנות את בית ה' בירושלים בהר המוריה.**
ורבותינו פירשו על שם שמשם הוראה יצאה לישראל.

The land of Moriah. Jerusalem. And thus in Chronicles (2 Chronicles 3:1): To build the house of God on the mountain of Moriah. And our rabbis interpreted: it is named thus because from there went out teaching to Israel.

Rashi's source here is Genesis Rabbah 55.7, which is a closer parallel to Jerome:

ר' חייא ור' ינאי חד אמר למקום שהורייה יצאה לעולם וחרנה אמר למקום שהיראה
יצאה לעולם. דכוותה ארון ר' חייא רבה ור' ינאי חד אמר למקום שהאורה יצאה לעולם
וחרנה אמר למקום שהמורא יצאה לעולם. דכוותה דביר ר' חייא ור' ינאי חד אמר למקום
שהדיבר יצאה לעולם וחד אמר למקום שהדבר יצאה לעולם.

Rabbi Hiya and Rabbi Yannai [disagree]: One [interprets the word *Moriah* as] "the place from which the teaching went out into the world," and the other says, "the place from which the awe went out into the world." Rabbi Hiya Rabbah and Rabbi Yannai similarly [disagree regarding] the word *aron*. One says, "the place from which the light went out into the world" and the other says, "the place from which awe went out into the world." They similarly interpret *dabir*. Rabbi Hiya and Rabbi Yannai, one says, "the place from which the commandments went out into the world" and the other says "the place from which the word went out into the world."

The shared language of Jerome and *Genesis Rabbah* leaves no doubt that they are related. Both connect *Moriah* with *dabir*, and both include etymologies related to "teaching," "word," and "light." This similarity suggests that Jerome had some access to this comment from *Genesis Rabbah*, although not necessarily in its final written form.

Although this example shows how a similarity in content between Rashi and the Gloss can derive from a patristic/midrashic exegetical encounter, there is also a convergent similarity that is not present in the source material. Rashi, the Gloss, and Jerome all quote 2 Chronicles 3:1, but *Genesis Rabbah* does not. These are ways in which Rashi and the Gloss on Genesis 22 are even more similar than Jerome and *Genesis Rabbah*.

The marginal gloss, with Jerome as its source, brings a second *hebrei* interpretation in its comment on Genesis 22:14:

Hoc apud hebreos exiuit in proverbium, ut in angustus constituti, et dei optantes auxilio sublevari, dicant: in monte dominus videbitur, id est, sicut abrahe misertus est, miserebitur nostri. Unde et in signum dati arietis, solent cornu clangere.

This is a proverb among the Hebrews. When they are found in a crisis, and wishing to be freed by divine aid, they say "the Lord will be seen on the mountain." That is, just as Abraham was granted mercy so may He be merciful to us. They are also accustomed to sound the horn a symbol for the ram that was sacrificed.

This is a nearly exact quotation from HQ on Genesis 22:14.[51] Jerome and the Gloss are describing a Jewish tradition of asking God for mercy and connecting this request to the story of the near-sacrifice of Isaac and to the phrase "God will see" (ה' יראה) in particular. Rashi explains Genesis 22:14 similarly:

. . . ומדרש אגדה: ה' יראה עקדה זו לסלוח לישראל בכל שנה ושנה ולהצילם מן הפורענות, כדי שיאמר היום ובכל' הדורות הבאים: בהר ה' יראה אפרו של יצחק צבור ועומד לכפרה.

And a midrashic statement is that "God will see" this binding to forgive Israel in every year and to rescue them from disasters, so that they might say today and in every future generation: On the mountain God will see the ashes of Isaac piled up and standing for atonement.[52]

Here again *Genesis Rabbah* is the common source for both Jerome and Rashi. In 56.10, *Genesis Rabbah* explains the phrase "God will see" (ה' יראה) through this prayer of Abraham:

כן יהי רצון מלפניך י"י אלוהינו בשעה שהיו בניו של יצחק באים לידי צרה תזכור להם אותה העקידה ותימלא עליהם רחמים.

May it be Your will Lord my God that when Isaac's children come to commit sins and bad actions, this binding may be remembered for them, and may You be filled with mercy for them.[53]

The common thread in all three interpretations is the idea that the phrase "God will see" sets up a connection between the binding of Isaac and God having mercy or forgiving sins in the post-biblical future. The sources articulate the relationship somewhat differently. Jerome takes from *Genesis Rabbah* the idea that Jews connect remembering the binding of Isaac with

God having mercy on Israel. He does not include the connection of the *Akedah* to sin and forgiveness, which is important in Rashi's adaptation. The sources also differ in the perspectives they adopt. *Genesis Rabbah* writes from the perspective of Abraham, and although Abraham makes his prayer, there is no guarantee that God will do what he asks. Jerome and the Gloss write from the perspective of the contemporary Jews, who invoke this story. Rashi writes from God's perspective, in that he does not mention anyone praying, but only says that God will see and remember.

In this case, as in the previous parallel, Rashi and Jerome (and the Gloss) have biblical material in common that is not present in *Genesis Rabbah*. While *Genesis Rabbah* tells the story of this prayer of Abraham as an interpretation of the words "God will see," it does not include these words in the story. Jerome includes these words in his interpretation, and so does Rashi.

Unasked Questions: Augustine in Rabanus and in the Gloss

Augustine's *Questionum in Heptateuchem Libri Septem* (QH) (written in 419[54]) is one of the most important sources for both Rabanus and the marginal gloss on Genesis 22.[55] Rabanus quotes the entirety of QH on Genesis 22 (comments 57–59). Manuscript G, following Rabanus, is very close to the text of Augustine as it appears in the *Corpus Christianorum* edition.[56] It places all of Augustine's comments in the marginal gloss, and names Augustine as the author of 1.1m. This is the only source attribution in manuscript G.

Manuscript A, representing the second recension, truncates and condenses all of Augustine's comments.[57] It subdivides Augustine's comments 58 and 59 and uses paraphrased pieces from them as interlinear glosses (12.1i, 14.2i, and 15.2i).[58] Manuscript A and almost all other manuscripts in the second recension name Augustine as the author of the marginal comments 1.1m and 12.1m,[59] but no manuscripts name Augustine as the author of interlinear comments 12.1i, 14.2i, or 15.2i, even when those manuscripts move the comment to the marginal gloss.

Augustine also deals with the story of the Binding of Isaac elsewhere in his writing. In his second sermon in *Sermones de Vetere Testamento*[60] he explains the story at much greater length than the few paragraphs from QH used here, and he discusses it as well in *De Civitate Dei* 16.32.[61] The Gloss quotes *De Genesi ad Litteram* [On the Literal Sense of Genesis][62] at length in its introduction, but in its commentary on Genesis 22 it only quotes QH. This is consistent with its pattern of using only one work from each author.

In his *Retractiones*, Augustine states that the purpose of QH was to call attention to and then resolve conceptual difficulties in the biblical text. As he writes in *Retractio* 2.55:

> Scripsi etiam libros quaestionum de libris eisdem divinis septem, quos ideo appellare sic volui, quia ea quae ibi disputantur magis quaerenda proposui quam quaesita dissolui, quamvis multo plura in eis mihi videantur ita pertractata, ut possint etiam soluta et exposita non inmerito iudicari.[63]

> I also wrote books of questions on those same seven holy books, which I wished to give this name, because in the matters disputed there I more propose matters to be investigated than solve questions, though it seems reasonable to me to judge that having been examined [in this way] they could be considered solved and explained.

Augustine states here that his original intention in this work was to call attention to the difficulties in the text. It was only in the process of writing that he saw that many of these difficulties could in fact be explained. Whether or not this accurately describes his writing process, it certainly describes the structure of his work. His commentary on Genesis 22, as is typical of QH, begins with questions and only then proceeds to answers.

The questions that Augustine asks on the binding of Isaac story are primarily theological. In question 57 he calls attention to the problem of God testing someone in light of the explicit contraindication in James 1:12–13.[64] In question 58 he asks how the Biblical text can say that God knows (22:12) and God sees (22:14), as if it were possible that God does not know or see.[65] In question 59 he asks why the angel says "you did not spare your beloved son from me" (22:12), when Abraham had not offered his son to the angel but to God.[66] Each discussion of Augustine's begins with a question.

If Augustine's purpose was to raise questions rather than give answers, the second recension of the Gloss gives answers rather than raising questions. Manuscript A only retains the question and answer structure in gloss 12.1m. Rabanus and manuscript G retain all three of Augustine's questions. This truncation of Augustine's comments, which takes place not between Augustine and Rabanus or between Rabanus and the first recension but between the first and second recensions of the Gloss, substantially recontextualizes Augustine's exegesis. Rather than asking questions, the marginal gloss is providing answers.

A Late Addition: Alcuin in the Gloss

The incorporation of Alcuin's comments into the marginal gloss is the strongest evidence for the evolution of the Gloss on Genesis 22 over the course of the twelfth century. Rabanus does not quote Alcuin, and neither does the earliest recension of the marginal gloss (as represented by manuscripts L, B, and G). Manuscript S has some comments by Alcuin, and the remaining manuscripts quote extensively from his *Interrogationes et Responsiones in Genesin* (RG). This indicates that Alcuin's comments were added to the marginal gloss in the mid–twelfth century, and that during this time the Gloss was still a dynamic, changing document. Together with the incorporation of Isidore, it may also suggest a growing willingness to rely on later exegesis.

Alcuin lived from 735 to 804, in England and France, which makes him the latest source to be cited by the Gloss on Genesis 22. His commentary on Genesis, RG, deals with the near-sacrifice of Isaac in questions 201 through 209.[67] RG is structured as a series of questions and answers. As it does with Augustine, the Gloss removes the rhetorical structure and never mentions the questions.

The Gloss does not quote all of Alcuin's commentary. Out of Alcuin's nine questions and answers, the Gloss only draws on five: 203, 204, 205, 206, and 209. Alcuin's other responses use exegesis by Augustine and Jerome already cited by the Gloss, which is likely the reason that the Gloss omits them.

Glosses based on Alcuin are 2.1m, 2.2i, 5.3m, 13.1m, and 17.1i-4i. The manuscripts cite Alcuin by name consistently in 2.1m, 5.3m, and 13.1m, but never in 2.2i or 17.1-4i.[68] This is consistent with the pattern that glosses with names attached do not move to the interlinear gloss. With the exception of 209 as cited in 17.1-4i, the Gloss stays very close to Alcuin's language.

It seems that glossators added Alcuin's commentaries sometime during the early twelfth century, between the two rescensions represented by manuscript G and manuscript A. Alcuin's material is in C, F, and Z, all of which are most likely dated prior to 1160. There is no obvious reason why the later glossators would choose to add Alcuin's commentaries (and no commentaries by anyone else) to those transmitted by Rabanus and the early form of the Gloss. If the glossators were consciously intending to reproduce the commentary of Rabanus and not the patristic authors, perhaps they saw Alcuin's mentorship of Rabanus as a reason to include his comments along with those of Rabanus. In any case the inclusion of Alcuin's comments points to a very high regard for Alcuin and his work.

Like Jerome's commentary, Alcuin's commentary introduces a parallel between Rashi and the Gloss which seems to be based on an earlier exchange between Jewish and Christian exegetes, although there is no evidence that Alcuin himself studied midrash with Jewish scholars.[69] Both Rashi and the marginal gloss, in their first comments on Genesis 22.13, explain that the ram that replaced Isaac had been made by God at the time of the creation of the world. In comment 13.1, Rashi writes:

והנה איל. מוכן היה לכך מששת ימי בראשית.

And behold, a ram. It had been prepared for this during the six days of creation.

Gloss 13.1m reads:

Alc. Aries qui pro ysaac immolatus est, non putativus, sed verus est. Ideo magis putatur angelum eum aliunde attulisse, quem ibi de terra post sex dierum opera dominum procreasse.

Alcuin. The ram which was sacrificed in place of Isaac was not imagined but real. Therefore it is thought, rather, that the angel brought it from elsewhere, where God had created it from the earth after the six days of creation.

This is a very close paraphrase of Alcuin:

Inter. 206. Unde aries iste, qui pro Isaac immolatus est (Gen. XXII, 13), venerit, solet quaeri: an [de] terra ibi subito creatus esset, vel aliunde ab angelo allatus?—Resp. Aries iste non putativus [Ms., putatus], sed verus esse credendus est. Ideo magis a doctoribus aestimatur, aliunde eum angelum attulisse, quam ibi de terra, post sex dierum opera, Dominum procreasse.[70]

Question 206. Whence came this ram, which was sacrificed for Isaac? People often ask whether it was suddenly created from earth there, or was it brought from elsewhere by the angel? Answer: This ram was not putative, but must be believed to be real. Therefore it is judged by the learned men more that the angel brought it from elsewhere than that the Lord brought it forth there from the earth after the six days of creation.

In Rashi, in the Gloss, and in Alcuin, the ram was miraculous and was created at the end of the six days of creation. This is a popular theme in midrashic literature. It appears in *Midrash Tanchuma* Shlach 14, *Bamidbar Rabbah* 56.8, *Pirkei de Rabbi Eliezer* 31, and the Palestinian Talmud Nedarim 1.3. It is however very unusual in patristic or Carolingian literature. Alcuin's source seems to be a commentary falsely attributed to Augustine, as follows:

> Sed iste aries requiritur unde in solitudine fuit: utrum, ut quidam asserunt, hunc in illa hora terra protulit, quomodo et in principio pecora gignit? An etiam, ne illud opus post diem sextum condidisse de terra Deus dicatur, istum arietem detulisse angelum aliunde credimus, quo modo et Philippum angelus ab eunucho transtulit in Azotum (Act VIII, 39), et ad Danielem in Babylonem Habacuc transtulisse ad lacum leonum fertur angelus (Dan. XIV, 35).[71]

> But it is asked from where in that isolated place that ram could have come, and if, as some assert, the earth brought it forth at that time, in the same way as it brought forth flocks in the beginning. But we believe that an angel carried that ram from another place, lest God be said to have created this work from earth after the sixth day, in the same way that an angel took Philip away from the eunuch to Azotus, and an angel is reported to have carried Habakkuk to Daniel in the lion's den.

This is not an exact parallel, since it seems to argue against the interpretation which Alcuin accepts. For pseudo-Augustine, it is important that the ram was brought from elsewhere to make clear that it was *not* miraculously brought into being.[72] It simply was miraculously transported, just like Philip (Acts 8:25–40) and Habakkuk (Daniel 14:35) were miraculously transported to where they were required. Alcuin has the ram brought from elsewhere, but still created miraculously *after* the six days of creation. Alcuin seems to conflate both these possibilities, the one that pseudo-Augustine accepts and the one that he rejects. In this way he brings the interpretation of pseudo-Augustine closely into alignment with that of *Genesis Rabbah*.

As in the case of Jerome, this example shows that, although there was no direct contact between Rashi and the Gloss, these two commentaries reflect the contact between their sources. This contact can be direct and through explicit quotation, as with Jerome and *Genesis Rabbah*. Conversely, it can be indirect and without citation of sources, as in the case of Alcuin's miraculous ram. Both cases show that Rashi and the Gloss share not only a common biblical text but some common interpretative traditions.

Isidore of Seville and the Integration of Anti-Judaism in the Gloss

All the anti-Judaism in the marginal gloss on Genesis 22 is based on quotations from Isidore. The choices by different manuscripts to emphasize or de-emphasize Isidore's commentary will therefore very much impact the importance of anti-Jewish exegesis in the marginal gloss. In some manuscripts Isidore's commentary is very prominent, to the extent that he is quoted more than any other commentator. In others his commentary is placed all in one block at the end, almost as an appendix.[73] These two choices lead to very different levels of anti-Judaism in the marginal gloss: the more reliant on Isidore, the greater the anti-Judaism.

Isidore lived from 570 to 636 in Visigothic Spain. He is best known for his *Etymologiae*, an encyclopedia of Greek and Roman philosophy and learning. As bishop of Seville he was involved in the eradication of Arianism among the Visigoths. He also wrote an anti-Jewish polemic, *De fide catholica ex Veteri et Novo Testamento, contra Judaeos* [About the Catholic faith from the Old and New Testament, against the Jews].[74] This work was very popular in the middle ages, and it goes beyond classic anti-Jewish polemics by describing Jews as deliberately deceptive.[75] He also advocated for decisions by the Fourth Council of Toledo calling for Jewish children to be removed from their parents' care and prohibiting Jews—and even Christians of Jewish descent—from holding public office.[76]

In the final form of the Gloss on Genesis 22, as represented by manuscript A, Isidore is the most quoted source. Out of its 16 marginal comments, Isidore is the source of seven, or almost half. Manuscripts G and L, representing the earlier recension, have all of Isidore's comments in a separate block at the end. This is consistent with how Rabanus quotes Isidore.[77] So over the course of the manuscript history of the Gloss on Genesis 22, the Isidore-based exegesis went from being attached separately at the end to being integrated with the rest of the commentary.[78]

All of the quotations from Isidore in the Gloss on Genesis 22 are from his *Quaestiones in Vetus Testamentum—In Genesim* (QV), Chapter 18, paragraphs 3–19.[79] In paragraphs 1 and 2, Isidore summarizes the narrative of Genesis 22, but the Gloss does not quote this at all. Paragraph 3 begins "Come, now, let us see what hides under the mystery of this sacrament," and the rest of the chapter describes the Christological significance of the events of Genesis 22. Isidore describes his Christ-centered interpretation as *mysterio*[80] and *sacramentum*,[81] and differentiates it from his first, presumably literal, interpretation. The marginal gloss does not quote Isidore's first interpretation at all, and while earlier manuscripts retain Isidore's terms indicating the spiritual sense, later manuscripts remove them. This removes the distinction between senses which is central in Isidore's commentary.[82]

There is no critical edition of Isidore's commentary on Genesis, and so it cannot be easily established which versions of Isidore's commentary were available to the glossators. Based on the versions of Isidore and Rabanus that appear in the *Patrologia Latina*,[83] it seems that the glossators of the earlier recension read Isidore directly as well as through Rabanus. The evidence for this is the presence of the last lines of Isidore's commentary on Genesis 22, which Rabanus omits:

> Immolato ergo Abraham pro Isaac filio suo, **vocavit nomen illius loci: Dominus vidit**, pro eo quod est, Dominus videri fecit, utique per incarnationem.

> Therefore, after Abraham sacrificed for Isaac his son, **he called the name of this place: "The Lord saw,"** which is, "The Lord caused to be seen," that is, through the incarnation.[84]

These last lines of Isidore's commentary (*Immolato . . . per incarnationem*) are included in manuscripts G, B, and L, which represent the earlier recension, but not the rest of the manuscripts. This seems to indicate that the earlier glossators copied directly from Isidore rather than indirectly from Rabanus.[85] The second recension follows Rabanus and omits these lines. This may be because they rephrase ideas already stated in glosses 12.2i and 14.2i, based on Augustine, and once the Isidore-based exegesis was incorporated with the rest of the Gloss the redundancy became obvious, or it may be that they were copying from Rabanus.

Following Rabanus, manuscripts G and L quote all the Isidore-based material in one block and stay very close to Isidore's text. Manuscript B is also very close to Isidore's text, but breaks it up in a way that is closer to A, the rest of the manuscripts, and the final form of the Gloss. The other manuscripts paraphrase Isidore and remove his rhetorical structures. For example, Isidore writes in paragraph 3:

> Age nunc videamus quod sub huius sacramenti lateat misterio. Abraham, quando unicum filium suum perduxit ad immolandum, habebat personam Dei Patris. Sed quid est, quod eum senex suscepit? non enim senescit Deus, sed ipsa praenuntiatio de Christo jam quodammodo senuerat, quando natus est Christus.[86]

> Come, now, and let us see that under this sacrament there may hide a mystery. Abraham, when he led his only son to be sacrificed, had the person of God the father. But what is that the old man received him? For God does not age, but the foretelling of Christ now aged in a certain way, when Christ was born.

Manuscripts B and L quote this comment almost exactly, with a slight variant in word order in L.[87] Aside from one transposition of words,[88] the only change between Isidore and manuscript G is the addition of the word *cornu* [horn] referring to the horns of the ram entangled in the thicket, which became necessary after removing paragraphs 1 and 2 in which Isidore summarizes the narrative.

Manuscript A, in its comment on Genesis 22.8, condenses Isidore's comment as follows:

> Isidore. Abraam filium unicum ducens ad immolandum, deum patrem significat. Abraam senex filium suscepit, deus autem non senescit, sed promissio de christo quodammodo senuerat, quando christus natus est.

> Isidore. Abraham, in leading his only son to be sacrificed signifies God the father. Abraham received his son as an old man; God, however, does not age, but the promise of Christ in a certain way aged when Christ was born.

Aside from the loss of rhetorical structure, *habebat personam* has become *significat* (in all manuscripts), and the words *mysterio* and *sacramentum* are removed. The word *sacramentum* (in some form) appears another five times in Isidore's commentary and in the first recension, and only once (in 3.1m) in the second recension. The final form of the marginal gloss, then, removes some of the contextual and textual cues that indicate a division between senses in Isidore's commentary.

Isidore is rarely cited by name in any manuscript. No manuscripts cite him as a source for comments 3.1m, 4.2m, 5.1m, 5.2m, 9.1m, and 14.2m. (In all manuscripts those comments are anonymous, except for manuscript N which misattributes comment 5.2m to Alcuin.) The single comment which is consistently attributed to him is 8.1m. (The exceptions are manuscripts W and Q, which do not name an author for this comment and P, which attributes 8.1m to Jerome.)[89] So although his comments make up the largest source of the marginal gloss in its final form, he is the source least often cited by name.

Although Isidore's comments are rarely attributed to him, they remain for the most part stable. 3.1m is only interlinear in two manuscripts, 4.2m is marginal in all manuscripts, 5.1m is interlinear in one manuscript, 5.2m is marginal in all manuscripts, 9.1m is marginal in all manuscripts, and 14.2 is absent in one manuscript but never appears in the interlinear gloss. None of these glosses are ever attributed to Isidore in any manuscripts.

The comments of Isidore, therefore, have a textual history that sets them apart from the rest of the Gloss. They began, in Rabanus and G, as a single passage set apart from the rest of the text, and over the course of the manuscript transmission the comments became rearranged according to the order of the verses alongside the commentaries of Augustine and Jerome. They also underwent substantial truncation and were integrated as anonymous sources into the marginal gloss.

VARIABLE GLOSSES

Most glosses in Genesis 22 are stable in their positions. Glosses that are marginal in one version tend to be marginal in all versions and glosses that are interlinear tend to remain interlinear. A few glosses that move between the marginal and interlinear position ("variable glosses") have certain characteristics that can explain their instability.[90]

The following fifteen glosses in Genesis 22 appear in at least one manuscript in the marginal gloss and in at least one in the interlinear gloss: 2.1i, 2.2i, 3.2i, 4.1i, 3.1m, 5.1m, 9.1i, 9.2i, 12.2i, 14.1i, 14.2i, 15.2i, 16.1-3i, 16.3i and

17.3i. Out of these glosses, the following eight appear in more than one manuscript in the interlinear position and in more than one manuscript in the marginal position: 2.2i, 4.1i, 12.2i, 14.1i, 14.2i, 15.2i, 16.3i, 17.3i.[91] Most of these comments paraphrase an earlier source but do not quote the source word for word. Comment 2.2i is a close paraphrase of Alcuin, and like his marginal comments is taken from RG. Comments 12.2i and 14.2i are a close paraphrase of Augustine, also like the marginal comments taken from his QH. Comment 14.1i does not appear in Augustine, but only appears in the marginal gloss joined with 14.2i. Comment 15.2i is a close paraphrase of two lines from Augustine 59, which is also the source for 12.1m. Comment 17.3i is related to Alcuin.

Mark Zier,[92] following Beryl Smalley,[93] has suggested that the organizing principle by which a gloss is assigned to a marginal or interlinear position is simply length. Longer glosses are assigned to the margins, shorter glosses are placed in the interlinear position, and glosses of two to three lines vary in their position.[94] In the Gloss on Genesis 22, most of the variable glosses are two to three lines. The single exception is 15.2i which is one line made up of two shorter comments. Length, however, does not fully explain the positioning of glosses on Genesis 22. Comments 3.2i, 6.1i and 7.1i, which are longer than 15.2i, are all stable in their position and either have no positioning variants or only one. Similarly, comment 3.1m is only two lines—shorter than 7.1i and the same length as 6.1i—but is nevertheless in the marginal position in all but two manuscripts. Comment 13.1m, which is only three lines long and shorter than 12.2i and 14.2i, never changes position.

Rather than length, attribution appears to be the deciding factor in the stability or instability of these comments. The critical edition of the Gloss on Genesis 22 (see Appendix A) shows a strong correlation between marginal placement and having an earlier source. This suggests that the glossators and copyists of the Gloss intended to keep sourced comments in the margins and original comments (or at least comments that are far removed from the original source) in the interlinear gloss.[95]

In Genesis 22, then, glosses that are sometimes marginal and sometimes interlinear are almost always paraphrases of comments from unnamed patristic or other earlier authors. The naming of the source seems to be an important factor in determining whether a marginal gloss will become a variable gloss and seems to be more important than the length of the comment. Marginal glosses may have represented earlier opinion, while interlinear glosses may have been clear enough continuations of the biblical text not to require a source. These variable glosses show the instability of the categories "sourced" and "unsourced," "patristic" and "original" for the Gloss scribes and readers.

CONCLUSIONS

The marginal and interlinear glosses use earlier material differently. The marginal gloss, in its final form, is an adaptation of the commentary of Rabanus (in turn made of quotations from Augustine, Jerome, and Isidore) with the addition of Alcuin. No new or original material is added. The marginal gloss uses the complete arguments of its sources, although in its final form it strips out a great deal of rhetorical structure, including most question-answer structures. The interlinear gloss consists of original comments, or at least comments phrased in new ways. Even when it takes ideas from earlier sources it paraphrases them. The only direct quotations in the interlinear gloss are biblical.

This difference between the marginal and interlinear glosses is clearly visible in most manuscripts. Names of patristic or Carolingian writers appear frequently (although not universally) in the marginal gloss and never in the interlinear gloss. Later manuscripts tend to add more attributions to the marginal gloss rather than stripping them out, even though they tend to condense and truncate the comments themselves.

This chapter has suggested that the marginal and interlinear glosses are two alternative strategies for generating meaning and locating authority. While the marginal glosses appear as a record of patristic and other earlier opinion and locate authority in Church tradition, interlinear glosses appear as an outgrowth of the biblical text and locate authority in the autonomous reader. In reading these two kinds of comments together a reader can easily see how tradition and autonomous reading lead to the same inevitable conclusion.

As a Christian anti-Jewish polemic, the dual commentary of the Gloss has a particular advantage. The marginal gloss represents Isidore's anti-Jewish polemic as authoritative and normative. By dividing up Isidore's commentary and naming him less than it names other sources, later versions of the Gloss obscure the origin of Isidore's anti-Jewish exegesis and give the impression that it represents the consensus of earlier opinion. At the same time, the interlinear gloss presents both anti-Judaism and a Christ-centered reading as the logical outcomes of an autonomous reading of the Bible as a self-glossing text. To a reader of the Gloss, both tradition and autonomous reading appear to lead to the same anti-Jewish conclusions.

Rashi and the Gloss as Selective Synthesizers

The previous two chapters have shown that Rashi and the Gloss alter their source materials in two ways. First, they merge and truncate sources to emphasize certain themes, and in particular the role of the "other" in the narrative. Second, both Rashi and the Gloss subtly change their source material in a way that seems stylistic but in fact reveals an important shift in ideas of textual authority. While rabbinic literature is obsessed with tracing the lineage of ideas through the names of the specific rabbis who taught or transmitted them, Rashi almost always omits these names. Without names of sources, the comments appear to the reader to be justified not by an appeal to authority but as an independent reading of the biblical text.

The *Glossa Ordinaria* similarly removes source citations. Patristic exegetical literature is always associated with a patristic author. Even anonymous writings tend to be ascribed to someone by later copyists. The marginal gloss, following Rabanus, strips away these names and then attempts to restore them. The interlinear gloss dispenses with the names of its sources and does not quote directly from their work. As in Rashi's commentary, this gives the impression of the glosses arising simply as a response to and continuation of the biblical verse.

By removing the names of their sources, as well as by recombining them, both Rashi and the Gloss allow the reader to imagine their commentaries as an original composition. At the same time, each commentary's occasional and vague citation of sources allows the reader to place Rashi and the Gloss in the context of Jewish and Christian tradition. This recombination (and paraphrase) without citation privileges the authority of Rashi and the Gloss as independent readers of the biblical text and obscures the diversity of midrashic and patristic exegesis, while at the same preserving the claims of Rashi and the Gloss to the authority of their sources.

CHAPTER FOUR

ISAAC ON JEWISH AND CHRISTIAN ALTARS: POLEMIC, FAITH, AND SACRIFICE IN RASHI AND THE GLOSS ON GENESIS 22

The structure of this book has been a four-way comparison between Rashi, the Gloss, and their respective sources. While previous chapters have highlighted the differences, this chapter will show that the most important elements in Rashi and in the Gloss on Genesis 22 are themes that they have in common. Both Rashi and the Gloss read the near-sacrifice of Isaac polemically, in a way that uses the story of Abraham as evidence for the greatness of Abraham—representing their own faiths—over "other" figures—different nations or religions. The Gloss specifically names Jews and polemicizes against them. Although Rashi does not name Christians, his interpretation emphasizes the polemical function as the main purpose of the story. Both retell the story of the near-sacrifice of Isaac in a way that has Abraham both participate in and foresee a future sacrifice: that of Christ and the Eucharist that reenacts it in the case of the Gloss and the Temple sacrifice in the case of Rashi. In doing this, each glossator sees Abraham as a participant in his own faith's religious rituals as they continue to be practiced into the future. Isaac becomes placed on the Christian altar in the Eucharist and on the Jewish altar through the Temple sacrifices and the rituals that replace them, and Abraham acts out the role of a faithful member of the Jewish or Christian religion whose example every follower should emulate.

This similarity, though, is intertwined with an important, paradoxical difference. Although both Rashi and the Gloss, following their own exegetical traditions, read this story as morally didactic and as an example of faith, Rashi describes Isaac's greatness and holds him up as a model for emulation, whereas the Gloss focuses entirely on Abraham and describes Isaac as a passive character. Further, the particular virtue of which Abraham sets an example is different. While the Gloss emphasizes his obedience, Rashi describes his love and enthusiasm (indeed, he is willing to argue with God).

Some of these similarities and differences show continuities between earlier (midrashic and patristic or Carolingian) exegesis and medieval interpretation. Abraham as an example of faith is common to early Jewish and Christian exegeses. Early Jewish exegesis consistently presents Isaac as a figure for the reader to identify with and emulate, but early Christian exegesis tends to de-emphasize Isaac's role.[1] Rashi and the Gloss follow their sources here, although as we will see, Rashi's description of the greatness of Isaac goes beyond even that of his sources. Rashi and the Gloss, though, develop the polemical significance of the near-sacrifice of Isaac far beyond what is in earlier Jewish or Christian exegesis, and in a way that reflects their shared eleventh- and twelfth-century context.

THE NEAR-SACRIFICE OF ISAAC AS PERFORMANCE AND POLEMIC

For Rashi, the purpose of the near-sacrifice of Isaac was to show the greatness of Abraham to "others." These "others" may be general and nameless, or they may be specific "others" who are outside of the lineage of the Patriarchs and therefore coded as non-Jews. The importance of this theme to Rashi is demonstrated by how frequently it appears in his commentary on Genesis 22. We find named or unnamed accusing "other" figures in comments 1.1 (twice), 2.1, 4.1, and 12.3. Ishmael and Eliezer also appear in 3.3, and Ishmael appears alone in 2.2. Both of Ishmael's appearances mention that he is secondary to Isaac. Satan also appears in 13.3, where he hides the ram in the thicket, although there Rashi does not describe him specifically as the intended audience of Abraham's act. Named or unnamed "others" appear as significant players in the story a total of seven times in Rashi's 34 comments, and appear both at the beginning and at the climax of the story.

As Michael Signer has observed, the idea of Abraham's superiority, for Rashi, is intertwined with the centrality of God's exclusive love for Israel. A key term for Signer is *hibbah*, or affection, which Rashi uses to describe God's relationship to Abraham as a result of this test.[2] This word appears in Genesis 22 primarily in the context of the theme of proving to "others" that Abraham is worthy of this love. In 2.1 God asks Abraham to stand in this test to prove to "others" his worthiness of God's love, and in 12.3 Abraham's worthiness of this love is proven.³ God's love for Abraham only appears outside of the context of proving Abraham's worthiness of this love to "others" once in this story, in 11.1.

In this polemical reading, Ishmael plays a pivotal role. He appears in 1.1 as Isaac's primary rival for divine affection. Then in 2.2, Abraham argues with God's implication that he only has one son, saying that he has two sons, each the only child to his mother, each beloved. Ishmael here is not excluded because of any intrinsic unworthiness. Still, it is clear, even over Abraham's objections, that God does not consider him to be Abraham's real son and heir. Ishmael appears again in 3.3 as one of Abraham's two servants (the other is Eliezer) who accompany Abraham on the journey but who remain at the foot of the mountain with the donkey. Rashi does not spell out the implications of this as David Kimhi does in his comment on verse 3: "you who are like the donkey, stay with the donkey." Still, Ishmael is clearly relegated to a secondary, servile role. In all these comments, Ishmael is a significant audience for the proof of Abraham's greatness.⁴

Ishmael's companion and counterpoint in Rashi's commentary is none other than Satan. In his first comment on the story of the *Akedah*, Rashi explains the rationale for the proposed sacrifice of Isaac through two stories. In the first story, Satan accuses Abraham of not offering sacrifices to God in his feast of thanksgiving for the birth of Isaac. To this God responds: "If I told him to sacrifice [Isaac] before me he would not delay." In this story, the purpose of the near-sacrifice of Isaac is to prove Abraham's worth to Satan. In the second story, Ishmael brags to Isaac that he was circumcised willingly at the age of thirteen, when he could have objected. Isaac answers: "With one limb you are trying to intimidate me? If God said to me, sacrifice yourself before me, I would not object." The combination of these two stories indicates that for Rashi the near-sacrifice of Isaac was a performance by Isaac as well as Abraham, by which both could prove Isaac's worth in the face of detractors as well as Abraham's. The parallel between Ishmael and Satan here makes clear that these detractors are human and concrete as well as abstract and theological. These two interpretations both use the story of the near-sacrifice of Isaac as a way to show Abraham and Isaac's superiority in the face of an external challenge.

Rashi returns to the theme of challenges from outside figures later in the story, but without specifically identifying Ishmael and Satan. In comments

2.1 and 4.1, Rashi interprets Abraham's actions as necessary in order to deflect challenges and questions of unnamed "others." In 2.1, we see that if it were not for the near-sacrifice of Isaac they might say that "the first ones had no substance." This is similar to the challenges that Satan and Ishmael bring against Abraham and Isaac in Rashi's commentary on verse 1. In 4.1, God forces Abraham to endure a three-day journey out of fear lest these "others" suspect that he acted out of confusion or temporary insanity. In 12.3, Rashi names these suspicious "others" as "Satan and the nations of the world," who wonder why God loves Abraham, and who have been answered by this test. The near-sacrifice of Isaac, then, is for Rashi primarily and centrally a response to external theological challenges.

For Rashi, the purpose of the near-sacrifice of Isaac was to refute the claims of "others" (including Christians) to divine election, and to justify the election of Israel. This theme of the near-sacrifice of Isaac as performance and polemic is thus for Rashi the most crucial theme in this section. It appears at both the beginning of the story, setting out its purpose, and at the climax, describing what Abraham, Isaac and God have accomplished.

The Gloss, like Rashi, emphasizes the role of the "other" in Genesis 22. The Gloss, though, clearly names and defines the "other": the Jews. The Gloss goes beyond its sources (including Rabanus) in polemicizing against the Jews.[5] Jews are mentioned in a total of thirteen glosses, showing their importance for the Gloss in constructing its narrative. These Jews are of two kinds: *iudei* and *hebrei*. When Jews are described as *hebrei*, typically in quotations from Jerome, they can be authoritative sources for the interpretation of scripture, and when they are described as *iudei* or *Israel* they are described as mistaken. Jews appear in interlinear glosses only as misguided *iudei*: four times explicitly (4.1i, 5.1i, 13.3i, and 19.1i.), four times by implication (3.2i, 17.3i, 17.4i, and 19.2i.). The marginal gloss uses both terms: Two instances refer to *hebrei* whose interpretations (as brought by Jerome) are authoritative (2.1m and 14.1m),[6] and three to *iudei* or *israel* who misunderstand everything (3.1m, 5.1m, and 5.2m).[7]

By referring to Jews as *iudei, israel,* and *hebrei*[8] the marginal gloss retains the terms of its sources: Jerome and Isidore. Jerome exclusively uses the term *hebrei* and in this section only refers to Jews as an authoritative source of information. Jerome's *hebrei* sources here are clearly post-biblical: In 14.1m Jerome writes in the present tense about a proverb of his contemporary Jews, who draw on the Abraham story in their current crisis. Isidore uses the terms *iudei* and *israel*, and all his references to Jews are negative and polemical. Of Isidore's two terms, *israel* appears in two glosses (5.1m and 5.2m), and only in direct quotations from scripture.[9] *Iudei* appear in 3.1m and 5.2m, and 5.2m identifies *iudei* with *israel* by bringing a prooftext about *israel* (and *iuda*) to make a point about *iudei*. The Gloss does not base the distinction between *iudei* and *hebrei* on time period, since Jerome is clearly referring to Jews of his own time period and not biblical Jews. It seems only to be based on the purpose for which the Jews are mentioned: as sources of information or objects of polemic.[10]

Just as the marginal gloss indirectly incorporates Jewish exegesis by quoting Jerome, it incorporates anti-Jewish polemic by quoting Isidore. In the Isidore-based material, Jews (who are always *iudei*, except in direct biblical quotations) are an important part of the story of the near-sacrifice of Isaac. Represented by the donkey and the two slaves, they participate in Abraham's journey but do not understand it.

Iudei first appear in the marginal gloss in gloss 3.1m, based on Isidore: *Asinus insensatam iudeorum stulticiam significat, qui portabat omnia sacramenta et nesciebat* [The donkey signifies the senseless stupidity of the Jews, as it was carrying all the sacraments and was unaware].[11] This "Jewish" donkey-like stupidity carries Christ, represented by Isaac. *Iudei* here are the Jews who understand nothing even though they have access to the biblical text. The marginal gloss continues this theme in 5.1m, which connects the "partial blindness" of the Jews in Romans 11:25 with the donkey in Genesis 22. Comment 5.2m also continues this theme and connects the two servants with the Jews, who were divided into Northern and Southern kingdoms. The polemic in all cases is that the Jews do not understand anything about their own scripture.[12]

The juxtaposition of the Isidore-based material with the Jerome-based material creates a paradox. On the one hand, by virtue of their language and customs, Jews understand things about scripture that Christians need to learn. On the other hand, Jews do not understand scripture at all. This leads to the conclusion that, for the Gloss, Jews may be useful for the sort of questions Jerome uses them to answer, such as defining the meaning of words and identifying locations, and their customs may even be interesting and have bearing on the interpretation of scripture, but when it comes to understanding the deeper meanings that Isidore proposes they are willfully blind. The Gloss expresses this dichotomy in the positive (*hebrei*) and negative (*iudei/israel*) terms for Jews.

The interlinear gloss, unlike the marginal gloss, does not quote sources and thus has more freedom to synthesize or select. As a result, it is more consistent in both its narrative and its polemical emphasis. The eight comments in the interlinear gloss tell a complete, coherent history of the Jews from the crucifixion through the present to the future redemption. The terminology is also more consistent: They are only named as *iudei*, with almost no manuscript variants that use any other names.[13] In 3.2i, the *iudei* are introduced in the context of their responsibility for the death of Christ, *quia duo populi in morte christi consenserunt et pater proprio filio non pepercit* [Because **two peoples** (Gen. 25:23) consented in the death of Christ, and **the father did not spare his own son** (Romans 8:32)]. The Gloss here connects the two youths accompanying Abraham (to Mount Moriah, which is the place of the crucifixion) with the "two peoples" responsible for the death of Christ.

Who are the "two peoples"? Reading this interlinear comment together with marginal gloss 5.2m, which describes the division of Israel into two kingdoms, suggests that the two peoples are the Northern Kingdom and the Southern Kingdom. This seems unlikely, though, in the context of allocating responsibility for the death of Christ. Further, the phrase *duo populi* is a quotation from the Vulgate translation of Genesis 25:23, where the Lord tells Rebecca that two peoples will come forth from her womb. The interlinear gloss on this verse explains that the two peoples are *Israel vel christianus populus*[14] [Israel and the Christian people].[15] The use of the phrase *duo populi* suggests that the interlinear gloss is leading the reader to understand these two servants as representing the Jews and Gentiles who were responsible for the death of Christ. The different methods of the marginal and interlinear glosses here produce different readings from the same sources.

The interlinear gloss repeatedly introduces anti-Jewish comments. In the interlinear gloss, the Jews not only consent to the death of Christ, they are both malicious (4.2i) and extremely stupid (5.2i). Still, the idea that they will be redeemed in the future is introduced in gloss 5.1i:

postquam adoraverimus revertemur ad vos. hoc erit in fine mundi cum plenitudo gentium intraverit.

After we have worshipped, we will return to you. This will be at the end of the world when the full number of the nations will have come in (Romans 11:25).

The Gloss here quotes Romans to explain the verse from Genesis. The full verse of Romans 11:25 in the Vulgate is as follows:

> nolo enim vos ignorare fratres mysterium hoc ut non sitis vobis ipsis sapientes quia caecitas ex parte contigit in Israhel donec plenitudo gentium intraret
>
> Brothers, I do not want you to be ignorant of this mystery, with the result that you should not be wise for yourselves, because a partial blindness has happened in Israel until the fullness of the nations will enter.

The interlinear gloss on Genesis 5 expects the reader to know the full verse from Romans from its partial quotation. Once the reader understands the context of Romans 11:25, it is clear that Abraham is speaking on behalf of the Christians to the Jews. Abraham, as the representative of the true faith, tells the servants and donkey—who represent Jews—that in the end of the world the true faith will return to them.

The interlinear gloss ends the story of the near-sacrifice of Isaac with both a statement of the inferiority of the Jews and a hope for their future redemption. In its exegesis of 22:17, the interlinear gloss picks up on the double blessing that God gives Abraham, and uses it to show the inequality between Jews and Christians. Here is the interlinear gloss as it appears interwoven with the biblical text:

> **sicut stellas caeli**
> spirituales, pauciores, fulgentes
> Israel dei
> **velut harenam quae est in litore maris**
> Israel secundum carnem quia erant et degeneres futuri, et de bona oliva in **oleastrum** transituri
> plures carnales sterilis

> **like the stars of the heaven**
> spiritual, fewer, shining
> Israel of God
> **like the sand that is on the sea-shore**

Israel in the manner of the flesh because they were and will be degenerate and will be transformed from the good olive to a **wild olive tree**
(Romans 11:17)

  many, fleshy, barren

The Jews, or "Israel in the manner of the flesh" here are secondary, and are
only like sand and not like stars. Still, they also have a place in the blessing.

The story in the interlinear gloss ends with the conversion of the Jews.
Just as in the end Abraham returns to the boys and the donkey, so in interlinear comments 19.1i and 19.2i:

  in fine mundi fideles de gentibus ad iudeos revertetur.
    tunc concorditer vivent in ecclesia

  in the end of the world the faithful of the nations will be returned to
  the Jews,
    then they will live harmoniously in the Church.

The conversion of the Jews here is the most important point for the conclusion of the narrative of Genesis 22. The placement of this theme at the end
of the story shows just how central it is for the Gloss.

The comments in the interlinear gloss can be constructed into a coherent story about the Jews. Once the Jews were with Abraham, but he left
them behind. They sinned, and were foolish, and became more like sand
than like stars, but in the end the faith of Abraham will return to them.

Non-Polemical Alternatives

Rashi and the Gloss adapt their sources to construct a polemic using non-
polemical (or only tangentially polemical) texts. Here, a few examples will
show how unusual this interpretation was even in the eleventh and early
twelfth centuries.

The only continuous Hebrew work on Genesis written in France prior
to Rashi is the late midrash *Bereshit Rabbati* of Rabbi Moshe ha-Darshan.
It mentions the idea of Abraham's test as a performance for other nations
only once, in its comment on Genesis 22:12

להודיע לאומות העולם שלא על חינם בחרתי בך הה"ד **עתה ידעתי**.[16]

To make known to the nations of the world I chose you for a reason:
This is what is meant by the words **now I know**.

This comment appears in the middle of a conversation between Abraham and God in which Abraham questions God's change of mind. It is relevant in *Bereshit Rabbati* only as one of many ways for God to justify the command to Abraham. Satan is a tempter and not an accuser.[17] There are accusers, but they have no identity or motivation, and the near-sacrifice of Isaac does not refute them.

The late midrashic collection the *Lekach Tov* was written by Tuviah ben Eliezer in the Greek Balkans in the late eleventh or early twelfth century.[18] Its commentary on Leviticus 22:23 refers explicitly to the massacre of the Jewish community of Mainz during the first Crusade of 1096, and it mentions the Christian siege of Jerusalem in its commentary to Numbers 24:17. Its approach to the near-sacrifice of Isaac is similar to Rashi's in that it describes the *Akedah* as a demonstration of both Abraham's and Isaac's greatnesses. It is not the nations of the world who are the audience, however, but the ministering angels. The most important role of the near-sacrifice of Isaac in the *Lekach Tov* is to allow God to forgive Israel in the future, as is discussed below.

Rashi's grandson Rashbam (1085–1160) explicitly intended for his commentary on the Pentateuch to build on and challenge that of his grandfather Rashi.[19] Accordingly, he continued Rashi's polemical reading but took it in a different direction. Rashbam's commentary introduces the story of the near-sacrifice of Isaac as Abraham's punishment for making a treaty with the king of the Philistines in the preceding verses. As Rashbam writes:

ויהי **אחר הדברים האלא.** כל מקום שנאמר **אחר הדברים האלא** מחובר על הפרשה שלמעלה. **אחר הדברים האלא** שהרג אברהם את המלכים אמר לו הק' **אל תירא אברם מן האומות. ויהי אחר הדברים האלא** שנולד יצחק ויגד לאברהם לאמור עוד **ובתואל ילד את רבקה.** וכן **אחר הדברים האלא** שהגיד מרדכי על בגתן ותרש **גדל המלך אחשורוש את המן** שרצה להרוג את מרדכי ולא הואיל לו מה שהציל את המלך ונתלה המן. אף כאן **אחר הדברים האלא** שכרת אברהם ברית לאבימלך לו ולנינו ולנכדו של אברהם ונתן לו שבע כבשות צאון וחרה אפו של הק' על זאת שהרי ארץ פלישתים בכלל גבול ישראל והק' ציוה עליהם **לא תחיה כל נשמה.**

And it came to pass after these things. Every place [the biblical text] says **after these things** it is connected to the preceding section. **After these things** (Gen. 15:1) [after] Abraham killed the kings God said to him, **Abram, do not fear the nations. And it was after these things** (Gen. 22:20), after Isaac was born, that it was told to Abraham that

Betuel begat Rebecca. And thus **after these things** (Esther 3:1), that Mordechai told about Bigtan and Teresh, **the king Achashverosh raised up Haman**, that he wanted to kill Mordechai and it helped him that he had saved the king and Haman was hanged. Also here **after these things** that Abraham made a covenant with Abimelech and his children and grandchildren and he gave him seven sheep and God was angered because the land of the Pelishtim was in the borders of the land of Israel and God had commanded them **Do not allow any to live** (Deut. 20:16).

Rashbam's innovative interpretation of the binding of Isaac as a punishment contradicts not only Rashi but the entire midrashic tradition praising Abraham's greatness. He presents himself as deriving Abraham's sin from the simple necessity of language: Since Genesis 22 begins with the words **after these things**, Abraham's test must be a direct outcome of the story preceding it, which is about Abraham's treaty. Rashbam concludes from this that Abraham sinned by making a treaty and had to atone by proving his faith. Abraham's sin, according to Rashbam, was implicitly recognizing the claim of another to the land of Israel by making a treaty. This is a step beyond Rashi's reading, in which the near-sacrifice of Isaac justifies God's exclusive love. In Rashbam's reading, not only is the exclusiveness of God's love assumed but Abraham is punished for doubting it.[20]

For the mid- to late-twelfth-century Jewish commentator Joseph ben Isaac Bechor Shor of Orleans, the story of the near-sacrifice of Isaac is not primarily about responding to others. Although he does mention accusers briefly in his comments on verses 1 and 12, they are not identified and are not central to the story. His Genesis commentary explicitly attacks Christianity in other places,[21] but does not seem to do so explicitly in Genesis 22.

The polemical emphasis in the Gloss on the near-sacrifice of Isaac is not typical of the interpretations in Latin exegetes from 1000 to 1150. It is completely absent from the commentaries of three monastic exegetes: Bruno of Segni (1040–1123), Guibert of Nogent (1053–1124), and Rupert of Deutz (1075–1129). It is also absent from the *Adnotationes elucidatoriae in Pentateuchon* [Explanatory notes on the Pentateuch][22] by Hugh of the Parisian Cathedral school of St. Victor, written between 1125 and 1140. None emphasize Jews, or any "other" figure. Guibert of Nogent's *Moralia in Genesin* [Ethics in Genesis][23] focuses exclusively on the moral lesson of Abraham's test, as is typical of monastic exegesis.[24] The donkey, for Guibert, is *corporis lasciviam* [the lasciviousness of the body] which the rational mind needs to restrain and discipline in order to fulfill the test.[25] The two youths that accompany Abraham and Isaac are *voluntas et affectus* [will and emotion] that accompany reason.[26] Thus, although he polemicizes against Jews elsewhere,[27] in his commentary on Genesis 22 he does not allow polemical considerations to distract him from his moral exegesis.

Like Guibert of Nogent, Bruno of Segni, a Benedictine monk, wrote a commentary on the Pentateuch[28] in the late 1080s or early 1090s that does not mention Jews in the context of the near-sacrifice of Isaac at all.[29] Isidore of Seville is one of his main sources, and he draws on Isidore for his allegorical reading of the near-sacrifice of Isaac, but he does not quote any of Isidore's anti-Jewish polemic. Bruno's conclusion to the story of the near-sacrifice of Isaac is similar to Rashi's:

> Nunc te tentando, te probando cognovi, id est, cunctis gentibus notum feci quod timeas Dominum: nisi enim Abraham tentaretur, ejus obedientia non cognosceretur.[30]
>
> Now I have known you by testing you, by proving you. That is, I made known to all nations that you fear the Lord. If Abraham had not been tested, his obedience would not have been known.

For Rashi, God needed to make Abraham's greatness known to the other nations in order to explain his exclusive love for Israel. Bruno's conclusion, although it seems similar to Rashi's, is different in that the purpose is not to prove that the other nations are unworthy or that Abraham is greater than they are. Abraham may merely serve as a model to them of faith and obedience. This is not a polemical reading.

Hugh of St. Victor's *Adnotationes elucidatoriae in Pentateuchon*[31] is part of his program, set out in his *Didascalion: de studio legendi* [Teaching: concerning the study of reading][32] and his *De scriptis et scriptoribus sacris* [Concerning the sacred writings and their authors],[33] a comprehensive program of study in which the literal sense of scripture is only the first step.[34] In this commentary he does not mention Jews in the context of Genesis 22 at all. He does not quote Jerome on this passage, and although he repeats Jerome's *hebrei*-based association of Mount Moriah with Jerusalem he does not ascribe it to him or his Jewish sources.

Unlike Guibert of Nogent, Bruno of Segni, and Hugh of St. Victor, Rupert of Deutz does mention Jews in one of his six sermons on the near-sacrifice of Isaac, his *De sancta trinitate et operibus eius* [On the holy trinity and its beneficences], which he began in 1112[35] and completed in 1117. Unlike the Gloss, however, he is not preoccupied with them. Although he describes them in hostile terms he mentions them only twice. Both are tangential, brief references to the Jews as the killers of Christ.[36] He does not read the Jews as characters in the story, and the donkey is a positive indication of Abraham's humility rather than a negative portrayal of an "other" figure.[37] Rupert quotes both of Jerome's *hebrei*-based interpretations,[38] but when he quotes Jerome in chapter 28 it is to reject as useless his Hebrew etymology of Moriah as the place of vision, calling it "etymologiam dubitabilem quaerere, aut ut opinabilem investigare" [seeking after doubtful etymology or investigating something imaginary].[39] He does, however, accept the second comment that Jerome takes from Hebrew sources. Elsewhere in his commentary on Genesis, he describes Jews as enemies of the church and covered with blood from the death of Christ,[40] so the de-emphasis of this theme from his commentary on the near-sacrifice of Isaac cannot be attributed to lack of hostility towards Jews.[41] It suggests, rather, that exegesis of the near-sacrifice of Isaac was not a common location for anti-Jewish polemic, even among authors who polemicized elsewhere.

The polemical reading developed by Rashi and the Gloss, then, was not the only possible interpretation, or even the most obvious one, in either the Jewish or Christian twelfth-century exegetical tradition. It does not appear in any of the contemporary commentaries, even in those of commentators who also wrote anti-Jewish polemics. It also does not appear in any of Rashi's sources. Of the sources of the Gloss, it only appears in Isidore.

Although the polemical reading of the near-sacrifice of Isaac is not found in other Genesis 22 commentaries, the Hebrew crusade narratives (as shown in chapter one) do read the near-sacrifice of Isaac (and the sacrifices of Jewish fathers and mothers who emulated Abraham by killing their children rather than allowing them to be forcibly converted) as, among other things, proof that the Jews are worthy of God's love and divine election. This is a close parallel to the interpretation of the near-sacrifice of Isaac developed by Rashi. Similarly, as shown in chapter one, the idea of Jewish willful ignorance and blindness was current among Christian anti-Jewish polemicists, including Pseudo-William of Laon. Rashi and the Gloss developed at the same time an original and innovative polemical reading of the near-sacrifice of Isaac. Living during the deterioration of the

Jewish/Christian relationship, each read the story as specifically excluding the other. In this reading, each gave the other a central place in this pivotal Biblical narrative. Rashi made the accusing "other" into the instigator and audience of Abraham's test, and the Gloss turned the donkey and the slaves, representing the Jews, into important figures in the story. It is precisely in the ways in which Rashi and the Gloss exclude each other's religious tradition from the Abrahamic covenant they show both their similarity and centrality of the Jewish/Christian relationship to their exegesis.

Rashi and the Gloss display this similarity precisely when they are most engaged in proving their difference. We see a similar process at work when we examine the question of allegory in the near-sacrifice of Isaac. We have already seen the Gloss describe the Jews as blind, donkey-like, and stupid for not understanding the Christological significance of the story. For Rashi as well the story of the *Akedah* signifies a future redemptive event.

WHAT ABRAHAM SAW:
ISAAC, CHRIST, AND THE TEMPLE SACRIFICES

Both Rashi and the Gloss read the near-sacrifice of Isaac as looking forward to a future redemptive event. For Rashi, this future event is the sacrificial cult of the Temple. Rashi looks forward to the Temple sacrifices, and then past it to the present-day prayers and rituals of the Jews in exile. The present-day prayers therefore evoke not only the Temple sacrifices but also the *Akedah*. This is similar to the interpretation of the Gloss, which connects the near-sacrifice of Isaac to the crucifixion and then to the eucharist.

As is typical in medieval Christian exegesis, the Gloss draws strong connections between the near-sacrifice of Isaac and the sacrifice of Christ. Gilbert Dahan writes that "the essential characteristic of medieval [Christian] exegesis is the transition to the spiritual sense,"[42] and accordingly the Gloss frequently inserts Christ into the narrative of the near-sacrifice of Isaac. The Gloss also brings the narrative forward and connects it, like Rashi, to contemporary rituals and the hope of redemption in the present. While connections between the near-sacrifice of Isaac and the crucifixion are traditional in Christian exegesis, the innovation of the Gloss is in the lengths to which it goes to differ from both its sources and its contemporaries by avoiding defining this connection as spiritual or allegorical.

The marginal gloss bases its connections between the near-sacrifice of Isaac and the future redemption through Christ on quotations from Isidore. Comment 8.1m, paraphrased from Isidore, states:

> Abraam filium unicum ducens ad immolandum, deum patrem significat.
>
> Abraham, in leading his only son to be sacrificed, signifies God the father.

The marginal gloss sections based on Isidore develop the allegory detail by detail, and every word of the earlier story is significant foreshadowing. In comment 9.1m, for example, the thorns of the thicket in which the ram is caught prefigure the thorns of the cross. But it is not only the crucifixion that is foreshadowed but the entire future history of redemption. Comment 4.2m, paraphrased from Isidore, draws this analogy:

> Triduum quo venerunt ad locum sacrificii, tres etates significat. Ante legem ab abraham usque ad moysen. Sub lege a moyse usque ad iohannem. Inde usque ad dominum et quidquid restat, tercius dies est gratie, in qua tercia etate sacrificium dei completum est.
>
> The three days in which they came to the place of the sacrifice signify three eras: Before the law from Abraham until Moses, under the law from Moses until John [the Baptist], then up until [the time of] the Lord, and whatever [time] remains is the third era, a time of grace, in which the sacrifice of God was completed.

The marginal gloss here, like Rashi, emphasizes the continuing redemptive significance of the near-sacrifice of Isaac up until the present day. The interlinear gloss, like the marginal gloss and like Rashi, extends the prefiguration well beyond the death of Christ into present history. For example 9.1i explains the altar on which Abraham bound Isaac as *figura altaris in quo consecrantur corpus et sanguis christi* [a symbol of the altar on which the body and blood of Christ is consecrated]. Here the concordance is between the biblical text and the present ritual. The Gloss connects the altar of Genesis 22 with the present-day altar of the eucharist.

The interlinear gloss uses the words *quia* and *hoc est*—as we see in the above two comments—to create ambiguity about the allegorical nature of these comments by using the same words in comments which are not allegorical. For example, 16.1i explains the words *per memet ipsum iuravi, dicit dominus* [I have sworn by myself, says the Lord], as, *quia maiorem non habui* [because I have nothing greater]. Here the word *quia* introduces a comment which appears to be a simple explanation of the words. Similarly, in 16.2i, *quia immutabiliter a deo statutum est* [because it is unchangeably decreed by God] seems only to be an explanation of what it means for God to swear. These words blur the distinction between spiritual and literal exegeses which are present in the sources of the Gloss. The story of the near-sacrifice of Isaac is about the future history it foreshadows to the same extent and in the same way that it is about Abraham and Isaac.

In addition to the stylistic technique of using the same vocabulary to introduce different kinds of exegesis, the interlinear gloss further complicates the distinction between literal and allegorical exegesis by introducing the element of prophecy. In the Gloss, Abraham foresees the future redemption through Christ. In 2.3i, the interlinear gloss explains that the purpose of the test was to give Abraham this revelation. Abraham had to journey to Mount Moriah *ubi tibi revelabitur quid hac immolatione portendam* [where it will be revealed to you [Abraham] what I will foretell with this sacrifice]. The idea that Abraham foresees the future redemption through Christ is central in the interlinear gloss, appearing in six comments on Genesis 22 (2.3i, 2.5i, 11.1i, 14.1i, 14.2i, 15.1i). This important idea does not appear in the marginal gloss at all, except in those manuscripts in which 14.2i (which is the continuation of 12.2i discussed above) is in the marginal gloss.

Abraham's vision seems to be an innovation that the interlinear gloss has constructed by reading its sources together. In Augustine's *Quaestionum in Heptateuchem* 58 he writes:

> Vox angeli de caelo ad Abraham: Ne inicias manum in puerum neque facias ei quidquam; modo enim cognovi quoniam times deum tu. Etiam ista quaestio simili locutione soluitur; hoc est enim: nunc cognovi, quoniam times deum tu, quod significat: "nunc te feci cognoscere." In consequentibus autem hoc genus locutionis euidenter adparet, ubi dicitur: et vocavit Abraham nomen loci illius "dominus vidit." ut dicant hodie: in monte dominus adparuit. "Vidit" pro eo quod est "adparuit," hoc est "vidit" pro eo quod est "videri fecit," significans per efficientem id quod efficitur, sicut frigus pigrum quod pigros facit.[43]

> The voice of the angel from heaven to Abraham: "Do not strike your hand against your son, and do not do anything to him. For now I know that you fear God." This question is explained in a similar way, which is this: now I know that you fear God means: "Now I have made known." This

kind of speech is obvious in the following, where it is said: And Abraham called the name of this place "God saw," so that they might say today: God appeared on the mountain. "Saw" means that something "appeared," in other words "saw" means "caused to be seen," signifying through the effect that which is effected, just like "sluggish cold" makes people sluggish.

The interlinear (variable) glosses 12.2i and 14.2i adapt this comment and use Augustine as a source for Abraham's prophecy about Christ. Augustine here introduces the idea that "saw" equals "caused to see," but Augustine, unlike the Gloss, does not connect it specifically to God showing anything to Abraham, or to God showing anything about the incarnation. If anything, it seems that God is appearing himself rather than revealing something else. The interlinear gloss in 14.1i specifically connects this to God showing Abraham something about the future: *quia ibi fecit abraham videre diem*[44] *suum* [because there he caused Abraham to see his day]. Here, unlike in Augustine, Abraham sees not God but God's day. God's revelation turns into a prophecy about the future.

The interlinear gloss joins Augustine's comments about Abraham's vision to Isidore's typological reading. Isidore's *Quaestiones in Vetus Testamentum* Chapter 18 describes at length the parallels between the near-sacrifice of Isaac and the crucifixion narrative. The crucifixion is the "mystery" hidden in this story. In Isidore, however, there is no hint of Abraham himself being aware of this. By bringing Augustine and Isidore together, the Gloss (both marginal and interlinear) constructs this narrative of God revealing to Abraham the foreshadowing of Christ.

In addition to the six comments in which Abraham explicitly receives a prophecy of Christ, it also is a possible reading of eleven comments (2.4i, 3.2i, 3.3i, 5.1i, 6.1i, 8.1i, 9.1i, 9.2i, 12.1i, 13.1i, 16.3i, 17.3i) in which an action or command of God's is explained using *quia* or *hoc est*, followed by a description of an event in the life and death of Christ which is parallel to the verse in question. It is not clear if the authors intended Abraham or only the reader to understand this identification or explanation.

Although the idea that Abraham foresees Christ is not present in any of the immediate sources of the Gloss, it is a traditional theme in Christian exegesis of the near-sacrifice of Isaac. John 8:56 (Abraham your father rejoiced that he might see my day, he saw it and was glad) already suggests that Abraham had some foreknowledge of Christ. Irenaeus was one of the first to associate this verse with the near-sacrifice of Isaac.[45] Origen further suggests on the basis of Hebrews 11:17–19 that Abraham believed in the resurrection of the dead and the future resurrection of Christ.[46] Ambrose rejects this idea and writes that if Abraham prophesied he did so unknowingly.[47]

Although the idea of Abraham's prophecy is traditional, it is not found in the immediate sources of the Gloss. It is also largely absent in the Gloss' contemporaries. Rupert of Deutz and Guibert of Nogent also do not ascribe any special vision of Christ to Abraham. Bruno of Segni follows Jerome in translating "Moriah" as *Mons visionis* [mount of vision],[48] which he explains as the place where *Deus monstraret quid per hoc sacrificium monstrare vellet* [God showed that which he wished to be shown through this sacrifice]. But although the language is similar, the intent is different: as discussed above, for Bruno what God wished to be shown was Abraham's greatness. Abraham is the one who is shown, not the one who sees.

The Gloss is also unusual in not drawing a clear distinction between literal and allegorical senses in its commentary on Genesis 22. Bruno of Segni, Rupert of Deutz, and Hugh of St. Victor make a clear distinction between literal and allegorical senses. Bruno of Segni expounds upon Genesis 22 twice, once literally and the second allegorically. His commentary distinguishes the literal and allegorical senses and discusses them separately.[49] The literal sense, for Bruno, teaches the monk about Abraham and Isaac's examples of faith, while the allegorical shows the connections between the near-sacrifice of Isaac and the crucifixion. Bruno's main source for his literal exegesis is Josephus's *Antiquities* 1.13.4,[50] from which Bruno derives his emphasis on Isaac's willing participation. Bruno's allegorical[51] interpretation matches up the details of the near-sacrifice of Isaac with the crucifixion of Christ. Isaac represents Christ's divine nature, which could not be killed, while the ram represents his human nature, which could be and was.[52] Still, not all Bruno's references to Christ are contained in his allegorical interpretation. Bruno's literal interpretation ends with the promise to Abraham:

> promittitur ei semen insuperabile, et in quo omnes gentes benedicantur; pro quo Christus intelligitur, in quo qui non benedicitur, non est benedictus.[53]

> Unconquerable seed (which is understood to be Christ) is promised to him, and through Christ are all nations blessed. The only legitimate source of blessing is Christ.

In this text, Christ is the promised descendant of Abraham in whom all nations shall be blessed. To Bruno, this is a literal interpretation. Christ is the literal descendant of Abraham and the only one who generates blessing for all nations. Bruno of Segni, therefore, provides an exegetical alternative that distinguishes between literal and allegorical senses and sees Christ in both.

Rupert of Deutz also draws a distinction between *secundum litteram* [following the letter] and *medullitus* [the deeper meaning] in his six essays.[54] The first two, which Rupert describes as literal, explain the etymology of Mount Moriah and Abraham's humility in riding a donkey. The later four discuss spiritual meanings of the story.

Guibert of Nogent and Hugh of St. Victor each explicitly deal with only one sense of scripture in their commentaries on the near-sacrifice of Isaac. Guibert of Nogent interprets all of Genesis according to his moral scheme.[55] In his preface, entitled *Quo ordine sermo fieri debeat* [In what way a sermon must be given][56] he states that the goal of the preacher is to draw on both experience and scriptural texts to produce an emotional transformation for the audience.[57] Allegory, he says, may be useful for disputing with Jews and heretics but is only of tangential value for the believing Christian seeking self-improvement.[58] Following his plan of explaining Genesis purely from a moral perspective, Guibert's *Moralia* outlines the internal struggle of the soul through the stories of Genesis.[59] The soul is divided between Reason, Will, and Affection, all in constant struggle for supremacy.[60] The various characters of Genesis represent these different aspects. The patriarchs typically represent Reason, their wives represent Will, and children or other characters are Affection, turning all of Genesis into one continuous spiritual narrative with different names taking on the same or similar roles.[61] Abraham, as a patriarch, represents Reason or Intellect.[62] At his birth, Isaac as the child of Abraham signifies joy or Affection.[63] In Guibert's commentary on Genesis 22, Isaac begins to take on his role as patriarch by signifying Reason (as opposed to the two slaves, who signify Will and Affection that need to be subordinated to Reason).[64] At the same time Isaac continues to signify Abraham's hope of *superna gaudia*, highest delights, which Abraham is willing to throw on the fire of the Sacred Word.[65]

The purpose and intended audience of Guibert's commentary is absolutely clear. While his introduction leaves open the possibility that another, allegorical commentary could be written that would be useful for proving the truth of Christianity, that is not at all his concern here. His commentary on Genesis, and on the near-sacrifice of Isaac in particular, is intended purely as a guide to using the scriptures to further one's progress along the monastic path.

Hugh of St. Victor's commentary on the near-sacrifice of Isaac in his *Adnotationes elucidatoriae in Pentateuchon* [Explanatory notes on the Pentateuch][66] (written between 1125 and 1140[67]) consists of four disconnected comments that focus exclusively on the literal sense. It reads not as a full commentary but as a collection of short explanatory notes on the Pentateuch. Hugh sets out in his *Didascalion: de studio legendi* [Teaching: concerning the study of reading][68] a comprehensive program of study in which the literal sense of scripture is only the first step.[69] The program prescribes that a student first read the books richest in history (such as Genesis, Exodus, Joshua, the Gospels, and Acts) with an eye to history and geography.[70] The student may then progress to the study of doctrine through books such as the Epistles and the Apocalypse, and finally proceed to the study of the foreshadowing of Christ in the Pentateuch, Isaiah, Ezekiel, Job, Song of Songs, and Psalms.[71] Hugh's commentary on Genesis 22, then, represents only his first step. He keeps his literal commentary free from allegorical interpretation because the two types of exegesis are appropriate for different kinds of students.[72]

Although, unlike the Gloss, these commentaries clearly state whether they are writing literal or allegorical exegesis, the boundary between them is not always clear. Even Hugh of St. Victor draws connections between the near-sacrifice of Isaac and the crucifixion, by arguing (in one of his only four comments) that the place of the sacrifice was the place of the crucifixion. Similarly, Bruno's comment that Christ is the descendant promised to Abraham in Genesis 22:18 is part of his literal interpretation. Rupert of Deutz's exegesis—both *secundum litteram* and *medullitus*—looks towards the future, but in different ways. In the first, literal part of Rupert's exegesis, God intended the test as a lesson to Abraham's future descendants.[73] Rupert, unlike Bruno and Hugo, does not mention Christ in his literal exegesis. In the latter part of his exegesis, defined as *medullitus*, Rupert explains that God arranged the near-sacrifice of Isaac so that in the future, when God sacrifices His own son, it would be out of justice rather than mercy. Rupert then draws out the parallels between the near-sacrifice of Isaac and the crucifixion, and between the near-sacrifice of Isaac and the Eucharist.[74]

In summary, although the Gloss does consistently draw parallels between the crucifixion and the near-sacrifice of Isaac, it does so without the distinction between senses found in both its sources and contemporaries. In this its approach is like that of Rashi, who similarly draws connections between the near-sacrifice of Isaac, future sacrifices, and the ongoing history of salvation.

Rashi shows how important the Temple sacrifices are to understanding the near-sacrifice of Isaac by repeating references to them in Genesis 22 both at the beginning and at the end of the story. The theme of the Temple sacrifices appears in five of Rashi's comments and is one of his most repeated themes. In 2.3, he identifies the land of Moriah as Jerusalem, the place where the Temple will be built. He makes this connection by citing a Biblical parallel from 2 Chronicles 3:1, which uses the phrase "Mount Moriah" to describe the location of the Temple. Rashi connects these locations based on 2 Chronicles 3.1:

ויחל שלמה לבנות את בית ה' בירושלים בהר המוריה אשר נראה לדוד אביהו.

And Solomon began to build the house of God in Jerusalem on Mount Moriah where God appeared (*nireh*) to David his father.

This verse connects the name of the place *Moriah* with the verb "to see" or "to appear," but links it with the David story rather than the Abraham story.[75] Rashi also cites both the Babylonian Talmud Taanit 16a and the Targum of Onqelos, which give two different explanations for the connection. While Rashi frequently gives two alternative explanations for other words and verses, there is no other example in Genesis 22 of him giving three alternative explanations for one word. That they are all different ways of justifying the same translation makes the redundancy stronger. This connection between the near-sacrifice of Isaac and the Temple sacrifices is so important for Rashi that he proves it three different ways.[76]

After Abraham completes the sacrifice, Rashi once again emphasizes the connection to the Temple and its location. "God will see," in verse 14, means, in comment 14.1 "God will choose and see for himself this place in order to cause his presence to dwell there so that sacrifices will be offered there." The name that Abraham gives to this place has as its meaning that the Temple will be built in that place. To connect the Temple with Abraham, Rashi's source here is the Targum of Onqelos on this verse, from which he derives the idea that "God sees" actually means "God will show." He also uses b. Berachot 62b, from which he derives the idea that what God will see, or choose, is the future Temple. So Rashi shows the importance of the connection between the Temple sacrifices and the near-sacrifice of Isaac by emphasizing it repeatedly, and citing multiple redundant sources to prove the connection, both at the beginning and at the end of the narrative.

The connection, for Rashi, between Abraham's near-sacrifice and the Temple sacrifices is not only one of place. Abraham enters into the reality of the Temple sacrifices, becoming, as it were, a Temple priest who sacrifices Isaac according to the laws of Leviticus. In 13.4, Abraham prays that the sacrifice of the ram in the place of Isaac should be considered

כאילו בני שחוט, כאילו דמו זרוק, כאילו הוא מופשט, כאילו הוא נקטר ונעשה דשן . . .

. . . as if my son were slaughtered, as if his blood were sprinkled, as if he were flayed, as if he were burned and made ashes.

The verbs לשחוט, לזרק דם, לפשט, להקטיר are all used in Leviticus 1 to describe the stages of the עולה [*olah*], burnt offering.[77] The similarity in language indicates that Rashi is describing Abraham's sacrifice of Isaac as completely consistent with the Temple ritual, and in fact part of it.

For Rashi the connection between the near-sacrifice of Isaac and the Temple sacrifices goes beyond the time of the Temple itself and into post-Temple times. In comments 14.1 and 14.3 Rashi explains the phrase **God sees** as follows:

ה' יראה. פשוטו כתרגומו, ה' יבחר ויראה לו המקום הזה להשרות בו שכינתו ולהקריב כאן קורבנות. . . . ומדרש אגדה: ה' יראה עקידה זו לסלוח לישראל בכל שנה ולהצילם מן הפורענות כדי שיאמר היום הזה ובכל הדורות הבאים, בהר ה' יראה אפרו של יצחק צבור ועומד לכפרה.

God will see. Its contextual (*peshuto*) meaning is according to the Targum: God will choose and see for himself this place to cause his presence to dwell there and to cause sacrifices to be offered there . . . And there is an aggadic Midrash: God will see this binding to forgive Israel in every year and to rescue them from disaster, so that in this day and in all future generations it will be said: "On the mountain God will see the ashes of Isaac piled up as an atonement."

Here Rashi makes two implicit identifications. One, as we have already seen, connects biblical verses to identify the site of the near-sacrifice of Isaac as the site of the future Temple sacrifices. The second interpretation connects the near-sacrifice of Isaac not with another biblical text but with the reality of the interpretive community. Michael Signer suggests that the very early and influential tradition of reading the story of the near-sacrifice of Isaac on the high holy day of Rosh Hashana motivated Rashi to make this connection.[78] This interpretation uses the powerful and evocative image of "the ashes of Isaac" to explain what God will see in the far future. It connects this story to the post-Biblical future of Rashi's present, when Israel is in trouble and needs to be rescued and forgiven.

Although Rashi quotes rabbinic sources for all his comments, the importance of the connection between the near-sacrifice of Isaac and the Temple sacrifices, for Rashi, was not based on his sources. As shown in chapter two, the midrashic literature on Genesis 22 connects the near-sacrifice of Isaac to many other biblical texts. Rashi omits almost all of this exegesis, with the exception of the material that connects the near-sacrifice of Isaac with the Temple sacrifices. Outside of other stories about Abraham, the Temple sacrifices are the only biblical material that Rashi mentions more than once. So while Rashi has midrashic sources for this exegesis, the importance that he gives it is not based on his sources. The importance of the Temple sacrifices for Rashi may connect to the importance of both the near-sacrifice of Isaac and the Temple sacrifices as models in the martyrological Crusade narratives, although the dates of both these chronicles and of Rashi's composite commentary are too unclear to suggest a specific influence with any certainty.

Bereshit Rabbati's reading is similar to Rashi's in that does look forward to future events, including hinting at the Temple sacrifices. Two of its stories about the near-sacrifice of Isaac connect between Abraham's sacrifice and the condition of Jews in the future. The first story connects the near-sacrifice of Isaac with the passages about Daniel and his companions in Daniel 1. In the story as told in *Bereshit Rabbati*,[79] Daniel tells his companions not to eat impure bread even though it had been prophesied (in Ezekiel 4:13) that the children of Israel would eat impure bread among the nations. They resolve to fast for ten days, and explain to the ministers that they can do this because they are protected by Abraham's ten tests.[80] Here the near-sacrifice of Isaac functions as a way to preserve Israel from God's judgments, and is strong enough that Israelites in exile can call on it to overturn a prophecy against them.

Like Rashi, *Bereshit Rabbati* imagines Abraham as a priest offering sacrifices, and describes Abraham as wondering why he is the appropriate person to offer sacrifices rather than Melchizedek or Shem.[81] Unlike Rashi, however, it does not invoke the Jerusalem Temple or the laws of sacrifices that were applicable there.

Bereshit Rabbati concludes, like Rashi, by bringing the sacrifice into the present day. On Genesis 22:14, it comments:

א"ר שמלאי נתעטף אברהם בתפילה ויצחק בנו. אמר אברהם גלוי וידוע לפניך שהיה לי מה להשיבך . . . ולא השיבותי לך אלא עשיתי עצמי כאלם וכחרש, כך כשיהיו בניו של יצחק נדונים ביום הזה אפי' יש להם כמה קטגורים מקטרגים אותם, כשם שדוממתי ולא השיבותי אותך, אף אתה לא תקבל מהם. הה"ד **ויקרא אברהם שם המקום ההוא ה' יראה** היאך דממתי ולא השיבותי אף הוא ידום ולא ישיב למקטרגים. **בהר ה' יראה**. אמר יצחק גלוי הוא לפניך שלא שור העליתי לפניך אלא עצמי ובשרי, אף כשיבוא בני לידי צרות וצוקות שיש להם כמה קטיגורים תזכור להם עקדתי, ויראה לפניך כאילו עפרי צרור ע"ג המזבח. הוי **בהר ה' יראה**, עקדתי שנעשית כבר ה' יראה לפניך לדורות. **אשר** יאמר היום מפני שראש השנה היה . . .

Rabbi Simlai said: Abraham wrapped himself in prayer with Isaac his son. Abraham said, "It is revealed and known before you that I was able to respond to you . . . but I did not respond to you, rather I made myself deaf and dumb, thus when Isaac's children are judged on this day, even though they may have several accusers accusing them, just as I was silent and did not refute you, thus you should also not receive any rebuke from them." This is as it is written, **and Abraham called the name of the place "The Lord will see"** how I was silent and did not respond and so He will be silent and not respond to accusers. **On the mountain God will see.** Isaac said, it is revealed before you that I did not offer before you an ox but rather my own bone and flesh. Thus when my children will fall into troubles and cry out that they have many accusers, remember for them my binding, and may it be seen before you as if my ashes are piled up on the altar. This is **God will see** the binding that was already done, **God will see** before you for generations. **On that day** because it was Rosh Hashanah.

Both Abraham and Isaac invoke their near-sacrifice as a reason for God to protect their descendants from accusers who might remind God that the Jews deserve to suffer.[82] The "ashes of Isaac" continue to remind God to be merciful in the future. The timing of this conversation on Rosh Hashana strengthens the connection between the near-sacrifice of Isaac and present-day rituals.[83] In *Bereshit Rabbati*, however, Abraham and Isaac have no special vision. The only hint of this is when they ask God to protect their descendants from future dangers, but these dangers are not specified.

Midrash Lekach Tov makes this connection even stronger and more explicit. It interrupts its interpretation of the near-sacrifice of Isaac for a lengthy digression on the laws and significance of blowing the shofar on Rosh Hashana which is as long as the entirety of the rest of its commentary on Genesis 22. This discussion begins by explaining that the reason for blowing the shofar is to remember the near-sacrifice of Isaac, and because God has promised to forgive Israel in its memory. Further, *Lekach Tov* connects the *Akedah* explicitly to the future redemption. Its explanation of the ram caught in the thicket is as follows:

סימן לישראל אחרית הגלות ישראל נסבכים בצרות, וסופן להגאל בקרניו של איל, הה"ד
וה' אלוהים בשופר יתקע ובראש השנה נוטלין שופר ומתריעין וסופן להגאל. ר' יוסי
דסכנין בש"ר לוי, לפי שהיה אבינו אברהם רואה את האיל ניטש מן חורש זה, והולך
ומסתבך בחורש אחר, א"ל הקב"ה כך עתידין בניך להסתבך במלכויות, מבבל למדי,
וממדי ליון, ומיון לאדום, וסופן להגאל בקרניו של איל.

It is a sign for Israel that in the end of days Israel will be caught up in troubles, and in the end they will be redeemed through a ram's horn. This is as it is written: **And the Lord God will sound a shofar** (Zachariah 9:14). On Rosh Hashana they take the shofar and sound it, and it is a sign that they will be redeemed. And Rabbi Yossi of Sachnin said in the name of Rabbi Levi: When Abraham our Father saw a ram break away from one thicket and become entangled in another God said to him, "Thus your children will become entangled with [various] kingdoms, from Babylon to Medea, from Medea to Greece, and from Greece to Rome, and in the end will be redeemed through a ram's horn.

For the *Lekach Tov*, the ram caught in the thicket represents the sufferings of Israel before the redemption. Conversely, the theme of the near-sacrifice of Isaac foreshadowing a future redemption is not mentioned at all by the commentators of Rashi's school: Rashbam and Bechor Shor.

Like the use of the *Akedah* as a vehicle for polemic, this description of Abraham sacrificing his son like a priest in the Temple is central to the Hebrew Crusade narratives, which—as discussed in chapter one—describe pious Jews killing their children to prevent their conversion using the both the language of the Temple sacrifices and imagery from the near-sacrifice of Isaac. Rashi makes explicit the implied comparison in the Crusade narratives: between Abraham and the Temple sacrifices. The martyrs can be like both Abraham and the priests in the Temple because Abraham and the priests in the Temple are like each other.

Rashi juxtaposes biblical verses with biblical words and post-biblical rituals to draw connections between the near-sacrifice of Isaac and the Temple sacrifices. Abraham, going to the place of the Temple and sacrificing the ram as he would have sacrificed Isaac, according to the laws of the Temple sacrifices, not only prophesies the future Temple through his actions and but even enters into its reality. At the same time, Rashi connects the near-sacrifice of Isaac to redemption from future suffering. Both these identifications allow Abraham to participate in a later historical reality.

Gilbert Dahan describes the two methods of Christian allegorical interpretation operating in the late eleventh and early twelfth centuries as follows.

1. Double signification.
    The basic medieval technique for reading Christ into an Old Testament narrative is signification. As Richard of St. Victor describes it, *non solum voces sed et res significativae sunt* [not only words but also things are signifying]. This is based on the assumption that the biblical text, as an inspired text, exists beyond human language.[84] The Bible is a text that requires interpretation in order to discover its codes.[85]

2. Exegesis by concordance.
    While exegesis through signification is based on the idea of multiple significances to divine speech, exegesis through concordance is based on a different basic presumption of medieval exegesis: that of the unity of the divine word.[86] It depends fundamentally on memory:[87] An exegete will be reminded of one passage while reading another, and note the correspondence between them.[88] This unity goes beyond the unity

of the Old and New Testaments as described by Henri DeLubac[89] and includes a unity of all revelation. The boundaries of this unity will thus differ for Jews and Christians.

Exegesis by concordance raises the question of the boundaries of revelation. Can revelation take place through history? Rashi and the Gloss both make connections between the near-sacrifice of Isaac and present-day reality, as well as present-day rituals.[90] But they do so through a two-step process: first connecting the near-sacrifice of Isaac to a later biblical event, and then connecting both biblical texts to the present day.

ABRAHAM'S EXAMPLE OF FAITH

Even if Christological exegesis was a method for Christians to draw the border between their approaches to the Bible and the Jewish approach, the moral example of Abraham was occasionally a place where Jews and Christians could see similarity. Rashi and the Gloss both emphasize Abraham as a moral example. For each of them, though, Abraham's example is of something quite different. While Rashi describes Abraham's eagerness and love for God, the Gloss most strongly emphasizes Abraham's obedience: Rashi's Abraham argues with God and even tests God in return, while Abraham in the Gloss shows faith in God's ability to keep contradictory promises. So although Abraham's example of faith was shared by Jews and Christians, Rashi and the Gloss read this example differently.

In the Gloss on Genesis 22, Abraham demonstrates perfection, faith, love and obedience. In the interlinear gloss, obedience is the most important. It appears three times, in 1.2i, 8.1i, and 12.3i. As shown above, on verse 1 the interlinear gloss even adapts the material from Augustine to shift the emphasis from love to obedience. The virtues of perfection and zeal appear once each, in the interlinear gloss only, in 1.1i and 6.3i. Love and faith appear primarily in the marginal gloss. Love appears twice, in 1.1m and in 2.2i (which is a quote from Alcuin and is marginal in most manuscripts). Faith appears only in 5.3m, which is a quote from Alcuin.

The later manuscripts which include marginal and interlinear glosses based on Alcuin are thus the main source for how the Gloss uses Abraham as a moral example. Comment 2.1m describes the journey of three days as a time of torment for Abraham, in which he anticipates the sacrifice at the end of the journey. Comment 2.2i (which is marginal in the vast majority of manuscripts) describes the traumatic effect on Abraham of being reminded of God's promise that "in Isaac your seed will be called" (Genesis 21:12). Comment 5.3m praises Abraham's faith, and describes its emotional power:

> Indubitanti animo mactare filium volebat, laudandus in constantia offerendi, et in fide suscitandi.

> He was willing to sacrifice his son with an undoubting soul, being praiseworthy in the constancy of offering and trusting in resurrection.

Because the earliest manuscripts do not include the Alcuin material, this theme is a slightly later addition to the Gloss's story of the near-sacrifice of Isaac. In the earliest version, Abraham's moral example plays only a minor role.

The Gloss is unusual among its contemporary commentaries in how little it emphasizes Abraham as a moral example. The monastic exegetes Bruno of Segni, Rupert of Deutz, and Guibert of Nogent stress Abraham as an example for the reader to emulate. For Bruno, Abraham's virtue was that *ne resisteret* [he did not resist God's command].[91] Rupert of Deutz's first essay on Genesis 22 is about Abraham as an example of faith and love.[92] Guibert of Nogent develops this theme in great detail, describing Abraham as a model of self-restraint and intellectual inquiry.[93] To Guibert, Abraham is an example of the just man from Proverbs 24:16 who falls seven times and rises by overcoming every test.[94] Despite the addition of Alcuin's comments, the relative lack of emphasis on this theme in the Gloss shows movement away from the monastic tradition of exegesis. It is another way in which the Gloss is more similar to Rashi's commentary than it is to contemporary Christian commentaries.

Like the Gloss, Rashi mentions Abraham's moral example, and also allots it less space than he does to his other concerns. For Rashi, unlike the Gloss, Abraham's most praiseworthy trait is not his obedience but his zeal. Rashi mentions Abraham's eagerness to fulfill God's command in three comments, and God's delay and consideration in giving those commands in another three comments.[95] In comments 3.1, 3.2, and 6.2, Rashi describes Abraham's way of fulfilling God's command. In comment 3.1, Rashi explains that Abraham rose early because he was "eager to fulfill the command." In 3.2, he explains that Abraham saddled his own donkey, and did not ask one of his servants to saddle the donkey for him because "love breaks down the line [i.e., the natural order of things]." In 6.2, he describes Abraham going to the sacrifice "willingly and happily." Rashi presents Abraham not as a model of obedience, faith, or fear of God, but as a model of eagerness and joy in performing God's commands out of love.

Rashi's depiction of Abraham's obedience further differs from that of the Gloss in his emphasis on Abraham's paradoxical resistance to God's command. While Rashi presents Abraham as eagerly obedient, Rashi also presents Abraham as arguing with God. For Rashi, following his sources *Genesis Rabbah* and *Midrash Tanchuma*,[96] Abraham may be willing but he is not passive. Abraham argues with God, and even tests God back. This theme appears in four of Rashi's comments on this chapter. In 2.2, Rashi explains the seeming repetition of "your son, your only one, whom you love, Isaac," by presenting Abraham as consistently refusing the divine implication that he only has one son, or only loves one son. Rashi here presents Abraham resisting the divine selection of Isaac for as long as he can.

In comment 5.1, Rashi introduces the counter-test.

עד כה. . . . ומדרש אגדה, אראה היכן הוא מה שאמר לי המקום **כה יהיה זרעך.**

Until there . . . and an aggadic midrash, I will see where it is that God [the Place] said to me: **Thus will be your seed.**

The reference is to Genesis 15:5:

ויאמר לו הבט–נא השמימה וספר הכוכבים אם תוכל לספור אותם ויאמר לו כה יהיה זרעך.

And he said to him: Look to the heavens and count the stars. Can you count them? And he said to him: Thus will be your seed.

God may be testing Abraham here, but Abraham is also testing God. God has made a promise to Abraham, and Abraham is testing God to see if this promise will be fulfilled.

Abraham continues the counter-test in 12.1. After God tells Abraham to stop and not kill his son, Abraham answers, "If so, I have come here for nothing. I will wound him and withdraw a little blood."[97] Abraham here argues with the part of God's command where one would not expect argument. Isaac becomes Abraham's hostage in his demand for an explanation.[98]

כי עתה ידעתי. אמר רבי אבא: אמר לו אברהם: אפרש לפניך את שיחתי. אתמול אמרת לי: **כי ביצחק יקרא לך זרע.** וחזרת ואמרת: **קח נא את בינך.** עכשיו אתה אומר לי, **אל תשלך**

ידך אל הנער. אמר לו קב"ה: לא אחלל בריתי ומוצא שפתי לא אשנה. כשאמרתי לך
קח, מוצא שפתי לא אשנה. לא אמרתי שחטהו אלא העלהו. אסקתיה, אחתיה.

Now I know. Rabbi Abba said: Abraham said to him [God]: I will set
my words before you. Yesterday you said to me: "**In Isaac will be called
your seed**" (Gen. 21.12). Then you went back and said: "**Take your son**"
(22.1). Now you say to me: "Do not send forth your hand against the boy"
(22.12). God [the Holy Blessed One] said to him: "I will not profane my
covenant and the utterance of my lips will not change" (Psalms 89:35).
When I said to you "take," the utterance of my lips will not change. I did
not say "slaughter him" but rather "bring him up." You brought him up,
now bring him down.

Abraham's obedience has given him the right to demand an explanation
from God. If Abraham needs to pass God's test and prove his obedience,
God has to pass Abraham's test and prove his trustworthiness, prove that
he is capable of keeping all his varied and contradictory promises. This
contrasts with the interpretation in the Gloss of Abraham's obedience as a
way of proving his faith in God's ability to keep the contradictory promises
about Isaac. For the Gloss (following Alcuin), part of what God is testing
is Abraham's ability to believe that God will find a way to both accept the
sacrifice of Isaac and make Isaac into Abraham's fruitful heir. While Rashi's
Abraham challenges God on the contradiction between the commands,
the Gloss's Abraham has faith that the contradiction will be resolved. In
both cases Abraham shows faith, but it is expressed differently in the two
commentaries.

The theme of the counter-test is not original to Rashi and is also found in
Genesis Rabbah[99] and *Midrash Tanchuma*.[100] Unlike his midrashic sources,
however, Rashi does not use Abraham's arguments as a way to call God's
goodness and justice into question. The only comment in which Abraham
seems to do so is the likely late 12.2.

Rashi and the Gloss both emphasize Abraham's obedience but describe
it in different terms. Rashi focuses on Abraham's emotions: his love, his
willingness, his eagerness. The Gloss primarily stresses the fact of Abraham's obedience rather than its motivations. And while Rashi's Abraham
argues with God and tests God, Abraham in the Gloss does not. This difference shows that while both Jewish and Christian exegetes regard Abraham

as an example of faith, the nature of this example is not necessarily shared between the two traditions.

A SIGNIFICANT DIFFERENCE: THE ROLE OF ISAAC

While a close examination of Rashi and of the Gloss shows that they diverge only somewhat in their portrayal of Abraham's faith and obedience, the difference in their portrayals of Isaac is more dramatic. Rashi's Isaac is tested, while Isaac in the Gloss is not. Isaac in Rashi goes willingly to be sacrificed, while in the Gloss he is passive. Isaac, for Rashi, is to be emulated to the same extent as Abraham, while the Gloss encourages the reader to identify exclusively with Isaac. Finally, in the end Rashi's Isaac is rewarded, while in the Gloss the reward may be passed through Isaac, but it is earned by Abraham alone.

For Rashi, the near-sacrifice of Isaac is as much a test of Isaac as of Abraham. Rashi presents Isaac as an active and willing participant, who also proves his worth and greatness through his obedience. This theme appears in comments 1.1, 6.2, 8.1, 17.1, and 17.2: at the beginning, climax, and end of the story.

In comment 1.1, as shown in chapter 2, Rashi presents the near-sacrifice of Isaac as a test of both Abraham and Isaac. Rashi's need to bring two alternative explanations indicates that for him neither is fully adequate. The near-sacrifice of Isaac cannot be understood simply as a test of Abraham, just as it is not only a test of Isaac. Rashi needs to explain how this was a test for both, and why both required such a test. The structure of this comment equates Abraham and Isaac. Rashi gives both are equal space and their tests equal weight.

In 6.2 and 8.1, Rashi further emphasizes the equality of Abraham and Isaac, along with Isaac's willing participation.

וילכו שניהם יחדיו. אברהם שהיה יודע שהולך לשחוט את בנו היה הולך ברצון ושמחה כיצחק שלא היה מרגיש דבר.

יראה לו השה. יבחר לו השה, ואם אין שה, **לעולה בני.** ואף אל פי שהבין יצחק שהוא הולך להשחט, **וילכו שניהם יחדיו** בלב שוה.

And the two walked on together. Abraham who knew that he was going to slaughter his son went willingly and joyfully like Isaac who did not sense anything.

Will see for himself a lamb. He will choose a lamb, and if there is not a lamb, **my son will be the sacrifice.** And even though Isaac understood that he was going to be slaughtered, **the two went on together,** with an equal heart.

It is not enough that, as in *Midrash Tanchuma* Vayera 23, Isaac knows that he is to be sacrificed. Nor is it even sufficient that, as in *Genesis Rabbah* 56.4, Isaac continues with Abraham after finding out the truth. Rashi adds to *Genesis Rabbah* the final two words בלב שוה [with equal heart]. Not only is the test equal for Isaac and Abraham, but both pass it equally. Comment 6.2, although a logical extension of 8.1, is one of Rashi's few comments in this chapter that are entirely original.

Rashi ends his commentary on the story of the near-sacrifice of Isaac by emphasizing that just as the test was equal for both Abraham and Isaac (as shown in 1.1) and just as their joy and willing submission was equal (as shown in 6.2), so their reward was equal:

ברך אברכך, אחת לאב ואחת לבן. והרבה ארבה, אחת לאב ואחת לבן.

I will surely bless you. One for the father and one for the son. **And I will surely increase.** One for the father and one for the son.

The Hebrew here repeats: "blessing, I will bless you" and "increasing, I will increase." Rashi explains that there were two blessings, one for Abraham and one for Isaac. This is Rashi's final comment on the story of the near-sacrifice of Isaac.[101] Rashi, then, emphasizes Isaac as an equal participant at both the beginning and end of the story.

The Gloss, unlike Rashi, minimizes Isaac's role. The only comment that might possibly refer to Isaac's greatness or obedience is 8.1i: *quia obedivit patri filius usquam ad mortem* [because the son obeyed the father even unto death]. This comment explains the following verses (22.7–8):

Isaac said to his father, "Father." And he answered, "Here I am, my son." He said, "Here are fire and wood, but where is the lamb for the sacrifice?" And Abraham said, "God will provide himself a lamb for the sacrifice, my son." So they went on together.

If Isaac (as opposed to, or in addition to, Christ) is the son to which the Gloss refers, perhaps in these verses he understood Abraham's intent to sacrifice him and consented to it.

As Jody Lynn Vaccaro has shown, early Christian exegesis of the near-sacrifice of Isaac tends to present the test as only Abraham's. While midrashic collections tend to develop the theme of Isaac's anguish and his willing obedience to God and his father, most early Christian commentators focus exclusively on Abraham's moral struggle. Vaccaro suggests that Isaac's identification with Christ precludes any other way in which he could serve as a model.[102]

We see this difference reflected in eleventh- and twelfth-century exegesis as well. Rupert of Deutz, Guibert of Nogent, and Hugh of St. Victor describe Isaac in exclusively passive terms. In a seeming exception to this pattern, Bruno of Segni describes Isaac's greatness in terms equal to that of Abraham. He writes:

> Sic enim Josephus ait: jam illius erat aetatis, ut patrem, si vellet, facile superare posset; sed postquam hoc Deum praecepisse cognoverat, sponte se ad immolandum dedit, ne Dei resisteret voluntati. Quis igitur in hoc, Abraham an Isaac, laudabilior sit, non facile apparet.[103]

> Thus Josephus says: Now he was of such an age that he could, if he wished, easily overcome his father; but after he knew that God had commanded it, he willingly gave himself to be sacrificed, lest he should resist the will of God. Therefore, whether Abraham or Isaac is more praiseworthy in this is not easily apparent.

Bruno here stresses Isaac's obedience, but does so through a quotation from the Jewish source Josephus in the section which he specifically marks as literal exposition.[104]

Other Jewish commentators typically also emphasize Isaac's role, although this emphasis is not universal. *Bereshit Rabbati* strongly emphasizes Isaac's role, although Rashi goes further in that Isaac is in every way equal to Abraham, and that his test precisely parallels Abraham's own. The twelfth-century Spanish Jewish exegete Ibn Ezra on the contrary claims that Isaac was bound against his will.[105] Rashbam does not mention Isaac at all. Bechor Shor mentions both alternatives: In his single use of midrash in this chapter, he gives the possibility that Isaac understood and consented, and describes this reading as midrashic.[106]

We have seen that Rashi and the Gloss, while they both regard Abraham as an example of faith, differ in their approaches to the character and role of Isaac. This difference seems to be based on the differing patristic and midrashic traditions about Isaac, and on consistency with traditions of Jewish and Christian exegesis. But just as Rashi and the Gloss continue the differences of their sources, so too they continue the similarities generated by the exegetical contacts between their sources.

CONCLUSIONS

Our comparison has shown that while some themes and reading techniques persist from patristic/Carolingian and midrashic sources to the twelfth-century commentaries, there are differences reflecting the changed historical context. Similarly, there are similarities between Rashi and the Gloss that are not accounted for by their sources. Despite their heavy reliance on earlier exegesis Rashi and the Gloss are both substantially different from the earlier commentaries which they manipulate and transform. The similarities between them and the differences between them and their sources show trends in the exegesis of the near-sacrifice of Isaac that are particular to twelfth-century France.

The comparison of Rashi with his sources has shown substantial differences. *Genesis Rabbah* and *Midrash Tanchuma*, Rashi's main midrashic sources, interrogate God's justice in testing Abraham and connect it to the question of why God tests the righteous. Rashi reads Abraham's test as primarily for the purpose of proving Abraham's greatness to a hostile, accusing, non-chosen other. In terms of reading strategies, while midrash is, in the words of James Kugel, exegesis of verses rather than stories,[107] Rashi is holistically interpreting this story and brings in other verses only when relevant to this one. While Rashi's midrashic sources quote multiple interpretations in the names of different rabbis, Rashi does not cite a source and tends not to give interpretations that are in contradiction with one another (although he may give alternative interpretations that are complementary). By not citing the names of rabbis, Rashi makes clear that he is no longer in the framework of the midrashic oral tradition. Instead, he attempts to show how his exegesis, whether or not it has a midrashic source, arises naturally from questions any reader might ask of the biblical text.

The comparison of the *Glossa Ordinaria* with its sources has shown that, by combining Isidore with Jerome and Augustine, the Gloss generates an anti-Jewish polemical reading of the near-sacrifice of Isaac that goes beyond its sources. Further, in stripping out names and attributions it creates an impression of uniformity in its late antique sources. The interlinear gloss is unsourced except for other biblical verses and obscures the influence of patristic literature, giving the impression that it is reading the Bible as a self-glossing text. The combination of the marginal and interlinear gloss leads the reader to understand that authoritative tradition and a straightforward reading both point to the same inevitable conclusion.

The comparison of Rashi and the Gloss has suggested that both, at least in their final manuscript versions, are polemical in a way that reflects the intensification of polemic and violence around the First Crusade. They both read the near-sacrifice of Isaac as a polemic against the other's religion and manipulate their sources to do so. It has also shown that their commentaries are constructed in a way that makes it appear as if their exegesis arises directly out of the biblical text. On the one hand their omission of citations, question-and-answer structures, markers of orality, and parables obscure the sources of their interpretations in earlier exegesis and give them the appearance of an autonomous reading of the Bible as a self-glossing text. On the other they both selectively cite sources to make themselves look as though they are relying on late antique authority. Through the process of selective citation they give the appearance of relying on different sources than they are: Rashi obscures the influence of *Midrash Tanchuma* and emphasizes the influence of the Targum, while the Gloss obscures the influence of Isidore, emphasizes the influence of Jerome, and renders invisible the formative role of Rabanus. So Rashi and the Gloss have two sources of exegetical authority: late antique scholarship, and their own (apparently) autonomous reading of the biblical text.

In the twelfth century, as shown in the first chapter, Christian anti-Jewish polemicists (including Pseudo-William of Laon, from the school that developed the Gloss) developed new techniques of rational argumentation against the Jews. Representing exegesis as an autonomous reading of scripture fits well with the new importance of rationality in the Jewish–Christian debate. If any rational, autonomous reader would draw Christological conclusions from the biblical text, any Jew who does not must be as unseeing, in the view of the Gloss, as Abraham's donkey. Sarah Kamin points out in her examination of the ambiguity of the meaning of the term "literal interpretation" that many scholars take it to mean "a commentary that I think correctly explains the Bible,"[108] and thus it can be a judgment rather than an evaluation. Beryl Smalley, looking backwards from modern scientific ways of reading the Bible, sees literality in commentaries that resemble modern scientific exegesis.[109] Rashi and the Gloss are indefinable as literal or nonliteral, as we see in the vast literature about the meaning of *peshat* in Rashi and in the parallels in method between Rashi and the Gloss. Based on the evidence presented in this study, I would suggest that their ambiguous strategies of constructing authority—both as autonomous readers and as representatives of patristic and midrashic authority—are a part of what generates this difficulty in definition.

This study has shown the following assumptions shared between Rashi (and the many scribes involved in the production of his commentary) and the various glossators of Genesis 22:

1. Authority of earlier exegesis.
   We see this exegetical assumption in the marginal gloss's compilation of patristic and Carolingian sources, and in Rashi's extensive use of midrashic exegesis.

2. Unified canon of earlier exegesis.
   Rashi and the Gloss both present the exegetical texts of their respective traditions as a unified canon. Although they may quote or paraphrase diverse voices from within their traditions, they use anonymous paraphrase to obscure the diversity of opinion rather than to highlight it. We have also seen in the textual development of Rashi and of the Gloss that later scribes add additional earlier material (such as Alcuin's commentary or the additional quote from *Midrash Rabbah* in Rashi on Genesis 12) to earlier versions of the commentary.

3. Some sources are more authoritative than others.
   Rashi and the Gloss tend to name some midrashic, patristic, and Carolingian authors (such as Onqelos and Jerome) more than others (such as *Midrash Tanchuma* and Isidore). They thereby obscure the role of later and more recent sources in constructing their commentaries and present their exegesis as primarily reliant on earlier sources.

4. The biblical text can be read autonomously as a self-glossing text.
   Through strategies such as truncation, paraphrase, and anonymous citation, Rashi and the Gloss create the impression of original authorship. This impression is strengthened by Rashi's statement to be

writing *peshuto shel miqra* and by the position of the interlinear gloss
between the lines of the biblical text. The frequent citation of biblical
verses in both commentaries leads the reader to imagine that the interpretations in Rashi and in the Gloss are an autonomous response to
the Bible as a self-glossing text.

5. The Bible is a weapon in polemical battle.
    The similarities between Rashi's commentary and the Gloss, as we
    have seen, did not generate kind feelings between the authors or read-
    ers of these commentaries. The polemic here arises despite the similar-
    ity, and perhaps even because of it.

    The story of the Jewish–Christian relationship in the formative
    twelfth century is one of polemic and debate, and one of mutual influ-
    ence, but also, as these texts show, one of similarity. Living in the same
    world and reading the same texts, they ask and struggle with the same
    kinds of questions.

APPENDIX A

A CRITICAL EDITION OF THE *GLOSSA ORDINARIA* ON GENESIS 22: OVERVIEW OF EXISTING EDITIONS OF THE GLOSS AND RATIONALE FOR PRESENT EDITION

Although two modern printed editions of the *Glossa Ordinaria* exist, neither emphasizes the elements of the Gloss most crucial to my reading of the text. The most easily available edition, in volumes 113 and 114 of Migne's *Patrologia Latina*,[1] completely omits the interlinear gloss. Following an early mistake, Migne ascribed the marginal gloss to Walafrid Strabo and the interlinear gloss to Anselm of Laon.[2] Migne's edition, printed under Strabo's name, includes only the marginal gloss, eliminating the interlinear gloss because Migne viewed it as a later addition. This is a distortion of the manuscripts and early printed editions, since in either form the marginal gloss has never been found separately from the interlinear.[3]

In Migne's edition, even the marginal gloss is not complete. Because Migne saw the Gloss as a collection of excerpts from patristic authors, he truncated marginal comments, often replacing them with a cross-reference to Augustine or Jerome. This editorial choice conceals the minor but often significant changes that the gloss editors made in their reproduction of patristic commentaries.

In its most misleading decision, the PL edition did not reproduce the traditional gloss format, with the interlinear gloss between the lines and the marginal gloss on the sides. This layout, present in every known gloss manuscript, even the earliest,[4] was one of the main innovations of the gloss. It is impossible to understand the *Glossa Ordinaria* without understanding the method and innovation of its unique layout. The PL *Glossa Ordinaria* is problematic not only because of its manner of handling the gloss material, but because it uses one of the early printings rather than the manuscript tradition.[5] Therefore I have not incorporated it into the critical edition presented below.

The Rusch edition—a facsimile of the 1480/81 *editio princeps* published by Adolph Rusch in Strassburg reproduced by Karlfried Froehlich and the late Margaret Gibson—is a great improvement over the Migne edition.[6] All eleven subsequent early printed editions were based on Rusch's original printing.[7] The manuscripts (there must have been many, since the gloss on the entire Bible was almost never produced in a single unit)[8] that Rusch drew on for this edition have never been identified. Mary Dove has suggested, based on the order of the books, that the Rusch edition of Proverbs, Ecclesiastes, Song of Songs, Wisdom, and Ecclesiasticus must have been printed from a single manuscript that followed the tradition of placing the books in that order. Since this sequence of books was only customary after 1170, she concludes that the Rusch edition must have been based on manuscripts from after 1170 and before 1250, which was the end of the period of intensive copying of the Gloss.[9] This edition, therefore, best represents the *Glossa Ordinaria* in its final form at the end of its late medieval process of development.

Although the order of the books proves nothing regarding the date of the *Glossa Ordinaria* on Genesis, the Rusch edition of Genesis physically resembles late-twelfth- or early-thirteenth-century manuscripts. Unlike earlier Gloss manuscripts that leave space between marginal glosses, this edition is tightly organized with almost no blank space. The Rusch edition identifies most of the patristic authors of the marginal glosses by name. It also includes glosses by Alcuin, which some earlier manuscripts omit. All three of these features are typical of later manuscripts. As few new Gloss manuscripts were produced after the mid-thirteenth century,[10] the Rusch edition was probably based on manuscripts from the late twelfth or early thirteenth century and is not very different from some twelfth-century manuscripts.[11]

Unlike the Migne edition, the Rusch edition follows the traditional Gloss layout as found in the manuscripts, with the interlinear gloss in the center of the page between the lines of Biblical text and the marginal gloss on the margins. It does not truncate any part of the Gloss and includes the full quotations from patristic sources that are present in the Gloss manuscripts.

In appearance it strongly resembles a thirteenth-century gloss manuscript, even down to the use of truncations and sigla.

While the Rusch edition represents the late, final form of the Gloss, it lacks the scholarly apparatus necessary to see the Gloss as a living, changing document. It presents a very late text and represents it as static and complete. Although the manuscripts in this edition have shown few significant variants that can be traced with certainty to the thirteenth century or later, in the twelfth century the gloss was a changing, dynamic text. The Rusch edition is not even an accurate representation of the final form of the Gloss on Genesis 22, as it also has many variants that are not present in the majority of the manuscripts, and includes two[12] complete glosses that are entirely absent in any other manuscripts known to me. It is therefore not adequate for this study.

The goal of this critical edition is not to recreate the words written by Gilbert the Universal[13] but to uncover the progression of the gloss in response to the changes taking place in northern France over the course of the twelfth century.[14] In particular I looked for differences between the early and late manuscripts relating to changing approaches to biblical exegesis and to Jewish–Christian relations in the twelfth century.

Preparing an edition of the Gloss built on its most influential mid-twelfth-century form allows the comparison with the commentary of Rashi to be as accurate as possible. Deborah Abecassis has shown that the text of Rashi's commentary on Genesis developed in the two generations after Rashi's death, and that significant portions of his comments were added by the Tosafists.[15] The text of Rashi's commentary did not stabilize until the mid-twelfth century, approximately the same time as the text of the Gloss. The second Gloss recension, as represented by Admont 251, represents like Rashi the result of at least half a century of textual development and scribal interventions.

The manuscript that I chose as my base is Admont 251 (manuscript A), an early version of the Gloss produced between 1140 and 1170. Admont 251 represents the most influential textual tradition of the Gloss on Genesis 22. Of a total of sixty-seven interlinear glosses present in any of the twenty-two extant manuscripts, fourteen are absent entirely from at least two manuscripts of the *Glossa Ordinaria*. (Another eight appear in the marginal gloss in at least two manuscripts.) Of a total of sixteen marginal glosses, four are absent in at least three manuscripts. Admont 251 has all the glosses that are present in the majority of manuscripts and none of the glosses that are only present in a minority.

A is occasionally nonrepresentative in the location of its glosses; that is, some of the glosses which normally appear in the marginal gloss appear in A's interlinear gloss or vice versa. The clearest example of this phenomenon is 2.2i (based on Alcuin) which is marginal in most manuscripts. Content considerations outlined in chapter 2 suggest that this gloss belongs in the marginal rather than the interlinear gloss. Comment 12.2i is marginal in twelve out of the twenty-two manuscripts, for reasons that will be suggested in chapter 2. Similarly, and for the same reasons, 14.2i is in the marginal position in eight manuscripts and absent in another six. In all other places the position of the glosses in A represents the majority reading.

Because I only took present/absent variants of entire glosses into account, A's minor variants of glosses are also sometimes nonrepresentative of the tradition in general. In 19.1i, seventeen out of the twenty-two manuscripts have *fides* rather than *fideles*. In 1.1m fifteen manuscripts have *experimento cognoscat* for *cognoscat experimento*. In 8.1m twelve manuscripts are missing the word *christus* in the phrase *quando christus natus est*. In 13.2i seventeen manuscripts choose other spellings for the name *teodotio*. These variants seem incidental, and do not lessen manuscript A's status as the most representative text of the Gloss on Genesis 22.

Ideally, a critical edition of the Gloss should reproduce the traditional Gloss layout, with the biblical text in the center, the interlinear gloss between the lines and the marginal gloss in the margins, since this would best represent how the Gloss has been read. For the current edition that has not proved practical, though it is my hope that some sense of the original formatting has been preserved.

In the apparatus I have tended not to mark minor spelling variants: e.g. where one text reads *Abrae* instead of *Abrahe*, or *tentat* as opposed to *temptat*. I have not marked punctuation variants, but have punctuated minimally for clarity. I have followed the order of glosses as it appears in A, which, as I have explained, is consistent with most manuscripts. I have reproduced the quoted biblical verse which introduces each comment as it appears in A. Although the biblical quotations within the comments are written in the same script as the rest of the text in the manuscript tradition, I have bolded them here for ease of identification.

The twenty manuscripts compiled here (plus the Rusch edition) represent only a fraction of the Gloss manuscripts that exist. A full stemma would require more manuscripts than this edition was able to include. Still, the range of manuscript variants in this critical edition shows how much the Gloss changes over the course of the twelfth century.

As the extant manuscripts demonstrate, the Gloss on Genesis 22 exists in two recensions.[16] One recension is attested in Lambeth 349, Salzburg, and BNF 183. Based on formal characteristics, Salzburg can be dated to before 1140. It is most likely the earliest manuscript in this edition. BNF 183 (B), produced before 1160, belongs to an early stage of the development of the Gloss, and Lambeth 349 (L) is from 1140–1170. The similarities between these manuscripts are strong enough, and mark them as different enough from the other manuscripts, that it seems reasonable to suggest that B and L were copied from G or a manuscript related to it.

This first recension is characterized by the complete absence of any of the material based on Alcuin that can be found in the marginal gloss in the other recension. The recension lacks 2.1m, 5.3m, 13.1m, and 2.2i, although it does include loose paraphrases from Alcuin in interlinear glosses 17.1-4i. This family is also unusual in its treatment of the material from Isidore. It places all the material from Isidore in one block at the end of the marginal gloss instead of interweaving it with the material from Jerome and Augustine. In style, the recension tends to retain the rhetorical structures of the Patristic authors, including the question and answer format.

Because of these variants, this first recension of the Gloss on Genesis 22, as attested in manuscripts G, B, and L, is more similar to the commentary of Rabanus on Genesis than it is to the marginal gloss in A. As explained in chapter 2, the marginal gloss in G is in fact nearly identical to Rabanus. This pattern suggests one of two possibilities. One is that the original form of the gloss was closer to A, but that copyists corrected based on Rabanus in the GBL family. The other is that GBL is the earliest form of the Gloss, and that therefore the earliest marginal gloss was taken from Rabanus. The early date of G suggests that the latter is the case.[17]

Manuscript S is influenced by the GBL family. It is missing 5.3m and half of 13.1m, which are based on Alcuin, although it includes the Alcuin-based glosses 2.1m and 2.2i. It is also missing 14.2m, which is based on Isidore, and may have been led to exclude this based on its unusual placement in the GBL family.

The second recension, attested by the other eighteen of the twenty-two manuscripts, includes all the Alcuin-based material and distributes the Isidore material throughout the commentary rather than isolating it in one block at the end. It also truncates and simplifies the material present in the first recension, and eliminates stylistic techniques such as rhetorical questions.[18]

DESCRIPTION AND DATING OF THE MANUSCRIPTS

A simple and readily evident method for dating Gloss manuscripts is by manuscript layout. Before the mid-twelfth century, Gloss manuscripts were written in two parts: the biblical text in a set column width with the Gloss surrounding it. Glosses in this period would be placed around the biblical text as necessary, so on pages where there were fewer comments a great deal of white space would remain on the page, leaving room for the reader.[19] The reader could use this space to add additional comments.[20] At this early stage, interlinear glosses that were too long to fit between the lines would continue into the margins, producing L-shaped glosses. (This may be a partial explanation for the variable glosses discussed in Chapter Five.)

Variable width of columns from page to page—but not within single pages—is characteristic of the mid–twelfth century from around 1140.[21] Also in this period, interlinear glosses too long for the space allotted them would continue on the next page, rather than in the margins.[22]

After about 1160, the width of the central column of biblical text could vary even within the page. Beginning around 1170 the page became very tightly organized, so that one gloss immediately followed the next and there was no room for the reader to add comments.[23] Instead, an extra outer margin was left for additional comments.

The Manuscripts

This edition is based on twenty manuscripts plus the Rusch edition (R). Many of these manuscripts are from the Bibliothèque Nationale de France collection, while others were transcribed from the Hill Museum and Manuscript Library microfilm collection, which microfilms manuscripts from monastic libraries in Europe.[24] Since I have read these manuscripts from microfilm, the physical descriptions are based on information provided by the BNF and HMML catalogs, and occasionally the number of pages and size of the original manuscript were not available to me.

This is far from an exhaustive list. Stegmüller has identified the following manuscripts of the Gloss on Genesis that I have been unable to consult for the present edition:

> Arras 188 (1004) (XII; Arras, Cathédrale) f. 2–43.
> Lund, Univ. Medeltid. 3 (XII; Domkyrka).
> Montpellier, Ecole de Médicine 298 (XII; Troyes s. Stephani) f. 1–151.
> Montserrat 804 (XIII): fragmenta.
> Clm. 3746 (XII; Augsburg, Dom. 46) f. 1–108.
> Torino, Naz. 429 (D II 26) (XIII) f. 1–144.[25]

The criteria that I have used for dating manuscripts are as follows:

1. Width of central column. In manuscripts written in the first third of the twelfth century, the width of the central column of biblical text tends to remain stable from page to page.[26] Between 1130 and 1150, the central column began to vary in width from page to page but not within a single page.[27] Between 1150 and 1170, the width of the column of biblical text began to vary even within the page.[28]

2. Blank space. Manuscripts from the first half of the twelfth century leave so much blank space that they can give the appearance of being incomplete.[29] Sometime between 1160 and 1170, gloss manuscripts began to be written on tightly ruled lines so that one gloss closely followed another.[30] This meant that no room was left for the reader to insert additional comments.[31] Mary Dove has found that very tightly written manuscripts, in which the pages are "a jigsaw of diversely-shaped blocks of text," were produced after 1200.[32]

3. L-shaped glosses. These are glosses that begin as interlinear glosses and continue into the margins. They are characteristic of the first half of the twelfth century.[33]

4. Script. Manuscripts written after 1160 tend to use a gothic script for the biblical text,[34] while earlier manuscripts use a protogothic script.[35] Distinguishing features of protogothic scripts include the *e* caudata (*e* with a notation beneath it) for *ae*,[36] open *a*,[37] and rounded letters (particularly *o*, *d* and *g*).[38] Distinguishing features of Gothic scripts include

a simple *e* for *ae*,[39] vertical alignment of all shafts,[40] frequent fusion of circular letters[41] and "round" *r* following letters other than *o*.[42] Since the protogothic scripts continued to be used in France and England through the early thirteenth century,[43] I have considered the type of script as corroborating evidence only and have dated the manuscripts more primarily based on their layout.

5. Presence or absence of chapter numbers. Chapter numbers first appear in Bibles in the first years of the thirteenth century and became common from around 1220. Chapter numbers were added to old Bibles as well as newly produced Bibles, so their presence does not necessarily prove that a specific manuscript is from the thirteenth century.[44] The presence of chapter numbers can, however, help support claims for a later date of production in combination with other evidence.

I have also noted any other unusual features about each manuscript. Manuscripts are listed in roughly chronological order, from earliest to latest. After the title of each manuscript I will note its sigla in parentheses.

1. Early Manuscripts (early twelfth century)
    Codex S. Petri Salisburgensis a.VIII.34 (G)
    Title: Liber Genesis cum glossa marginali et interlineari
    Library: Stiftsbibliothek Sankt Peter, Salzburg
    Description: Gloss on Genesis. 92 ff., quarto

Fixed width columns with a great deal of blank space, more than in any other manuscript consulted for this edition. L-shaped glosses. Protogothic script, with very many abbreviations and truncations. The scripts of the marginal and interlinear glosses are the same size. All the marginal glosses based on Isidore is in one block at the end, and there are no marginal glosses based on Alcuin. There are no chapter numbers. Based on all these factors this seems to be the earliest gloss manuscript that I have found, and is certainly from no later than 1150. The HMML catalog dates it as thirteenth century.[45]

    BNF 63 (C)
    Title: Genesis cum glossa ordinaria
    Contains: 122 ff. 335 X 225 mm[46]

The biblical text is written in fixed-width columns. Some interlinear glosses are L-shaped. There is a great deal of empty space in the margins, and many abbreviations are used. Protogothic script. No chapter numbers. All these features indicate that this manuscript is from before 1150. This manuscript has exactly the same glosses in the marginal and interlinear as A, and in language is very close to A. It may be one of A's sources.

BNF 183 (B)
Title: Genesis cum glossa ordinaria
Contains: 120 ff., 265 X 180 mm. From the library of Gaston of Noailles, Abbot of Haute-Fontaine and then bishop of Châlons from 1669 to 1720.[47]

Fixed column width, a moderate amount of blank space, many abbreviations and contractions, and L-shaped glosses. The letter size in the marginal gloss is very slightly larger than the letter size in the interlinear gloss. Protogothic script. No chapter numbers. These features suggest a date of before 1160. The BNF catalog dates it as twelfth century.[48] Most of the Isidore material (with the exception of 14.2m) is in one block in the middle.

Codex Zwettlensis 147 (Z)
Title: Liber Genesis glossatus
Library: Zisterzienserstift, Zwettl
Description: 230 ff. (f. 3a-96a), folio

Columns fixed in width from page to page. No L-shaped glosses. Moderate amount of blank space. Protogothic script. These features suggest a date between 1140 and 1160. The HMML catalog dates it as twelfth century.[49]

Cod. 349 (L)
Title: none supplied
Library: Lambeth Palace Library, London[50]

Columns stable in width from page to page. No L-shaped glosses. A great deal of blank space. Protogothic script. No chapter numbers. These features suggest a date of 1140–1150.

2. Mid–twelfth century

BNF 66 (F)

Title: Genesis cum glossa ordinaria—Radalphus Flaviacensis

Contains: Gloss on Genesis, and a fragment of a commentary by Raoul of Flaix on Romans. 156 ff., 300 X 200 mm.[51]

Fixed column width, a great deal of blank space, many abbreviations and contractions, and L-shaped glosses. Protogothic script. There is no difference in letter size between the marginal and interlinear gloss. All the Isidore-based material in the marginal gloss is collected together. Chapters are numbered, possibly in a different hand. These features suggest a dating of around 1150. The BNF catalog dates it as thirteenth century.[52] This is a corrected manuscript, notable for its large number of transcription mistakes with dots under them, followed by the corrected word.

BNF 367 (H)

Title: Genesis cum glossa ordinaria

Contains: 133 ff., 245 X 165 mm[53]

In this manuscript the width of the central column varies from page to page but not within the page. There is a moderate amount of blank space. The marginal gloss is the same letter size as the interlinear, but both are noticeably smaller than the biblical text. There are no chapter numbers. Protogothic script. These features indicate that this manuscript is from the middle period of the development of the Gloss, 1140–1170. The BNF catalog dates it as thirteenth century.[54] This manuscript is noteworthy for the wordiness of its interlinear gloss.

Codex Admontensis 251 (A)

Title: Liber Genesis cum glossa ordinaria

Library: Stiftsbibliothek, Admont (Austria)

Description: Gloss on Genesis. 106 ff., folio.

Central columns vary in width from page to page but not within a page. No L-shaped glosses. There is a moderate amount of blank space. Protogothic script. Script in marginal gloss slightly larger than script in interlinear gloss. No chapter numbers. These features place it in the middle of the development of the gloss, between 1140 and 1170. The HMML catalog gives a date of thirteenth century.[55]

Codex 3–5 (D)
Title: Biblia. Glossa ordinaria in Genesim
Library: Biblioteca del Cabildo, Toledo
Description: 225 ff.

Columns vary in width from page to page but not within a page. L-shaped glosses are common. Very little blank space. Space between lines of biblical text expands to fit longer interlinear glosses. Protogothic script. No chapter numbers. These features suggest a date of around 1150. The HMML catalog dates it to the thirteenth century.[56]

Ms. O.5.i (O)
Title: none supplied
Library: Cathedral Library, Hereford[57]

Columns vary in width from page to page but not within each page. Moderate amount of blank space. Gothic script. No L-shaped glosses. No chapter numbers. These features suggest a date of 1150–1160.

3. The final form of the Gloss (1170 through the mid–thirteenth century)
Codex Vindobonensis Palatinus 1204 (V)
Title: Biblia Sacra: Genesis et Exodus (textus Vulgatae), cum glossa ordinaria et interlineari
Library: Österreichische Nationalbibliothek, Wien
Description: 284 ff., folio

Columns vary in width on the page. No L-shaped glosses. Tightly organized with no blank space. Protogothic script. Chapter numbers. These features suggest a date in the thirteenth century, although the early script raises the possibility that it could be earlier. The HMML catalog dates it as thirteenth century.[58] The unusual feature of this manuscript is that each paragraph of the marginal gloss is numbered with numbers beginning again on each page.

BNF 65 (N)

Title: Genesis cum glossa ordinaria, pars I

Contains: Gloss on Genesis 1:1–49:10. 135 ff., 340 X 230 mm. A sixteenth-century hand labels it as from the Fulcarmont Abbey in the diocese of Rouen.[59]

Tightly written, with central columns of biblical text that vary in width within the page and allow for little blank space. No L-shaped glosses. Gothic script. Chapter numbers. This indicates a dating of thirteenth century. The BNF catalog dates it as twelfth to thirteenth century.[60] The grouping of the marginal glosses is unusual, with all the glosses by Alcuin placed together and all the glosses by Isidore placed together.

BNF 368 (I)

Title: Vetus Testamentum cum glossa ordinaria, pars I

Contains: Gloss on Genesis and Exodus. 206 ff. 480 X 282 mm.[61]

Tightly organized, with columns that vary in width within the page and little blank space. Gothic script. Chapter numbers. These features indicate a thirteenth century date. The BNF catalog dates it as late thirteenth to early fourteenth century.[62]

BNF 370 (J)

Title: Biblia sacra cum glossa ordinaria, pars I

Contains: Gloss on Genesis and Exodus. 223 ff., 460 X 325 mm.[63]

Tightly organized, with columns that vary in width within the page and little blank space. Marginal letter size larger than interlinear. Very small, standardized writing. Gothic script. Chapter numbers. These features indicate a thirteenth century date. The BNF catalog dates it as late thirteenth to early fourteenth century.[64]

Ms. P.9.iv (P)

Title: none supplied

Library: Cathedral Library, Hereford[65]

Central columns very in width within the page. No L-shaped glosses. Very tight jigsaw-like organization. Gothic script. No chapter numbers. Most likely early thirteenth century.

Codex 3–6 (X)
Title: Biblia. O.T. Genesis. Commentarius.
Library: Biblioteca del Cabildo, Toledo.
Description: 116 ff.

Columns vary in width within the page. No L-shaped glosses. The space between lines of the biblical text varies to accommodate large interlinear glosses. Very tightly organized. Gothic script. No chapter numbers. A blank outer margin with occasional additional comments in a different hand. These features suggest a date of early thirteenth century. The HMML catalog dates it as thirteenth century.[66]

Ms. 104 (S)
Title: none supplied.
Library: Cathedral Library, Salisbury.[67]

Columns vary in width within the page. No L-shaped glosses. Very tight organization, with marginal glosses surrounding each other in complicated patterns. Gothic script. Blank outer margin with occasional comments in a different script. Chapter numbers. These features indicate a date after 1250.

Codex Dominicanorum Vindobonensis 219 (185) (W)
Title: Glossa in Genesim et Exodum
Library: Dominikanerkloster, Wien
Description: 226 ff., folio.

Columns vary in width within the page. No L-shaped glosses. No blank space. Gothic script. No chapter numbers. These features suggest a date in the early thirteenth century. The HMML catalog dates it as thirteenth century.[68]

BNF 11943 (Q)
Title: Genèse et Exode, avec glose

Columns vary in width on the page. No L-shaped glosses. Tightly organized with no blank space. Gothic script. Chapter numbers. These features
suggest a date in the thirteenth century. The BNF catalog dates it to the
second half of the thirteenth century.[69]

BNF 15186 (M)
Title: Genèse et Exode, avec glose

Columns vary in width on the page. No L-shaped glosses. No blank space.
Gothic script. Chapter numbers. These features suggest a date of thirteenth
century. The BNF catalog dates it to the thirteenth century.[70]

4. Manuscripts consulted but not included in the apparatus
Codex 3–4
Title: Biblia. Glossa in Pentateuchum.
Library: Biblioteca del Cabildo, Toledo
Description: 290 ff.

Columns vary in width within the page. No L-shaped glosses. Very tightly
organized with no blank space. Gothic script. It has chapter numbers.
These features suggest a date later than 1200. The HMML catalog dates
it as thirteenth century.[71] Not included in the edition because it is nearly
impossible to read. Its distinctive feature is the presence of a second gloss
in the outside margins. This second gloss quotes from Origen, as well as
including material omitted from Jerome and Isidore in the regular marginal gloss. It is written in a different script, in smaller letters than the regular marginal gloss, and does not fill up all the space in the second margins.

BNF 371
Title: Vetus Testamentum cum glossa ordinaria, pars I
Contains: Gloss on Genesis and Exodus. 180 ff., 420 X 295 mm. Has a
note of sums paid by Raollus li Perciminer and Ramondus de Figiaco.[72]

Columns vary in width within the page. Gothic script. Too illegible to
transcribe. The BNF catalog dates it as late thirteenth to early fourteenth
century.

Other Editorial Notes

As already mentioned, throughout this book I have bolded all biblical quotations to make it easier to see where the biblical quotation ends and the exegesis begins. In the critical edition I have identified all biblical citations in the apparatus, and in the rest of the book I have included biblical citation references in the body of the text. Along with the interlinear gloss I have included the Vulgate Latin text of the Bible passages as they appear in manuscript A. For ease of identification I have added the number of each interlinear gloss after the word which it begins above in manuscript A. In other manuscripts these interlinear glosses may appear above the word before or after, but I have not noted these variations.

List of Abbreviations

add.   addidit/addiderunt
corr.   correctio, -ionis etc., correxit/correxerunt
interl. interlinearis
marg.   marginalis
om.   omisit/omiserunt

Abbreviations for Primary Sources

Quaest. Hept. Aurelius Augustinus, *Quaestionum in Heptateuchem Libri Septem*, I. Fraipoint, ed., Corpus Christianorum Series Latina 33, (Turnholt: Brepols, 1958).

Hebr. Quaest. Hieronymus, *Hebraice Quaestiones in Libro Geneseos*, Pavli de Lagarde, ed., Corpus Christianorum Series Latina 72, (Turnholt: Brepols, 1959).

Quaest. Vet. Isidore of Seville, *Quaestiones in Vetus Testamentum*, PL 83, 207–288.

Resp. Gen. Alcuin, *Interrogationes et Responsiones in Genesin*, PL 100, 515–570.

Comm. Gen. Rabanus Maurus, *Commentariorum in Genesim Libri Quatuor* PL 107, 439–670

THE *GLOSSA ORDINARIA* ON GENESIS 22:1–19

Que postquam gesta sunt temptavit (1.1i) (1.2i) Deus Abraham et dixit ad eum Abraham ille respondit assum (1.3i).

1.1i   ut notificaret eius perfectionem quam ipse non ignorabat.

notificaret] notificaret ei R notam faceret S G B H notum facit temptationem qui probat L | eius] *om.* M | eius perfectionem] perfectionem eius B | non] *om.* R Z N | ignorabat] ignorat G temptatione quam probat *add.* S G H temptatione comparabat *add.* B

1.1i Based on Aug. *Quaest. Hept.* 57 (CCSL 22). cf. 1.1m.

1.2i   ut probaret quam promptus esset ad obediendum.

ut probaret] et inquam apparet L hinc apparet B | esset] sit L B | obediendum] obedientiam R W X V P M J Q obedienciam

1.3i Some manuscripts add the following additional gloss:

In manuscript S: hoc apparet quod promptus esset ad obediendum.

In manuscript G: huic apparet quid promptus sit. ad obediendum.

In manuscript H: hinc apparet quod promptus esset ad obediendum.

1.1m   Aug. **Que postquam gesta sunt tempt. d. a. etc.** Jacobus dicit quod neminem temptat deus sed usualiter temptare pro eo quod est probare dicimus. Jacobus autem dicit de ea temptatione qua quisque peccato implicatur. Unde: **Ne forte temptaverit vos is qui temptat.** Alibi enim scriptum est: **Temptat vos deus vester, ut sciat si diligatis eum.** Id est, vos scire faciat. Vires enim dilectonis sue homo ignorat nisi cognoscat experimento.

Aug] *om.* S | peccato implicatur] peccatorum probatur S | Unde] *om.*C | vos deus vester] vos deus vos deus vester C dominus deus vester H | vos scire] scire vos X scire V P S M J I H ut vos scire C F |

1.1m Aug. *Quaest. Hept.* 57 (CCSL 22), Rab. *Comm. Gen.* 3.3.12 (PL 107 col. 566 B-C).

neminem temptat James 1:12-13.

Ne forte 1 Thessalonians 3:5.

Temptat vos Deutoronomy 13:3.

experimento B *add*: Augustinus. Est temptationem quam deus immittit ad probandum hominem hominem. ut non se ipsum cognoscat. vel quantum deum diligit. Unde scriptum est. Temptat vos deus vester. ut sciat id est scire faciat si diligantis eum. est alia temptatio quam immittitur a diablo et a concupiscentia hominis. quae sit ad decipiendum. hac temptatione deus neminem temptat.

experimento G *add*: Aug. Que postuam gesta s.t.d.a.etc. Queri solet hoc quam verum sit. cum dicat in epistola sua iacobus. quod deus neminem temptavit. nisi quod locutionem scripturarum solet dici. temptat. pro eo quod est probat. Temptatio vero de quam iacobus dicit. non intellegitur. nisi quod quisque peccato inplicatur. Unde apostolus dicit. Ne forte temptaverit vos is que temptat. Nam et alibi scriptum est: Tentat vos dominus deus vester. ut sciat si diligantis eum. Et iam hoc genere locutionis ut sciat. dictum est. ac si diceretur. ut scire vos faciat. Quam vires dilectonis suae homo latent. nisi experimento etiam eidem innotescant.

Ait illi tolle (2.1i) (2.2i) filium tuum unigenitum quem diligis Isaac et vade in (2.3i) terram visionis atque offer ibi holocaustum (2.4i) super unum montium (2.5i) quem monstravero tibi.

2.1i **sic dilexit deus mundum ut filium unigenitum daret.**

sic] sic mistice *add.* W V D M J I Q | dilexit deus] deus dilexit R C Q deus diligit ysaac dilexit mundum P enim deus dilexit L G enim dilexit deus B enim dilexit H | filium] suum *add.* R X Z L G B filium . . . daret] filium suum daret unigenitum W V P D J I Q

2.1i John 3:16.

2.1i *marg.* I.

2.2i caritatis admonitione et nominis recordatione temptatio cumulatur et paternus affectus movetur ex memoria promissionis quia dictum est **in ysaac vocabitur tibi semen.** tanquam si ille occideretur tota spes promissionis frustraretur.

admonitione] ammonitione V | affectus movetur] movetur affectus N | movetur] et *add.* R | si] *om.* P | frustraretur] etc. *add.* Q

2.2i cf. Alc. *Resp. Gen.* 203 (PL 100 cols. 544 D—545 A). Quem diligis ysaac. *add* W X V P D J I Q Ex *add.* R W O X De *add.* V P M J I Q.

2.2i *marg.* in all manuscripts except A Z C F (L-shaped in F).

in ysaac Romans 11:18 (**dictum est quia in Isaac vocabitur tibi semen**), Genesis 21:12 (**Isaac vocabitur tibi semen**).

2.3i ubi tibi revelabitur quid hac immolatione portendam.

ubi tibi revelabitur] quia ibi revelabitur tibi L G B | hac] in hac F | portendam] portendatur R W X V P D S J N

2.4i signum veri holocausti.

signum] in holocaustum in signum L | signum] signam L in figura H | signum veri holocausti] signum holocausti veri R X V P D J I Q in figuram veri holocausti S L G B *om.* F

2.5i eminentiam fidei quam revelabo tibi.

eminentiam] in eminentiam S L G B | eminentiam] eminentia L G B eminenciam I | revelabo] revelaturus sum S L G B H

2.1m Alc. Non statim iussus est abraham filium occidere, sed triduo ad immolandum ducere, ut longitudine temporis temptatio augeretur. Per triduum enim crescentibus curis paterna viscera cruciantur, et prolixo spacio pater filium intuetur, cibum cum eo summit, tot noctibus pendet puer in amplexu patris, cubat in gremio, et per singula momenta in paterno affectu dolor occidendi filium cumulatur.

Alc.] Aug. S | statim] *om.* V P *corr.* Q | filium occidere] occidere filium W D | longitudine] per longitudinem N | enim] *om.* X D | pendet] pandet D | in amplexu patris] *om.* S | in] *om.* X | filium] filii O I | cumulatur] incumulatur R W O P

2.1m Alc. *Resp. Gen.* Inter. 204 (PL 100 col. 545 A).

2.1m *om.* L G B.

2.2m [2.2i appears here in the marginal position in manuscripts H, D, O, N, I, J, P, X, S, W, V, Q, M]

2.3m Jer. **Vade in terram .u. etc.** Aiunt hebrei hunc montem esse in quo postea templum conditum est in area orne iebusei. Unde in paralipomenon:

Ceperunt edificare templum mense secundo, secunda die mensis, in monte moria, qui idcirco illuminans interpretatur, et lucens, quia ibi est dabir, hoc est oraculum dei, et lex, et spiritus qui docet homines veritatem et inspirat prophetas.

Jer.] *om.* G | aiunt] tradunt S H dicunt B N | conditum] edificatum R W D | templum conditum est] templum est conditum B conditum est templum G | templum conditum est] templum est conditum B conditum est templum G | area] archa G | orne] hornam B area orne] *om.* F | orne] hornam B area orne] *om.* F | Unde] Sic B | paralipomenon] scriptum est *add.* G | paralipomenon] et *add.* G | illuminans . . . lucens] illuminans et lucens interpretatur X | est] *om.* G | dei] *om.* B | et] *om.* M | lex] lux P | spiritus] spiritus sanctus B | docet homines] homines docet R | inspirat prophetas] prophetias inspirat R

2.3m Jer. *Hebr. Quaest.*22.2 (CCSL 26), Rab. *Comm. Gen.* 3.3.12 (PL 107 col. 566 C).

Ceperunt 1 Chronicles 3:1–2.

Igitur **(3.4i) Abraham de nocte consurgens stravit (3.1i) asinum (3.5i) suum ducens secum duos (3.2i) iuvenes et Isaac filium suum cumque concidisset ligna (3.3i) in holocaustum abiit ad (3.6i) locum quem preceperat ei Deus.**

Igitur (3.4i) Manucript Z has the following additional gloss: stulticiam significat que portabat omnia sacramenta et nesciebat.

asinum (3.5i) Manuscript Z has the following additional gloss: asinus insensatam iudeorum.

abiit ad (3.6i) Some manuscripts have as an additional gloss: calvarie V P S L G B M J I H Q.

3.1i   preparavit necessaria holocausto.

preparavit] paravit B | holocausto] holocausti R W X D holocausta S

3.2i   quia **duo populi** in morte christi consenserunt et **pater proprio filio non pepercit**.

quia] *om.* W X D | morte] mortem N | consenserunt] assenserunt L | pater] deus S deus pater L G B J I | proprio] *om.* N

duo populi Genesis 25:23.

pater Romans 8:32.

3.3i   quia duobus lignis compacta est crux christi.

quia] ex *add.* N | lignis] *om.* Z | est] *om.* G

3.3i cf. Isid. *Quaest. Vet.* 18.10 (PL 83 cols. 251 A-B).

3.1m   Asinus insensatam iudeorum stulticiam significat, qui portabat omnia sacramenta et nesciebat.

insensatam] insensatus Q | iudeorum stulticiam] stulticiam iudeorum R X | que portabat] que portabat que Q | Asinus . . . nesciebat] Asinus ille insensata est iudeorum stulticiam que portabat omnia sacramenta et nec intellegebat. B

3.1m Isid. *Quaest. Vet.* 18.7 (PL 83 col. 250 C).

3.1m *interl.* Z N.

Die (4.1i) autem tertio elevatis oculis vidit (4.2i) locum procul.

4.1i   feria quarta de proditione cum iuda pactum est quinta comprehensus
est tercia die id est parasceve crucifixus.

proditione] christi *add.* P L M J I H Q | quinta] feria *add.* L G B | tercia] sexta V P C M
J I tercia sexta Q *fort.* sexta *vel* tervia H | die] *om.* P M J I F Q | crucifixus] crucifictus
est R W crucufixus est V P L G B M J N I Q vel sexta *add.* G B

4.1i *marg.* W X V P G M J I.

4.2i   longe existens a malicia iudeorum.

4.2i *om.* G N.

4.1m   Jer. **Die autem tercio etc.** Notandum quia de geraris usque ad montem
moria id est sedem templi iter trium dierum sit, et abraham illuc die
tercio die tercio pervenisse dicitur. Male ergo putant abraham illo tempore habitasse apud quercum mambre, cum inde ad montem moria vix
unius diei plenum iter sit.

Jer.] *om.* G | quia] quod S G F | id est] usque ad *add.* Z | trium dierum] dierum trium
W P S G H | abraham illuc die tercio] abraham tercio die illuc W N consequenter die
tercio B consequenter die tercio illuc G | habitasse] abitasse I | apud] ad C iuxta N aput
I | putant . . . mambere] quidam dicitur ad quercum mambre. putant illo tempore habi-
tasse. G | plenum iter] iter plenum B G

4.1m Jer. *Hebr. Quaest.* 22.4 (CCSL 26), Rab. *Comm. Gen.* 3.3.12 (PL 107 col. 566 D).

4.1m After this gloss, the following interlinear glosses are added in some manuscripts:
3.2i W 4.1i W X V P G M I.

4.2m   Triduum quo venerunt ad locum sacrificii, tres etates significat. Ante
legem ab abraham usque ad moysen. Sub lege a moyse usque ad iohan-
nem. Inde usque ad dominum et quidquid restat, tercius dies est gratie
in qua tercia etate sacrificium dei completum est.

ab] *om.* Z | tercius dies est gratie] tercius est dies gratie C | sacrificium dei] sacrificium
christi W O X Z D C N F christi sacrificium S M J I H Q | Triduum . . . completum est]
Triduum quo venerunt ad locum immolationis significat terciam etatem. qui est sub
gratia. qua sacrificium christi est completum. B dei . . . est] completum est christi R

4.2m Isid. *Quaest. Vet.* 18.9 (PL 83 col. 251 A), Rab. *Comm. Gen.* 3.3.12 (PL 107 col.
569 A -B).

Dixitque ad pueros suos expectate (5.1i) hic cum asino ego et puer illuc usque properantes postquam adoraverimus (5.2i) revertemur ad vos.

hic Manuscript O adds marginal gloss 5.1m here as an interlinear gloss.

asino Manuscript N adds here marginal gloss 3.1m as an interlinear gloss.

postquam R has cum instead of postquam and adds postquam as an interlinear gloss.

5.1i   quia iudei a summa tarditate non intellegunt mysterium crucis.

quia] perfidi *add.* V P S L G B M J I H Q | non] *om.* W | intellegunt] intellexerunt P L G
M J I intellegunt N christi *add.* V L G B M J I H christi etc. *add.* Q | crucis] christi *add.*
V L G B M J I H christi *add.* etc. Q

5.2i   hoc erit in fine mundi cum **plenitudo gentium intraverit.**

hoc] quod L G B H | cum] postquam B | plenitudo] plenitudine V | gentium] *om.* G N |
intraverit] etc. *add.* Q

5.2i cf. Isid. *Quaest. Vet.* 18.8 (PL 83 col. 250 D).

plenitudo Romans 11:25.

5.1m   **Expectate hic .c. a. etc. Caecitas ex parte contigit in israel,** hoc
est: **cum asino.** Ut plenitudo gentium intraret, hoc est: **postquam
adoraverimus.** Ubi sacrificium crucis per gentis fuerit predicatum,
hoc est: **ut plenitudo gentium intraret. Revertemur ad vos,** hoc est:
Et sic omnis israel salvus fiet.

ut] ubi R cum O | intraret] *om.* P intraverit R | israel] israhel H | salvus fiet] salvus H.
Duo . . . fiet] Quod dicitur. expectate hic cum asino. hoc est quod apostolos dicit. cecitas contigit in israel. ut plenitudo gentium intraret. Postquam adoraverimus. id est ubi
sacrificium dominice passionis per gentium erat predicatum. tunc revertemur ad vos.
quia tunc omnis israel salvus erit. B

5.1m Isid. *Quaest. Vet.* 18.8–9 (PL 83 col. 250 C—251 D), Rab. *Comm. Gen.* 3.3.12 (PL
107 col. 569 A).

5.1m *interl.* in O.

Caecitas Romans 11:25–26.

5.2m   Duo servi dimissi nec perducti ad locum sacrificii, iudei sunt qui serviliter viventes, et carnaliter sapientes, non intellexerunt humilitatem
et passionem christi. Duo quidem, quia in duas partes dividendi, quod
factum est peccante salmone, quando divisus est populus loco regni
non errore impietatis, quibus dicitur: **Adversatrix israel, et prevaricatrix iuda.**

humilitatem et passionem christi] humilitatem christi et passionem Q | non] et X
| Duo servi . . . prevaricatrix iuda.] Duo servi qui dicitur. nec perveniunt ad locum
sacrificium. ideorum populum significat. qui in duo regna dividendus erat per peccato salmonis. qui populus serviliter vivunt. et carnaliter sapit. non intellegens christi
himilitatem et passionem. totaquam ad locum sacrificii non pervenit. B

5.2m Isid. *Quaest. Vet.* 18.7 (PL 83 col. 250 C), Rab. *Comm. Gen.* 3.3.12 (PL 107 col.
568 D). Alcuinus N.

Adversatrix Jeremiah 3:8.

5.3m   Alc. **Ego et puer etc.** Indubitanti animo mactare filium volebat. Lau-
dandus in constantia offerendi, et in fide suscitandi. Sciebat enim cer-
tissime deum fallere non posse, et licet puer occideretur, promissio-
nem tamen dei salvam permanere. Unde apostolus: **Fide abraam non
hesitavit, cum unicum offeret, in quo acceperat repromissionem,
quia a mortuis potens est suscitare deus.**

mactare filium] filium mactare H | volebat] vo P | tamen dei] dei tamen N | credens
add. R sciens *add.* F | quia] quia et R W X V P N et quia D | suscitare] *om.* C | po-
tens . . . deus] suscitare potens est deus O Z H F potens est deus suscitare X M *om.* D

5.3m Alc. *Resp. Gen. Inter.* 205 (PL 100 col. 545 B).

5.3m *om.* S L G B.

Fide abraam Hebrews 11:17.

Tulit quoque ligna holocausti et inposuit (6.1i) super Isaac filium suum. Ipse vero portabat in manibus (6.2i) ignem (6.3i) et gladium (6.4i). Cumque duo pergerent simul.

6.1i   quia christus angariatus est portare crucem unde factus est principa-
tus super humerum eius.
> quia] et *add.* G H | crucam] suam *add.* L G B | factus] factum Z | principatus] principa-
> tum Z | unde . . . eius] *om.* L G B
> **6.1i** cf. Isid. *Quaest. Vet.* 18.6 (PL 83 col. 250 B).

6.2i   operibus.
> operibus] in operibus X
> **6.2i** cf. 2 Thess. 1.11.

6.3i   bonum zelum.

6.4i   quia separat patrem et filium.
> quia] qui R | separat] separant V P separabat Z
> **6.5i** *om.* C.

dixit Isaac patri suo Pater mi. Et ille respondit. Quid vis fili ecce inquit ignis et ligna. Ubi (7.1i) est victima holocausti.

7.1i   quantum ad innocentiam suam ignorare videtur christus cur patiatur,
unde **Congregata sunt super me flagella et ignoravi.**
> cur] cur avidis L G H quare avidis B | unde] scilicet illud L G B secundum illud H | et
> ignoravi] et ignoravi et ignoravi. C etc. *add.* Q
> **Congregata** Psalms 34:15.

Dixit Abraham Deus providebit sibi victimam holocausti fili mi. Perge-bant (8.1i) ergo pariter.

8.1i   quia obedivit patri filius **usquam ad mortem.**
> obedivit patri] consensit voluntati patris S L H consensit patris voluntati G concordat
> voluntati filius B | filius] *om.* O | usquam ad mortem] *om.* L G B
> **usquam ad mortem** Philippians 2:8.

8.1m   Isidore. Abraam filium unicum ducens ad immolandum, deum patrem
significat. Abraam senex filium suscepit, deus autem non senescit, sed
promissio de christo quodammodo senuerat, quando christus natus est.
Inchoavit ab adam quando dictum est **Erunt duo in carne una** et completa est sexta etate seculi. Senectus sare in plebe dei, hoc est in multitudine prophetarum, hoc idem significat: quia in fine temporum ex plebe
sanctarum animarum natus est christus. Sterilitas eius significat, quod
in hoc seculo spe salvi facti sumus, et in christo tanquam in ysaac omnis

nati sumus, quem partum ecclesia in fine temporum gratia non natura procreavit. Abraham ergo deum patrem significat. ysaac christum. Sicut enim abraham unicum et dilectum filium victimam deo obtulit, sic deus pater unigenitum filium pro nobis tradidit, et sicut ysaac ligna portabat, quibus imponendus erat, sic christus crucem, in qua figendus erat.

Isidore] *om.* W Q Jer. P | filium unicum] unicum filium R Z C unicum filium suum S H | filium unicum ducens] qui ducit unicum filium B | quodammodo] quomodo P | christus] *om.* R O X V P Z D C I H F Q | Abraham . . . natus est] quem quasi in senio suscepit quando post prenuntiatem de christo longe ante factam quando natus est christum. B | Inchoavit] Inchoata si quidem est B | inchoavit ab] abraham *add.* Z | quando dictum est] ubi dicitur B | et] *om.* B | completa] completum P | seculi] quamvis in senio abrahe B | Senectus] et senectu B | sare] sarre W X D | in] *om.* B | plebe] ple O | hoc] id B | ex] ex ipse B | eius] sare B enim *add.* W etiam *add.* D M J I H | significat] etiam figurat P intimat B | spe] sepe C | omnis] omnes N | omnis nati summus] omnes sumus nati Q | quem partem] in *add.* O | ecclesia] *om.* N | gratia non natura] non natura sed gratia R W D J I Q mirabili dei gratia non naturali fecundate B | abraham . . . christum] *om.* R B | enim] ergo B | victimam deo] deo victimam O unicum . . . victimam deo] unicum et dilectum filium B | sic deus . . . pro nobis] ita dominus christum pro omnibus B | quibus imponendus] in quibus ponendus H | imponendus erat] erat imponendus B | sic christus . . . erat] ita christus lignum in qua crucifigendus erat B *om.* C

8.1m Isid. *Quaest. Vet.* 18.3–6 (PL 83 cols. 249 D—250 B), Rab. *Comm. Gen.* 3.3.12 (PL 107 col. 568 B—568 D).

erunt duo Genesis 2:24, Ephesians 5:31–32.

veneruntque ad locum quem ostenderat ei Deus in quo edificavit altare (9.1i) et desuper ligna conposuit. Cumque conligasset (9.2i) Isaac filium suum posuit eum in altari super struem lignorum.

9.1i   hoc est figura altaris in quo consecratur corpus et sanguis christi.
hoc] altare hoc S L G B H | est figura] figura est L G B nostri *add.* V P S L G B M J I H Q | corpus . . . christi] corpus christi et sanguis V P S L G B M J I H Q

   9.1i *marg.* I.

9.2i   quia vinctis manibus ante presidem ductus.
ductus] est X V P L G B N H Q christus X

   9.2i *marg.* I.

9.1m   Ysaac ligatis pedibus altari superponitur, et christus cruci affigitur. Sed quod figuratum est in ysaac translatum est ad arietem, quia christus ovis. Ipse enim filius quia natus, aries quia immolatus. In vepribus heret aries, crux cornua habet. Si enim duo ligna compingantur, crucis species reditur. Unde: **Cornua in manubus eius.** Cornibus ergo haerens aries, christus crucifixus est. Vepres autem spine. Spine inqui, qui dominum suspenderunt inter spinas enim peccatorum suspensus est. Unde ieremias. **Spinis peccatorum suorum circundedit me populus hic.** Alii hunc arietem in vepribus ligatum, intellegunt christum ante immolationem spinis coronatum.

altari superponitur] superponitur altari V D | christus] christo D | christus cruci] cruci
christus S | in] per R W P | heret aries] heret aries cornibus W Q aries heret cornibus P
| compingantur] compungantur Z compinguantur P | christus crucifixus est] crrucifixus
est christus N | suspenderunt] crucifixerit N | iermias] hiermias R | peccatorum . . . spi-
nis] *om.* P Z | intellegunt] *om.* R | coronatum] intellegunt *add* R.

9.1m Isid. *Quaest. Vet.* 18.10–11 (PL 83 col. 251 A-B), Rab. *Comm. Gen.* 3.3.12 (PL 107
col. 569 B-C).

9.1m 9.1i, 9.2i are present here as a marginal gloss in I.

Cornua Habakkuk 3:4.

Spinis This verse does not exist in the Vulgate, although there is a very loose parallel
in Psalms 117:10–12: "omnes gentes circumdederunt me et in nomine Domini ultus
sum eas circumdederunt me et obsederunt me sed in nomine Domini ultus sum
eas circumdederunt me quasi apes extinctae sunt quasi ignis spinarum in nomine
Domini quia ultus sum eas." Christopher Hohler in his study of Calixtus suggested
that this verse may have been fabricated as a joke or as a way to force the reader to
become better acquanited with the Prophets. See Christopher Hohler, "A Note on Jacobus," *Journal of the Warburg and Courtauld Institutes*, Vol. 35. (1972), 78.

9.1m In manuscript B: Ysaac ligatis pedibus et manibus superponitur altari. et christus cruci affigitur. Non ysaac sed aries mactatus. quia non christus secundum quod
est verbum patris. sed secundum quod de matre est ovis vel agnis. immolatur. aries
in veperes heret cornibus. ita christus in cornibus crucis suspenditur a peccatoribus.
qui per spinas significantur. alii dicunt hunc arietem in veperibus cornibus alligatum.
intellegunt christum ante immolationem a iudeis coronatum.

Extenditque manum et arripuit gladium (10.1i) ut immolaret filium suum.

10.1i   quo separaverat omnem carnis affectum.

> quo] hoc est gladius qui S hic est gladius qui L G B hic est gladius quo H | separaverat]
> superaverat Z separat S L G B | carnis] cordis B H | affectum] effectum F

Et ecce angelus (11.1i) Domini de caelo clamavit dicens Abraham Abraham. Qui respondit adsum (11.2i).

> **11.2i** Manuscript H adds as an additional gloss: Quia caro christi potuit occidi, divini-
> tas non potuit tangi.

11.1i   prophetia prenuncians cuncta que de christo ventura.

> prophetia] angelus hic prophetam significat S angelus hic prophetiam significat L G B
> H | prenuncians] prenunciatem L G B H dominus *add* V | cuncta de christo] *om.* P |
> ventura] erant ventura Z futura erant L B ventura erant G H sunt ventura N

Dixitque ei non (12.1i) extendas manum tuam super puerum neque facias illi quicquam nunc (12.2i)(12.4i) cognovi quod (12.5i) timeas Dominum et non peperceris (12.3i) filio tuo unigenito propter me.

> **Illi** Manuscripts V P D M I have ei in the text and vel illi as an interlinear gloss.

> **12.4i** Manuscript L has two additional glosses: (1) Nunc cognovi quod timeas domi-
> num. (2) probatum est.

> **12.5i** Manuscript L has an additional gloss: iterum posteam.

12.1i   quia caro potuit crucifigi: divinitas non potuit tangi.

caro] christi *add.* S L G B | crucifigi] occidi S B occidit G | divinitas] autem *add.* L

12.2i   cognoscere feci te, similiter in sequentibus dicitur, **vocavit nomen loci illius** dominus **videt** id est videri fecit, significans per efficientem id quod efficitur: ut frigus pigrum quod pigros facit.

Nunc cognovi *add.* W O X V P M Nunc Cognovi id est *add.* I | cognoscere feci te] feci te cognoscere P I | videt] vidit C | pigrum] dicitur *add.* W X D dicitur eo V P I cognoscere . . . pigros facit] cognoscere feci W X V P D M J I cognosci feci F Q nunc te et alios feci cognoscere de te quod prius ignorabatis. B

12.2i *cf.* Aug. *Quaest. Hept.* 58 (CCSL 22).

12.2i *marg.* W O X V P D S L G M J I *om.* B.

12.3i   obedientiam meam

obedientiam] id est obedientiam R O id est propter W X V P D M J I propter S L G B N H Q

12.3i Manuscript R has an additional gloss: vel pepercisti.

12.1m   Aug. **Non pepercisci .f. t. u. etc.** Nunquid non pepercit abraam filio suo propter angelum, sed in angelo dominus figuratus est, qui deus est, et **magni consilii angelus**, erat enim in angelo deus, et ex eius persona loquebatur. Hoc magis in sequentibus apparet ubi dicitur: **et vocavit angelus domini abraam iterum de caelo dicens: Per memet ipsum iuravi dicit dominus.** Non enim facile invenitur, christus patrem dominum dicere, tanquam suum dominum, presertim ante incarnationem. Nam secundum carnem hoc congrue dicitur, secundum quam in psalmo dicitur: **Dominus dixit ad me .f.m.e. etc.** Quod autem dictum est: **Dixit dominus domino meo,** ad prophetam refertur, qui loquitur, sicut illud **Pluit dominus ab domino.** Id est, dominus noster, scilicet filius a domino nostro scilicet patre.

Aug] Ieronymus B *om.* G | non] *om.* M J I | dominus figuratus est] figuratus est dominus R | in angelo deus] deus in angelo N | ex] *om.* S | Sed . . . scilicet patre] et non propter deum. angelus significari potuit. qui est magni consilii angelus. Vel qui deus erat in angelo. et ex persona dei loquebatur angelus. B | apparet] apparebit V P M I | ubi] cum R D M J I Q | iterum] secundo R W D M J I Q | christus] christum R X V D christo S christum corr. christus W | dixit dominus] dominus dixit N | prophetam] hoc *add.* R W D Q | sicut illud] secundum P secundum illud J I Q | ad] a C | dominus noster] noster dominus O C | scilicet] sed S secundum M id est Q | patre] etc. *add.* Q. | scilicet patre] patre scilicet R id est a patre D.

12.1m Aug. *Quaest. Hept.* 58 (CCSL 22), Rab. *Comm. Gen.* 3.3.12 (PL 107 col. 567 B).

12.1m Gloss was cut off in the margins in H, and so could not be transcribed.

magni consilii Isaiah 9:5.

Dominus dixit Psalms 2:7.

Dixit dominus Psalms 110:1.

Pluit dominus Genesis 19:24.

12.1m In manuscript G: Aug. **non pepercisti** inquit **.f.tuo dilecto.p.m.** Nunquid abraham non pepercit filio suo propter angelum; et non propter deum; aut ergo angeli nomine dominus christus significatur est. qui sine dubio dominus est. et manifeste a propheta dictus magni consilii angelus. aut quod deus erat in angelo. et ex persona dei angelus loquebatur. sic in propheta etiam solet. Nam in consequentibus hoc magis videtur apparere. ubi legitur. **Et vocavit angelus dei ab iterum de caelo. per memet ipsum. i.d.d.** Non facile enim invenitur dominus christi patrem dominum dicere. tamquam suum dominum. illo presertim tempore tanquam sumeret carnem. Nam secundum hoc quod formam servi accepit. non incongruenter dici sed videtur. Nam secundum huius rei futurae prophetiam. illud est in psalmo. Unde dixit **ad me f.m.e.t.** Nam neque in ipso evangelio facile invenitur aut christo. deum patre dominum appelatus. quod ei dominus esset. quamvis deum inveniamus illo loco ubi ait. **vado ad patrem. m.et patrem .u.d.m.et.d.u.** Quod autem scriptum est. **Dixit dominus domino meo**. ad ipsum qui loquebatur refertur id est **dixit dominus ad domino .m.** pater scilicit filio. et **pluit dominus ab domino**. Qui scribebat dixit ut dominus eius a domino eius id est dominus noster a domino nostro pluisse intelligatur. filius a patre.

Levavit Abraham oculos viditque post (13.1i) tergum (13.2i) arietem inter vepres (13.3i) herentem (13.4i) cornibus. Quem assumens optulit holocaustum pro filio (13.5i).

13.1i   quia longe post veritas huius umbre decleranda.

longe post] post longa tempora S L G B H | decleranda] claranda erat S declaranda erat L G B H

13.2i   tanquam ovis ad occisionem ductus est.

occisionem] occidendum Q

13.2i In manuscripts SH: de quo dicitur tanquam ovis ad occisionem ductus est qui inter veperes id est iudeos exasperantes inter duo brachia crucis suspensus est.

In manuscript L: dequam dicitur tanquam ovis ad occisionem ductus est. qui inter veperes id est iudeos exasperantes inter duo brachia crucis suspendus est.

In manuscript G: de quo dicitur. tanquam ovis ad victimam ductus est. quia inter veperes id est iudeos exasperantes inter duo brachia crucis suspensus est.

In manuscript B: de quo dicitur tanquam ovis ad occasionem ductus est. qui inter duos id est iudeos exasperantes. inter duo brachia chrucis suspensus est.

13.3i   iudeos exasperantes.

iudeos exasperantes] *om.* R S

13.3i cf. Isid. *Quaest. Vet.* 18.11 (PL 83 col. 251 B).

13.4i   inter duo brachia crucis suspensus est.

crucis suspensus est] *om.* C

13.5i   vice filii.

vice filii] *om.* R Z C Q

13.1m   Alc. Aries qui pro ysaac immolatus est, non putativus, sed verus est. Ideo magis putatur angelum eum aliunde attulisse, quem ibi de terra post sex dierum opera dominum procreasse.

putativus] putativus est F | attulisse] tulisse W X V P Q adtulisse Z | dominum] *om.* R | dominum procreasse] etc. *add.* Q dominum procreasse] dominum creasse V P M J I procreasse dominum N. Ideo . . . procreasse] *om.* S

13.1m Alc. *Resp. Gen.* Inter. 206 (PL 100 col. 545 C).

13.1m *om.* L G B.

13.2m Jer. **Arietem inter vepres .h .c. etc.** Aquila veprem vel spinetum posuit, et ut vim verbi interpretemur condensa et inter se complexa virgulta. Unde simachus eadem opinione ductus ait: et apparuit aries, post hec rententus in rete cornibus. Sed .LXX. et teodotio videntur melius interpretari: qui ipsum nomen sabeth posuerunt. In virgultis sabeth cornibus suis. Quia enim sicheon sive retae quod aquila posuit, et symachus per sin litteram scribitur, hic vero samech littera posita est. Unde patet non interpretationem stirpium condensarum et in modum retis inter se virgulta contexta verbum sabeth. Sed nomen sonare virgulti, quod ita hebraice dicitur.

Jer] *om.* G | veperem] veperes H | et] *om.* W D I | vim] *om.* R veri Z | interpretemus] interpretatio est R interpretatio D | simachus] symachus P V S M J N Q | teodotio] theodocio R W O X V P S F Q theodotio Z D C M J N I H | nomen sabeth] nomen sabech W nomen sabet Z | virgultis sabeth] virgultis sabech W virgultis sabet Z | Quia enim] Et enim R W O X V P Z S N I Q unde D | sicheon] sycheon M N I | rete] rethe I Q | symachus] simachus R W O X Z D C H | sin] syn W X P D M N I absent J sim F | samech] samec D sameh S | retis] rethis M | verbum sabeth] verbum sabech W M I verbum sabet Z S | dicitur] etc. *add.* Q | quod ita hebraice dicitur] *om.* C quod ita dicitur hebraice N

13.2m Jer. *Hebr. Quaest.* 22.13 (CCSL 27), Rab. *Comm. Gen.* 3.3.12 (PL 107 col. 567 D—568 A).

13.2m In manuscript B: Ieronymous. Notandum quod Aquilae habet veperem vel spinetum. symachus ponit. et apparuit aries retenitis in rete cornibus suis. septuaginta et theodotion dicunt. in virgulta sabech. Sabech in ebreo idem sonat. quod virgultum. Ex quo intellegitur quod aries in virgulto tenebatur. non in stirpibus veprium. et modum retibus contextum. sic sonat interpretatio aquilae et symachi.

In manuscript G: **Levavitque.o.a. usque optulit holocaustum pro filio.** Notandum quod factum aquilae interpretationem veprem vel spinetum habens. qui ut veri verbi interpretemus verbo greco condensa et inter se inplexa uirgulta significunt. Unde et simachus in eadem ductus opinionem. et apparuit ait aries post hoc in retentus in rete. cornibus hesit suis. Uerum quibusdam dum taxat in hoc loco melius viditur interpretati esse.LXX et theodicion. qui ipsum nomen sabeth cornibus suis. Et etiam [something illegible, probably Greek] sive rete. quod aquila posuit. et simachus per syn litteram scripsit. Hic vero samech littera posuit. tamen ex quo manifestum esse non interpretationem stirpium condensarum. et in modum retis virgulta inter se contexta verbum sabeth. sed nomen virgulti. quod ita hebraicae dicitur.

13.2m 12.2i appears here in the marginal position in manuscripts W O X V P S M I.

Add. O F: **Nunc cognovi quod timeas dominum** id est feci te cognoscere. cui simile est. In monte dominus videbit. id est videre faciet. et significans per efficientem quod efficitur. ut frigus dicitur pigrum quia pigros facit.

Add. Z C N F: **Nunc cognovi quod timeas deum** id est feci te cognoscere. cui simile est. in monte dominus videbit id est videre faciet. et significatur per efficientem quod efficitur ut frigus pigrum dicitur quod pigros facit.

Add. G: **Cunque conligasset .f.s.**usque **Et non pepercis.f.t.u.** Cunqua ista questio simili locutione soluitur. hoc est enim. Nunc cognoui quoniam timeas deum . quod significat. nunc te feci cognoscere. In consequentibus autem hoc genere locutionis euidenter apparet, ubi dicitur. vocabit nomen abraham loci illius dominus vidit. ut dicatur hodie. in monte dominus apparitur. vidit per eo quod est apparuit. si vidit per eo quod est vidi fecit. Significans per efficientem id quod efficitur. sicut frigus pigrum quod pigros facit.

Appellavitque nomen (14.1i) loci illius Dominus (14.2i) videt. Unde usque hodie dicitur in monte Dominus videbit.

14.1i   quia ibi fecit abraham videre diem suum.

ibi fecit] fecit ibi S G B | videre diem suum] videre dominum V P I videre dominum suum W X Q diem suam videre G videre ergo hic ponitur pro apparere. *add.* B *om.* J

14.1i *om.* R, *marg.* W V P M J I Q.

14.2i   ubique **dominus videt**, sed **vidit** dixit pro apparuit id est videre fecit. sicut illud, **nunc cognovi quod timeas dominum** id est cognosci feci per efficientem enim significatur id quod efficitur, sicut pigrum frigus dicimus eo quod pigros facit.

ubique dominus] *om.* J | videre fecit] facit videre S H | sicut] ut R secundum S H | congonsci] cognoscere te S | enim] *om.* N | id] *om.* I | pigrum] *om.* J | frigus dicimus] dicimus frigus Z | eo quod] quia S H

14.2i cf. Aug. *Quaest. Hept.* 58 (CCSL 22).

14.2i *om.* W L G B, *marg.* O V P S M J N I Q

14.1m   Jer. **Appelatur.n.l. etc.** Pro eo quod hic habetur videt, in hebreo videbitur scriptum est, hoc apud hebreos exiuit in proverbium, ut in angustus constituti, et dei optantes auxilio sublevari, dicant: in monte dominus videbitur, id est, sicut abrahe misertus est, miserebitur nostri. Unde et in signum dati arietis, solent cornu clangere.

Jer] *om.* G | hic habetur] ponitur hic B hic habet C | videbitur] videtur N | videbitur scriptum est] scriptum est videbitur S H | hoc] hinc B hoc autem G | exiuit in proverbium] proverbi exiuit B | ut] si quando *add.* G | ut in angustis constituti] ut si quando in angusta constituti sunt B | dei optantes] domini optant B deum optant G | videbitur] videbit P N F videbitur corr. videbit Q | id est] hoc est G | misertus est] est misertus P ita *add.* P J I | solent] etiam *add.* B

14.1m Jer. *Hebr. Quaest.* 22.14 (CCSL 27), Rab. *Comm. Gen.* 3.3.12 (PL 107 col. 568 A-B).

14.1m Various manuscripts insert the following glosses here: 14.1i W O V P M J I Q | 14.2i W V P S M J I Q | 15.2i X V P D M J I Q | 16.1-3i S | 16.3i X V P D M J I Q.

Add. manuscript B: Per memet. hoc per maiorem se iurat. deus quia maiorem non habet. per se ipsum iurare dicitur (cf. 16.1i).

Add. manuscript B: ubique dominus videt, sed vidit dixit pro apparuit id est videre fecit. sicut illud, nunc cognovi quod timeas dominum id est cognisci feci per efficientem enim significatur id quod efficitur, sicut pigrum frigus dicimus: eo quod pigros facit.

14.2m Peracto sacrificio dicitur abrahe **In semine tuo benedicentur omnis gentes.** Quod factum est, cum aries dixit **Foderunt manus meas, et pedes etc.** Peracto enim sacrificio dictum est **Convertentur ad dominum universi fines terre** et: **Adorabunt in conspectu eius et universe etc.** Immolato ergo ariete, vocavit abraham nomen loci illius dominus vidit, id est, videri fecit, per incarnationem, scilicet.

abrahe] *om.* J ad abraham N | cum] quando B | dixit] dicit W | Peracto enim sacrificio] Unde etiam peracto B | dictum est] dicitur R | Convertentur . . . terre] Commemarabuntur et convertentur universe familie gentium. B | eius] tuo R | et universe] *om.* R | ergo] enim D | vocavit abraham] abraham vocavit B | vidit] videt W | dominus vidit] *om.* C | videri] se *add.* W D C M H Q se per *add.* Z | videri fecit] dominus videre fecit utique B | scilicet] pro ysaac filio B. 14.2m *om.* S

14.2m Isid. *Quaest. Vet.* 18.12 (PL 83 col. 251 B-C), Rab. *Comm. Gen.* 3.3.12 (PL 107 col. 569 C-D).

Foderunt Psalms 22:16.

Convertentur Psalms 22:17.

Adorabunt Revelations 15:4.

Vocavit (15.1i) autem angelus (15.2i) (15.3i) Domini Abraham secundo de caelo dicens.

15.3i Manuscript R adds an additional gloss: christus.

15.1i replicat prophetia ventura de christo.

15.1i *om.* G.

15.2i christus **magni consilii angelus.** vel angelus in persona dei loquebatur.

christus] *om.* R | angelus] *om.* R O N | angelus] angelus ipse W V P D J I ipse angelus R O Z C N H F | dei] domini M

15.2i cf. Aug. *Quaest. Hept.* 59 (CCSL 22).

magni consilii cf. Isaiah 9:5.

Permemetipsum (16.1i) (16.2i) iuravi dicit Dominus quia (16.3i) fecisti rem hanc et non pepercisti filio tuo unigenito.

16.1i **quia maiorem non habui.**

16.1i cf. Hebrews 6:13.

16.1i *marg.* S B *om.* G.

In manuscript B: Per memet. Hoc per maiorem se iurat. deus quia maiorem non habet. per se iurare dicitur. *marg.*

16.2i quia immutabiliter a deo statutum est.

de christo *add.* G | statutum] constitutum W X V D M J I Q institutum N

16.3i quia pater filium tradidit **dedit ei nomen quod est super omne nomen, ut in nomine ihesu omne genu flecatur.**

quia] per eo quod S L G H | filium tradidit] tradidit filium P et *add.* P | est] *om.* M | quod est . . . nomen] *om.* S | ihesu] eius R domini M *om.* I .i.e. Q | genu] *om.* C

16.3i Phillipians 2:9–10.

16.3i *marg.* W X V P D S J I.

benedicam tibi et multiplicabo semen tuum sicut stellas (17.1i) (17.2i) celi et velut arenam (17.3i) (17.4i) que est in litore maris possidebit (17.5i) semen tuum portas inimicorum suorum (17.6i)

17.1i–4i cf. Alc. *Resp. Gen. Inter.* 209 (PL 100 col. 546 B).

17.1i   spirituales pauciores fulgentes.

spirituales pauciores fulgentes] plurales sicut stellas fulgentes S H *om.* L G B

17.2i   israel dei.

id est *add.* L B H

17.2i *om.* W V P D G M J I Q.

17.3i   **israel secundum carnem** quia erant et degeneres futuri, et **de bona oliva in oleastrum transituri.**

in *add.* G id est *add.* H | israel secundum carnem] id est israel qui est scilicet arenam L | et] *om.* W X V P quidam S L G B | et degeneres futuri] degeneres J | transituri] etc. *add.* Q

17.3i *marg.* O V P M N I *om.* L.

israel secundum carnem 1 Cor. 10:18.

de bona oliva Romans 11:17.

17.4i   plures carnales steriles.

17.4i *om.* L G B F.

17.5i   quia descendit christus infernu spoliaturus.

infernu] inferos W X V P D C M J N I F Q ad inferos S L G B H | spoliaturus] eos *add.* L G B H

17.6i   catecizabuntur id est baptizabuntur.

in christo *add.* L | catecizabuntur] catezizabuntur R S C cathecizabuntur W B N cathezizabuntur O V D G M J I H F cathezizabuntur X chatezizabuntur P catchezizabuntur Z catacizabuntur L chathecizabuntur Q | id est] vel V P M et L G B N F | baptizabuntur] babtizabuntur W baptizantur V

et benedicentur in semine (18.1i) tuo omnes (18.2i) gentes terrae quia obedisti voci mee.

18.1i   christo.

christo] christo est J in christo H

18.1i *om.* P D S L G B.

18.2i   predestinati de omnibus gentibus.

predestinati de omnibus gentibus] de omnes gentibus predestinati S predestinati de omni gente L de omni gente predestinati G B H

Reversus (19.1i) est Abraham ad pueros suos, abieruntque (19.2i) Bersabee simul, et habitavit ibi.

19.1i   in fine mundi fideles de gentibus ad iudeos revertetur.

quia *add.* L G B H | in fine . . . revertetur] in fine mundi de omnibus gentibus F |
mundi] *om.* S christi L G B H | fideles] fides R W O X V P D S L G B C M N I H Q |
de] *om.* O L | de gentibus] gentium C | ad iudeos] *om.* M | de gentibus . . . revertetur]
reverterur . . . iudeos X H christi a gentibus revertetur ad iudeos et tunc concorditer
vivent in ecclesia. S de gentibus revertetur ad iudeos G B 19.1i *om.* Z

19.2i   tunc concorditer vivent in ecclesia.

et *add.* S L G B H

19.3i   [17.3i i appears here in manuscripts O, V, P, S, M, J, I]

*The following block represents the first recension's rendering of Isidore,
which is substantially different from the second recension and cannot be represented accurately by simply marking variants. For a discussion of the two
recensions and their differences see pages 128–129. I have used G as the main
representative of this first recension because it is both most like the others and
earliest, and I have marked variants in L and B.*

Age nunc videamus quid sub huius cornu sacramenti lateat misterio.
Iste enim abraham quando filium suum unicum perduxit ad immolandum
habebat personam dei patris. Sed quid est quod eum senex suscepit? Non
enim senescit deus sed ipse prenuntiatio de christo iam quodammodo
senuerat quando natus est christus. Inchohata est ab adam ubi dictum est **et
erit duo in carne una.** Sacramentum illud magnum in christi et in ecclesia.
et completa est VI etate seculi, quae se subiecta significatur abrahe quia ipsum sacramentum dei iam longevum erat. Et senectus sare in plebe dei, hoc
est in multitudine prophetarum, hoc idem significat: quia in fine temporum ex ipsa plebe sanctarum animarum natus est christus. Sterilitas autem
eius intimat quod in hoc seculo sepe salvi facti sumus. et in christo tanquam in isaac omnis nati sumus. Quem partum ecclesia in fine temporum
mirabili dei gratia. non naturali fecunditate procreavit. Iam inde sequen-
tis historie sacramentum quid imaginarie portendebat inspiciendum est.
Quis ergo in abraham ut predictum est per immolationem figurabatur nisi
pater excelsus? Quis in isaac nisi christus? Nam sicut abraham dilectum et
unicum filium victimam deo optulit. ita dominus unigenitum filium suum
pro omnibus nobis tradidit. Et sicut isaac ipse ligna sibi portavit quibus
ipse erat imponendus, ita et christo gestavit in humeris lignum crucis sue
in quo ipse erat crucifigendus. Duo autem servi dimissi et non perducti
ad locum sacrificii iudeos significabant qui cum serviliter viverent et carnaliter saperent, non intellegebant humilitatem christi; non pervenerunt
ad locum sacrificii. Cur autem duo servi? Nisi quia populus ipse in duas

partes dividendus erat, quod factum est salmone peccante quando divisus est idem populus in loco regnum, non errore pietatis. Quibus etiam per prophetas dicitur: **adversatrix israel et prevaricatrix iuda**. Asinus autem ille insensata est stulticia iudeorum. Ista insensata stulticia portabat omnia sacramenta et quod ferebat nesciebat. Iam quod dictum est eis **expectante cum asino. Postquam .a.re.a.vos?** Apostolum audi. **cecitas**. inquit. **ex parte in israel facta est**. Quid est cecitas? **Expectate hic cum asino. Ut plenitudo inquit gentium intraret**. hoc est **postquam adoraverimus**. Ubi sacrificium crucis dominice inpletum. per gentes fuerit predicatum. hoc est **ut plenit.g.intraret**. Quid est et **revertemur ad vos? Et sic omnis israel salvus fiet**. Triduum autem illud in quo venerunt ad locum immolationis. tres mundi etates significant: unam ante legem, aliam sub lege, terciam sub gratia. Ante legem, ab adam usque ad moysen. Sub lege, a moise usque ad iohanem. Inde ad domino et quicquid restat tercius dies est grace, quod in tercia etate quasi post triduum. sacramentum sacrificiis christi completum est. Deinde isaac ligatis pedibus altari superponitur et dominus in ligno suspensus cruci affigitur. Sed illud quod figuratum est in isaac traniectum est in arietem. Cur? Quia christus ovis. Ipse est enim filius, ipse est agnus. Filius quia natus. Agnus quia immolatus. Sed quod est in vepribus herebat aries ille? Crux cornua habet. Sic enim duo ligna coniunguntur simul et speciem crucis redditur. Unde et scriptum est de eo. **Cornua in manibus eius sunt**. Cornibus ergo herentem arietem crucifixus significat. Vepres autem spine sunt. Spine iniquos et peccatores significat qui suspenderunt dominum in cruce. Inter spinas itaque peccatorum iudaiorum suspensus est dominus sic per iheremiam idem dicit. Spinis peccatorum suorum circumdedit me populus hic. Alii hunc arietem cornibus in veperibus obligatum eundem christum senserunt. antequam immolaretur spinis a iudeis coronatum. Peracto ergo sacrificio dicitur abrahe. **in semine tuo .b.o.g.** Quando enim hoc factum est? nisi quando dicit ille aries. **foderunt manus .m.** etc. hoc enim quando peractum est. illud in psalmis sacrificium tunc in ipso psalmo dictum est. **Commemorabuntur et convertentur ad dominum .u. fines t. et adorabunt in conspecto eius et relictus**. Immolato ergo abraham pro isaac filio suo vocavit nomen loci illius dominus videt pro quod est dominus videre fecit utique per incarnationem.

perduxit ad immolandum] ad immolandum perduxit L | subiecta] senecta L | nati]
om. L | inde] deinde L | portendebat] portendat L | predictum est per] illam *add.* L |
dilectum et unicum] unicum et dilectum L | omnibus nobis] nobis omnibus L | lignas]

sibi ligna L | ipse] absent L | duo autem] illi *add.* L | non intellegebant . . . sacrificii] non intellegens christi humilitatem et passionum totaquam ad locum sacrificium non pervenit B | per prophetas] sepe per prophetas L | sacraficiis] sacraficium L | isaac ligatis pedibus] ligatis pedibus ysaac L | translatum] transgestum L | ipse est enim filius] ipse enim filius L | ipse est agnes] ipse agnes L | quod est] quid est quod L | coniuguntur simul] conpinguntur fecit L | et scriptum] conscriptum L | et relictus] *om.* L | videt pro] eo *add.* G

Commemorabuntur Psalm 22:27.

TRANSLATION OF THE *GLOSSA ORDINARIA* ON GENESIS 22:1–19

After these things God tested (1.1i) (1.2i) Abraham and spoke to him. Abraham responded, "I am here." (13.1i)

1.1i   in order to make known to him his perfection, of which he himself was not unaware

1.2i   in order to investigate how quickly he would obey

1.1m   Augustine. Augustine. James says that **God does not test anyone** (James 1:12); rather, usually we say "test" when what we mean is "prove." However, James was only talking about a test in which someone is implicated in a sin, whence: **"Lest by chance he who tests should test you"** (1 Thess. 3:5). Indeed, elsewhere it is written: **"Your God may test you, that he may know if you love him"** (Deut. 13:3). That is, that he may cause you to know. A man is unaware of the strength of His love for him, unless he comes to know it from experience.

He said to him, "Take (2.1i) (2.2i) your only-begotten son Isaac whom you love and go to (2.3i) the land of vision and offer him as a sacrifice (2.4i) on one of the mountains (2.5i) which I will show you."

2.1i   **God so loved the world that he gave his only son.**

2.2i   By the reminder of love and the mention of the name the test is piled high, and the fatherly emotion is moved by the memory of the promise: because it was said that **in Isaac your seed will be called** (Genesis 21:12, Romans 11:18), so if he would be killed, all the hope of the promise would be frustrated.

2.3i   where it will be revealed to you what I will foretell with this sacrifice

2.4i   a sign of the true sacrifice

2.5i   the eminence of the faith which I will reveal to you

2.1m   Alcuin. Abraham was not commanded to kill his son suddenly, but to lead him for three days to the sacrifice; thus the test would be intensified because of its time length. For three days his paternal instincts were tortured by increasing concern. During that long time, the father looked at his son when he took food to him, and for so many nights the boy lay in his father's arms, resting in his bosom, so that at every moment he felt sadder about killing his son.

2.3m   Jerome. **Go to the place etc.** The Hebrews say that this is the mountain on which the Temple was later built, in the land of Orna the Jebusite, whence in Chronicles: **They began to build the Temple in the second month, in the second day of the month, on mount Moriah** (1 Chronicles 3:1–2) which is interpreted to mean "illuminating" and "lighting," which refers to the *dabir*, which is the word of God, and both the law and the spirit which teaches people the truth and inspires prophecies.

So Abraham rose in the night and saddled (3.1i) his donkey taking with him two youths (3.2i) and Isaac his son, and when he had cut wood (3.3i) for the sacrifice he went on his way to the place which God had commanded him.

3.1i   he prepared the requirements for the sacrifice
3.2i   because **two peoples** (Gen. 25:23) consented to the death of Christ, and **the father did not spare his own son** (Romans 8:32)
3.3i   because the cross of Christ was made of two pieces of wood
3.1m   The senseless stupidity of the Jews is signified by the donkey, which was carrying all the sacraments and was unaware.

And on the third day (4.1i), lifting up his eyes, he saw (4.2i) the place far off.

4.1i   On the fourth day of the week, the deal was made with Judas to betray [Christ]; on the fifth, he was arrested; on the third day, that is the eve of the Sabbath, he was crucified.

   third day ie. after the betrayal. Other manuscripts have "on the sixth day."

4.2i.   being far away from the malice of the Jews
4.1m   Jerome. It should be noted that from Gerar to Mount Moriah, the place of the Temple, would be a journey of three days, and Abraham is said to reach there on the third day. Those who think that Abraham dwelled in that time near the oak of Mamre are therefore incorrect, since from there to Mount Moriah the journey would be scarcely one full day.
4.2m   The three days in which they came to the place of the sacrifice signify three eras: before the law from Abraham until Moses, under the law from Moses until John [the Baptist], then up until [the time of] the Lord and whatever [time] remains, the third era is of grace, in which third era the sacrifice of God was completed.

And he said to his youths, "Wait (5.1i) here with the donkey, I and the boy will go quickly over there, and after we have worshipped (5.2i), we will return to you."

5.1i   because Jews, through great slowness, do not understand the mystery of the cross

5.2i   This will be at the end of the world **when the full number of the nations come in** (Romans 11:25).

5.1m   **Partial blindness befalls Israel** (Romans 11:25), that is, with the donkey, **in order that the fullness of the nations may come in** (Romans 11:25), that is, and later we will worship. Where the sacrifice of the cross for the nations was predicted, this is, **until the fullness of the nations may come in,** (Rom. 11:25). We will return to you, that is, **and thus all of Israel will be saved** (Rom. 11:26).

5.2m   The two servants who were sent away and not led to the place of the sacrifice are Jews, who live slavishly, and, thinking in a carnal way, do not understand the humiliation and suffering of Christ. Two, because of their division in two which happened after the sin of Solomon, when the people was divided in the location of their government, although not in the error of impiety. From which it is said: **Israel the adversary, Judah the liar** (Jeremiah 3:8).

5.3m   Alcuin. The boy and I: He was willing to sacrifice his son with an undoubting soul, praiseworthy in the constancy of offering and in his trust in ressurection. For he knew with greatest certainty that God could not fail, and although the boy might be sacrificed, God's saving promise would yet endure. Whence the Apostle: **Abraham did not hesitate in his faith, when offering his only son in whom he received the promise, believing that God was able to revive him even from death** (Hebrews 11:17–19).

And he took the wood for the sacrifice and put it (6.1i) on Isaac his son, and he himself carried in his hands (6.2i) fire (6.3i) and a sword (6.4i). And then the two went on together.

6.1i   because Christ was forced to carry the cross on his shoulder from where it was originally made

6.2i   by works

6.3i   a great zeal

6.4i   which separated the father and son

Isaac said to his father, "My father." And he answered, "What do you want, son?" "Here," he said, "are fire and wood. Where (7.1i) is the victim for the sacrifice?"

7.1i   It is seen how much Christ seems to be unaware why he suffers for his own innocence, whence: **They gathered against me with a whip and I did not know** (Psalms 34:15).

And Abraham said: "God will provide himself a victim for a sacrifice, my son." So they went on (8.1i) together.

8.1i   because the son obeyed the father even unto death

8.1m   Isidore. Abraham, in leading his only son to be sacrificed, signifies God the father. Abraham received his son as an old man; God, however, does not age, but the promise of Christ in a certain way aged when Christ was born. It began from Adam, when it was said: **There were two in one flesh** (Gen. 2:24, Eph. 5:31–32), and it was completed in the sixth era of the world. The old age of Sarah is in the people of God, that is, in the multitude of the prophets. This signifies the same thing: that in the end of days Christ was born out of the people of holy souls. His infertility signifies that in this era we are made only through the hope of salvation, and in Christ we are all born just as in Isaac. Which birth not nature but grace created for the Church at the end of times. Therefore Abraham signifies God the father and Isaac Christ. Thus just as Abraham offered his only and beloved son as a sacrifice to God, thus God the father gave his only son for us, and just as Isaac carried the wood on which he was put, so Christ the cross on which he was fixed.

And they came to the place which God had shown him, where he built an altar (9.1i), and arranged the wood on it, and when he had bound (9.2i) his son Isaac, he set him on the altar on the pile of wood.

9.1i   This is a symbol of the altar on which is consecrated the body and blood of Christ.

9.2i   because he was led with bound hands before the governor

9.1m   Isaac was placed with bound legs on the altar, and Christ was affixed to the cross, but what was prefigured by Isaac was transferred to the ram, because Christ is a sheep. He himself is a son because he was born, [and he is] a ram because he was sacrificed. The ram caught in thickets, the cross has a thorn. For if the two pieces of wood were joined together the appearance of the cross is given. Whence: **Thorns in his hands** (Habakkuk 3:4). Therefore the ram caught in thorns is Christ crucified. The thorn-bushes are also spines. It says "spine," for Christ was hung between the spines of sinners. Whence Jeremiah says **This people surrounded me with the spines of their sins**. Others understand this ram bound in the thorn-bush as Christ crowned with thorns before the sacrifice.

And he reached out his hand and took the sword (10.1i) to sacrifice his son.

10.1i   by which he had separated all affection for the body

And behold an angel (11.1i) of the Lord from heaven called to him, saying: "Abraham, Abraham." And he answered: "Here I am."

11.1i   pronouncing all prophecies concerning the coming of Christ

And he said to him, "Do not (12.1i) lay your hand on the boy and do not do anything to him. Now (12.2i) I know that you fear God and have not spared (12.3) your only begotten son from me."

12.1i   because while the flesh could be crucified, divinity could not be touched
12.2i   "I have caused you to know": Similarly, it says later, **He called the name of this place The Lord Sees**, meaning that he caused to be seen, attributing an effect to its effector, as in "the sluggish cold," which is actually a cold that makes people sluggish.
12.3i   my obedience
12.1m   Augustine. It is not that Abraham did not spare his son for the sake of an angel; rather, in the angel the Lord is figured, who is God, and **an angel of great council** (Isaiah 9:5), for God was in the angel, and He spoke through his person. This is clear in what follows, when it is said: **And the angel of God called Abraham a second time from heaven, saying "By myself I have sworn, says the Lord"** (Gen. 22:15–16). Indeed, it is not easily found that Christ calls the Father "Lord," as though being his lord, especially before the incarnation. For according to his physical state this is rightly said, according to what is said in the Psalm: **The Lord said to me** etc. (Ps. 2:7). That which moreover was said **The Lord said to my lord** (Ps. 110:1), this refers to the prophet, who speaks, just like this: **The Lord rained [. . .] from the Lord** (Gen. 19:24) that is, **our Lord**, namely the Son, **from the Lord**, namely the Father.

Abraham lifted up his eyes, and saw behind (13.1i) him (13.2i) a ram among the thickets (13.3i) caught (13.4i) by its horns, which he took and offered for a sacrifice in place of his son (13.5i).

13.1i   because long after the truth must be declared by his shadow
13.2i   just as the lamb was led to the slaughter
13.3i   inciting Jews
13.4i   he was hung between two arms of the cross
13.5i   or, "of the son"

13.1m   Alcuin. The ram which was sacrificed for Isaac was not imagined but real. Therefore it is thought, rather, that the angel brought it from elsewhere, which he created there from the earth after the first six days of creation.

13.2m   Jerome. Aquila wrote "veprem" [thorn-bush] or "spinetum" [spike], so we interpret that the force of the word means that bush was thick and entangled in itself. So too Symmachus, being led to the same opinion, says: "And a ram appeared, after these things, having been restrained by the horns in a net." But in the Septuagint and Theodotion they are better interpreted, where the word *sabeth* itself is written: "[caught] **in bushes (***sabeth***) with its horns.**" When Aquila and Symmachus write "suchnon" or 'tree,' which is normally written with the letter "sin," indeed the letter "samech" is written. From this it is clear that the interpretation of the word "sabeth" is not the explanation that the dense plants and bushes tangled among themselves like a tree, but rather to use the Hebrew name of the shrub.

And he called the name (14.1i) of that place, "The Lord (14.2i) sees." Whence until this day it is said, "In the mountain the Lord will see."

14.1i   because there he caused Abraham to see his day

14.2i   Wherever it says "the Lord sees" or "saw," it means that something appeared, that is, He caused to see. Likewise, "**Now I have known that you fear God**" means "I have caused to be known." It is the idiomatic attribution of an effect to its effector, as in "the sluggish cold," which is actually a cold that makes people sluggish.

14.1m   Jerome. Although it says here "**He will see,**" in the Hebrew it is written "He will be seen." This among the Hebrews has emerged as a proverb; when they are found in a crisis, and want to be rescued by the help of God, they say "God will be seen on the mountain," that is: "Just as Abraham was granted mercy, so may He be merciful us." Thus as a sign of the ram that was given, they are accustomed to sound the horn.

14.2m   It was said to Abraham when the sacrifice was completed, **In your seed is blessed all nations** (Gen. 22:18). That was done when the ram said: **They stab my hands and feet** (Ps. 22:17). For when the sacrifice was completed it is said: **All the ends of the earth will be converted to the Lord** (Ps. 22: 18) and **will worship in your presence** (Revelations 15:4). Therefore after the sacrifice of the ram, Abraham called the name of this place "The Lord saw," that is, he made to be seen, namely, through the incarnation.

And called (15.1i) the angel (15.2i)of the Lord to Abraham a second time from heaven, saying:

15.1i   he repeats the prophecy of the coming of christ.
15.2i   Christ is **the angel of great council** (Isaiah 9:5). Alternatively, the angel spoke for God.

"I have sworn by my own self (16.1i) (16.2i)," says the Lord, "because (16.3i) you have done this thing, and have not spared your only begotten son for my sake,

16.1i   because I have nothing greater
16.2i   because it is unchangeably decreed by God
16.3i   because the father gave up his son he gave to him a name which is above every name, such that in the name of Jesus every knee is bent (Philippians 2:9–10)

I will bless you, and I will multiply your seed as the stars (17.1i) (17.2i) of heaven, and as the sand (17.3i) (17.4i) of the seashore, your seed will possess (17.5i) the gates of their enemies (17.6i)."

17.1i   spiritual, fewer, shining
17.2i   Israel of God
17.4i   Israel after the flesh because they will be degenerate and will be transformed from the good olive to a **wild olive tree** (Romans 11:17)
17.4i   many, fleshy, barren
17.5i   because Christ descended to the underworld to pillage it
17.6i   catechized, that is, baptized

And in your seed (18.1i) will all (18.2i) the nations of the earth be blessed, because you have obeyed my voice.

18.1i   Christ
18.2i   the predestined of all nations

Abraham returned (19.1i) to his youths, and they went (19.2i) to Bersabee together, and he lived there.

19.1i   At the end of the world the faithful of the nations will be returned to the Jews.
19.2i   Then they will live harmoniously in the Church.

The following is the quotation of Isidore from GBL as represented by manuscript G:

Come, now, and let us see that under the horn of this sacrament hides a mystery. This Abraham, when he led his only son to be sacrificed, figuratively stood for God the father. But what does it mean that he was an old man? For God does not age, but considering the prophecy of Christ, in a way He aged when Christ was born.

This began with Adam, about whom it was said **and there were two in one flesh**. This sacrament is great in Christ and in the Church, and it was completed in the sixth era of the world, which having revealed itself was signified by Abraham, because that same sacrament of God yet was aged. And the age of Sarah in the people of God, that is in the multitude of prophets, signifies the same thing, because Christ was born in the end of days out of the people of sanctified souls. His sterility hints that in this age we are all made with the help of salvation, and in Christ just as in Isaac we all are born, which birth the Church made in the end of days by the miraculous grace of God, not by natural fecundity.

Now the sacrament in the following history, and what it foretells with its imagery, should be examined. Who was figured in Abraham so that it [the crucifixion] was predicted through this sacrifice, if not the High Father? Who in Isaac if not Christ? For as Abraham offered his beloved and only son as a sacrifice to God, so the Lord gave his only-born son for us all. And as Isaac himself carried the wood on which he himself was placed, so also Christ bore in his arms the wood of his own cross on which he himself was crucified. Moreover, the two servants who were sent away and not led to the place of sacrifice signify Jews, who live slavishly and think carnally and do not understand the humiliation of Christ. They did not arrive at the place of sacrifice. Why, moreover, two slaves, if not because this people was divided in two parts, which happened when Solomon sinned, when this same people was divided in place of government, although not in error of piety? About this, the prophet said, "**Israel the enemy, Judah the liar.**" That donkey, moreover, represents the irrational stupidity of the Jews. This irrational stupidity carried all the sacraments, yet it was not aware of what it was carrying.

Now what was said: **Wait here with the donkey, after we will worship we will return to you,** [means] listen to the apostle. **Partial blindness,** he says, **befalls Israel**. What is this blindness? He says, **"Wait here with the donkey": that the fullness of the nations may come in.** That is, **"and later we will worship"** where the Lord's sacrifice fulfilled by the cross for the nations was predicted. That is, **until the fullness of the nations may come in**. What is **"we will return to you"**? **And thus all of Israel will be saved.**

Moreover, these three days in which they came to the place of the sacrifice signify three eras of the world, one before the law, another under the law, the third under grace: before the law, from Adam continually until Moses, under the law, from Moses all the way until John. From the time of the Lord and on remains is the third day of grace, that in the third day as if after three days the sacrament of the sacrifice of Christ was completed.

Then Isaac was placed with bound legs on the altar, and the Lord, having been hung on the wood, was fixed to the cross. But that which was figured in Isaac was transferred to the ram. Why? Because Christ is a sheep, for as he himself is a son, he himself is a lamb. A son because he was born, a lamb because he was sacrificed. But what is this ram that was tangled in the thickets? The cross has thorns. The cross has thorns, for when two pieces of wood are joined together at the same time, it has the appearance of the cross. Whence it is also written about this, **thorns were in his hands**. Spines signify the wrongdoers and sinners who hung the Lord on the cross. Between thorns, accordingly, of the Jewish sinners, the Lord was hung. Thus he likewise says through Jeremiah, **This people surrounded me with the spikes of their sinners**. Others thought this ram bound in the thickets is the very same Christ before he was sacrificed crowned with thorns by the Jews. Therefore after the sacrifice it was said to Abraham: **In your seed all nations will be blessed**. For when was this done? Was it not when this ram said **they bound my hands**? For thus when it was completed that sacrifice in Psalms was then spoken of in the psalm itself: **They will be recalled and they will be converted to the Lord . . . and they will worship in his presence**. Therefore Abraham, for Isaac his son having been sacrificed, called the name of that place **the Lord sees**. For truly, how God made to see was through the incarnation.

APPENDIX B

MAJOR MANUSCRIPT VARIANTS IN RASHI'S COMMENTARY ON GENESIS 22: EXISTING EDITIONS AND RATIONALE FOR PRESENT EDITION

The first modern critical edition of Rashi's commentary on the Torah is that of Avraham Berliner, which was published in 1866 and further revised in 1905,[1] based on one hundred manuscripts. In his edition, Berliner selected what he considered the best text from all the available manuscripts, but did not provide a critical apparatus with the variant readings or explain the reasoning behind his choices. This raises the possibility that he simply went with the most familiar and comfortable reading.[2] The critical edition of Rashi on Genesis 22 by Hayim Dov Chavel[3] includes a reprint of the Berliner edition, Rashi variants found in the commentary of Nahmanides to the Pentateuch, and some variants from later commentaries on Rashi. It also includes variants from the first printed edition,[4] and from the Oxford manuscript (Bodleian 2440) which he doubts was included in Berliner's hundred manuscripts because it includes unusual variants.[5] *Rashi HaShalem*[6] reproduces four early printed editions of Rashi's commentary. Venice 1524 is the main text, and Rome 1470, Reggio di Calabria 1475, and Guadelajara 1476 are reprinted in the back in parallel columns. *Mikraot Gedolot Haketer*, as yet incomplete and published by Bar Ilan University volume by volume starting in 1992, is based on six Ashkenazic manuscripts but does not contain a critical apparatus.

These critical editions represent at best a late form of Rashi's commentary and do not allow for the reconstruction of its early twelfth-century form. This late form of Rashi should be understood to be a composite document, much of which was composed in the mid-twelfth century. To speak of Rashi as the author of his commentary is as much of a metaphor as to speak of a single, individual glossator writing the *Glossa Ordinaria*. What can be seen in the existing critical editions is a form of Rashi's commentary roughly parallel and comparable to the final form of the Gloss as represented by manuscript A.

To supplement the existing critical editions I have examined the following thirty-one Rashi manuscripts:

Berlin 14 (Ms. Or. Fol.121) פירוש התנך Microfilm of MS from Munich at Institute of Microfilmed Hebrew Manuscripts (Jerusalem). n.d.

Istanbul Topkapu Serai G.1.611 פירוש התורה לרשי Microfilm of MS from Munich at Institute of Microfilmed Hebrew Manuscripts (Jerusalem). Fourteenth to fifteenth century.

Leipzig (B.H. fol) 1 תורה הפטרות וה' מגילות Microfilm of MS from Munich at Institute of Microfilmed Hebrew Manuscripts (Jerusalem). Thirteenth to fourteenth century.

Munich (Cod. Hebr.) 5. "Perush Rashi." Microfilm of MS from Munich at Institute of Microfilmed Hebrew Manuscripts (Jerusalem).1233.

Oxford- Bodleian 1 Arch. Seld. A. 47 Dated 1304.

Oxford- Bodleian Heb. d. 102

Oxford- Bodleian 20 (Opp. 14 (ol. 102)) Dated 1340

Oxford- Bodleian 21 (Opp. add. 4to 47). Early thirteenth century.

Oxford- Bodleian 26 (Can. or. 62) Dated 1472.

Oxford- Bodleian 186 (Opp. 34). פרוש תורה נביאים כתובים. Thirteenth century.

Oxford- Bodleian 187 (Mich. 384) פרוש התורה Dated 1399.

Oxford- Bodleian 188 (Opp. 35) פרוש התורה Dated 1409.

Oxford- Bodleian 189 (Can. 81) פרוש התורה Dated 1396.

Oxford- Bodleian 190 (Opp. Add. 4to 53) Dated 1566.

Oxford- Bodleian 195 (Opp. Add. 4to 77) n.d.

Oxford- Bodleian 2440 (Corpus Christi Coll. 165) פירוש התנך n.d.

Oxford- Bodleian 2546 (Opp. Add. fol 69) Fifteenth century.

Paris Heb. 37 תורה ה' מגלות והפטרות Fourteenth century.

Paris Heb. 42 תורה Dated 1472.

Paris Heb. 48 תורה הפטרות וחמש מגילות Fourteenth century.

Paris Heb. 68 תורה Fourteenth or fifteenth century.

Paris Heb. 55 תורה והפטרות Fifteenth or sixteenth century.

Paris Heb. 156 פרוש התורה מאת רשי Thirteenth or fourteenth century.

Paris Heb. 157 פרוש התורה מאת רשי Thirteenth or fourteenth century.

Paris Heb. 158/1 פרוש התורה מאת רשי Fourteenth or fifteenth century.

Paris Heb. 159 פרוש התורה מאת רשי Fourteenth or fifteenth century.

Parma 181/9 (3204) רשי פרוש התורה Twelfth or thirteenth century.

Parma 459 (2760) פרוש התורה לרשי Fourteenth century.

Parma 682 (3256) פרוש התורה לרשי Dated 1312.

Parma 1082 (2986) פרוש התורה לרשי Dated 1370.

St. Petersburg Russian State Library Evr. ii.A 118/1 פרוש התורה לרשי Fifteenth
   or sixteenth century.

Uppsala (O. Cod. Hebr.) 1. תורה ה מגילות הפטרות Fourteenth century.

Berkeley Banc. UCB 124, Perush Rashi al ha-Torah, Fifteenth century.

Vienna (Wien) Oesterreichische Nationalbibliothek Cod hebr. 12a, פרוש
   התורה לרשי Fourteenth or fifteenth century.

Vienna 24 (Hebr. 3) פרוש התנך לרשי Fourteenth or fifteenth century.

Because of the number and late date of the manuscripts I have not compiled a full critical edition of all variants. Rather, I have identified the substantive differences, that is, those that impact the meaning of the comment.

1.1

In the first half of the comment, while the early printed editions are consistent, the manuscripts show a significant variant.

אחר הדברים האלא. יש מרבותינו אומרים, אחר דבריו של שטן, שהיה מקטרג ואומר,
מכל סעודה שעשה אברהם לא הקריב לפניך פר אחד או איל אחד. אמר לו, כלום עשה
אלא בשביל בנו, אלו הייתי אומר לו זבח אותו לפני לא היה מעקב.

After these things. Some of our rabbis say, after the words of Satan, who
would accuse and say, "From the whole feast that Abraham made he did
not sacrifice before you even one heifer or ram." He [God] said to him,
"He did nothing except for the sake of his son. If I were to tell him to
sacrifice him before me he would not delay."

A variant in Ms. Paris Heb. 157 reads:

יש מרבותינו אומרין אחר שקטרגה מדת הדין לפני הקב''ה.

Some of our rabbis say, after the [divine] attribute of justice accused
before the Holy One, Blessed be He . . .

I have found similar variants in Ms. Paris Heb. 37, Ms. Paris Heb. 157, Ms. St. Petersburg Russian State Library Evr. ii.A 118/1 and Ms. Vienna 24. This variant is discussed at length in chapter two.

In the second half of the comment, the Rome edition shows a significant variant. In the printed edition Isaac responds to Ishmael's boasting about his circumcision by declaring his willingness to sacrifice himself:

אילו אמר לי הקב"ה זבח עצמך לפני לא הייתי מעכב.

If the Holy One, Blessed Be He were to say to me "sacrifice yourself before me" I would not delay.[7]

In the Rome edition there is a longer variant that adds another piece of dialogue between Isaac and Ishmael:

אילו אמר לך הב"ה קרב עצמך לפני אתה זבח אמר לו חס ושלום אמר לו יצחק מיד אני זובח לפניו.

[Isaac asked Ishmael:] "If the Blessed One said, 'Sacrifice yourself before me' would you sacrifice [yourself]?" [Ishmael] said to [Isaac], "Heaven forefend." Isaac said to him, "I would sacrifice [myself] immediately before him."[8]

This variant is also attested in Ms. Parma 682 (3256) and Ms. Paris Heb. 159. The addition sharpens the contrast between Isaac and Ishmael. Not only is Isaac willing to make a greater sacrifice than Ishmael has made, it is clear that Ishmael would not be willing to make such a sacrifice. This additional dialogue does not appear in any of Rashi's sources.

Two fourteenth- to fifteenth-century manuscripts make Rashi's condemnation of Ishmael even more explicit, by adding the word רשע [evil one] at the beginning of this line, so that Isaac directly calls Ishmael "wicked one" in his refutation of him.

1.2A (ADDED AFTER COMMENT 1.2)

Ms. Oxford- Bodleian 2440 and Ms. Oxford- Bodleian 269 Can. Or. 23 add this comment:

והאלוהים נסה את אברהם. יי צדיק יבחן.

And God tested Abraham. God will test the righteous.

This variant is also attested in Perush Yakov ben Shabti and is discussed in detail in chapter two.

1.3

Most manuscripts describe God asking Abraham to perform the test so that שלא יאמרו הראשונות אין בהן ממש [they will not say that the earliest ones did not have substance]. Ms. Vienna 20/12 adds the word אומות [nations] making explicit that God is particularly concerned about other nations doubting Abraham's greatness.

2.2

Ms. Oxford-Bodleian 195 gives an alternative explanation for the term Moriah: מוריה לשון מורים מים [from the words "raising water"] instead of מוריה שיש בה מור ושער בשמים [Moriah, because it contains myrrh and other fragrances], which is found in all other manuscripts and in the printed editions.

3.1 AND 3.2

Most manuscripts have the comment וישכם. נזדרז למצוה [[Abraham] rose early eager to perform the commandment]. This comment is absent in Ms. Oxford-Bodleian 195 (Opp. Add. 4to 77). The absence of this comment greatly undermines Abraham's role as a model for behavior, since this is the only time that Rashi presents Abraham as acting in a way that the reader could emulate. Similarly, while most manuscripts follow this with an additional comment illustrating Abraham's zeal, הוא בעצמו ולא צוה לאחד מעבדיו [And [Abraham] saddled: he himself, and did not command his servants]. Ms. Oxford-Bodleian 195 as well as Ms. Oxford-Bodleian 21 and Ms. Oxford-Bodleian 186 eliminate the reference to servants.

8.1

יראה לו השה. יבחר לו השה, ואם אין שה, לעולה בני. ואף על פי שהבין יצחק שהוא הולך להשחט, וילכו שניהם יחדיו, בלב שוה.

God will see for himself a lamb. He will choose for himself a lamb, and if not **my son will be the sacrifice**. And even though Isaac understood that he was going to be slaughtered, **the two went on together**, with an equal heart.[9]

This is a key passage, as it is the only piece in Rashi that describes Isaac's motivations. The Guadalajara 1476 edition significantly alters it by removing the phrase שהבין יצחק שהוא הולך להשחט [Isaac understood that he was going to be slaughtered].[10] That Isaac understood can probably still be inferred from this comment, however it is nowhere near as strong a statement of Isaac's willingness. This omission is not found in the manuscripts.

11.1 AND 12.1

Almost all manuscripts have comment 11.1 and 12.1 as follows:

אברהם אברהם לשון חיבה הוא שכופל' את שמו. **אל תשלך (ידך)** לשחוט.

Abraham Abraham. It is a term of affection that he repeats his name. **Do not stretch forth your hand** to slaughter.

Manuscript E replaces these two comments with a lengthy quotation from *Midrash Tanchuma* Vayera 23:

וכן **יעקב יעקב**. ומדרש אגדה למה שני פעמים. שהיה ממהר והולך לשוחטו כשאמר לו **על תשלך** אמר לו מי אתה אמר לו מלאך אני אמ' כשאמר **קח נא** בעצמו אמר לי ואם הוא אבקש הוא ואמ' מיד **ויקרא מלאך שנית** שלא רצה לקבל מן הראשון. **ויאמר אל תשלך.**

It is similar to **Jacob Jacob** (Genesis 46:2). And an aggadic midrash asks, why two times? Because he was hurrying to slaughter him. When he [the angel] said "**do not send forth** [your hand]," [Abraham] said to him, "Who are you?" [The angel] answered, "I am an angel." [Abraham] said, "When [God] said to me 'Take [your son]' he himself said it to me, and if he [wants me to stop] let him ask." And it says immediately following this, **and the angel said again**, since [Abraham] did not wish to accept it from the first, and it said "**Do not send forth [your hand]**."

This addition is not attested in any other manuscripts, which suggests that the copyist of this manuscript added it because he considered it to be consistent with Rashi's approach.

12.1

After God commands Abraham to stop the sacrifice, Rashi describes Abraham as wanting to continue:

אמר לו אם כן לחינם באתי לכאן. אעשה בו חבלה ואוציא ממנו מעט דם. אמר לו על
תעש בו מאומה, אל תעש בו מום.

He [Abraham] said to him [God], "In that case I came here for nothing. I will wound him and take some blood from him." [God] said to [Abraham], "**Do not do anything to him**, do not make in him a blemish."[11]

The phrase אל תעש בו מום [do not make in him a blemish] (which would make him ineligible as a sacrifice) is only included in the Alkabetz and Venice editions,[12] and is not found in any of the manuscripts that I have consulted. This changes the significance of the comment. Without this phrase it seems that Abraham is trying to wound Isaac, to make at least a partial sacrifice, and that God is forbidding him from doing so. With this phrase, it seems that Abraham was intending to wound Isaac to make him ineligible as a sacrifice, and God was telling him that this was unnecessary.

12.2

אמר אברהם אני אשפך לפניך את שיחתי אתמול אמרת לי **כי ביצחק יקרא לך זרע**
חזרת ואמרת **קח נא את בנך** עכשיו אתה אמר **אל תשלך ידך אל הנער** אמר הקב"ה
לא אחלל בריתי ומוצא שפתי לא אשנה לא אמרתי שחתיהו אלא העליהו. איסיקיתיה
אחתיה.

Abraham said, "I will pour my speech before you. Yesterday you said to me '**for in Isaac will your descendants be called**.' You retracted it and said, '**Take your son**.' Now you say, '**Do not send forth your hand against the lad**.'" The Holy One, Blessed be He said, "**I will not profane my covenant and the utterance of my lips I will not change.** I did not say 'kill him,' only 'bring him up.' You brought him up; bring him down."

This comment is present in the Rome edition and absent in the Alkabetz and first editions.[13] Of the manuscripts I have seen, it is only found in Oxford-Bodleian 187, Oxford-Bodleian 195, Paris Heb. 37 and Paris Heb. 157. Oxford- Bodleian 189 has this comment in the margin of a Rashi manuscript. Chavel[14] points out that the early commentaries on Rashi do not comment on this, which indicates that it is a later addition. It is taken directly from *Genesis Rabbah* 56.8.

12.3

כי **עתה ידעתי**. מעתה יש לי מה להשיב לשטן ולאומות התמהים מה היא חיבתי אצליך,
יש לי פתחון פה שרואים **כי ירא אלוהים אתה**

Now I know. Now I have something to answer Satan and the nations of the world who wonder why I love you. I have something to say, now that they know **that you fear God.**

This comment varies substantially from manuscript to manuscript. Eight manuscripts (Ms. Oxford-Bodleian 187, Ms. Oxford-Bodleian 190, Ms. Paris Heb. 37, Ms. Paris heb. 157, Ms. Paris Heb. 159, Ms. Parma 682, Ms. Vienna 24, Ms. St. Petersburg Russian State Library Evr. ii.A 118/1) have "the divine attribute of justice" (מדת הדין) instead of Satan, but still include "the nations of the world" as the intended audience for Abraham's test. Ms. Parma 181/9 has "the divine attribute of justice" (מדת הדין) and omits "the nations of the world." This substantially changes Rashi's explanation of not only this verse but of the entire purpose of the near-sacrifice of Isaac, by making it about proving Abraham's greatness to God alone rather than to a hostile and accusing other. Seven manuscripts (Ms. Istanbul Topkapu Serai G.1.61, Ms. Oxford-Bodleian 195, Ms. Oxford-Bodleian 197, Ms. Paris Heb. 42, Ms. Paris Heb. 68, Ms. Paris Heb. 158/1, Ms. Parma 1082) do not mention either Satan, the divine attribute of justice or the nations of the world, leaving it unclear who God is now able to answer.

13.1

Ms. Oxford-Bodleian 187 ascribes the authorship of this comment to Rabbi Abba (א״ר אבא). This is the only case that I have found in which a manuscript of Rashi's commentary on Genesis 22 introduces a named rabbi as the author of a midrash.

13.1A

Three late manuscripts (Oxford-Bodleian 187 from the 14th century and Oxford-Bodleian 190 from the 15th century, and 26 can. or. 62 from 1472) add the following comment after Rashi's comment 13.1:

ר' יוסף ברבי שמעון פרש **אחר נאחז בסבך** שנקל לקחתו משם שאם נאמר וירא והנה
איל ולא בסבך בקרניו היה נראה שצריך לחזר אחריו. וכך נהגי כל הכתובים על כל מילה
שעתידין הבריות לחלק הוא מייתר הלשון ומיישר הדרך לפניהם.

Rabbi Yosef son of Rabbi Shimon explains: The Verse says **after [the
ram] was caught in a thicket** to show that it was easy to take it from
there. For if it were written, "He saw, and there was a ram" without saying explicitly "caught by its horns in a thicket" it would appear that he
had to go back after it. This is the way of all Biblical texts: to prevent
people from disputation in the future, it adds words and straightens the
way before them.

The significance of this addition is discussed in chapter two. These two
manuscripts follow up this change with an alteration in Rashi's second
comment on verse 13:

אחר. אחרי שאמר המלאך אל תשלך ידך ראהו כשהוא נאחז ... בסבך אילן בקרניו
שהיה רץ אצל אברהם והשטן סובכו ומעכבו באילנות כדי לעכבו.

After. After the angel said, "**Do not send forth your hand,**" [Abraham]
saw [the ram] caught . . . in the thicket of a tree by its horns, since it was
running to Abraham and Satan turned it around and delayed it in a tree
in order to delay [Abraham].

Oxford-Bodleian 187 and Oxford-Bodleian 190 has סבבו המלאך וערבבו באילן
כדי שיקחינו אברהם משם [an angel turned it around and delayed it in a tree
in order that Abraham would take it from there]. The change from Satan
to an angel, and from a hindering figure to a helping figure, completely
eliminates the midrashic Satan, who hinders and tempts Abraham rather
than accusing him.

13.2

The Alkabetz edition adds another explanation to the word אחר [after], in
addition to the one brought in other versions:

ולפי הגדה אחר כל דברי המלאך והשכנה ואחר טענותיו של אברהם.

And according to the aggadah, after all the words of the angel and the
divine presence and after Abraham's arguments.[15]

It is unclear what this explanation adds. It is based on *Midrash Tanchuma Vayera* 23.[16]

The above variants in seventeen out of Rashi's thirty-four comments on the near-sacrifice of Isaac show that Rashi's commentary remained a dynamic and changing document through fifteenth century and the early printed editions. Many of these variants are stylistic, but others produce substantially different comments. This limited study of the manuscript history shows significant divergence among Rashi manuscripts, but Abecassis' observations on the textual history of Rashi's commentary suggest that the true number of variants circulating in the twelfth century was even greater.

NOTES

INTRODUCTION

1. Christopher De Hamel, *Glossed Books of the Bible and the Origins of the Paris Booktrade* (Suffolk: Brewer, 1984), xiii.

2. The classic study of the role of the *akedah*, the binding or near-sacrifice of Isaac, for Jewish Crusade-era martyrs is Shalom Spiegel, *The Last Trial: On the Legends and Lore of the Command to Abraham to Offer Isaac as a Sacrifice: the Akedah* (Woodstock: Jewish Lights, 1993).

3. For examples see Avraham Grossman, "The School of Literal Jewish Exegesis in Northern France," in *Hebrew Bible/Old Testament* ed. Magne Sæbø vol 1, part 2, *V 1, Pt 2, From the beginnings to the Middle Ages (until 1300)* (Göttingen: Vandenhoeck & Ruprecht, 2000), 321–371.

4. For a study of Rashi's influence on Herbert, see Deborah L. Goodwin, *Take Hold of the Robe of a Jew: Herbert of Bosham's Christian Hebraism* (Leiden: Brill, 2006).

5. See Rainer Berndt, "The School of St. Victor in Paris," in *Hebrew Bible/Old Testament V 1, Pt 2, From the Beginnings to the Middle Ages (until 1300)* (Göttingen: Vandenhoeck & Ruprecht, 2000), 467–495.

6. See Herman Hailperin, *Rashi and the Christian Scholars* (Pittsburgh: University of Pittsburgh Press, 1963). Also see Deanna Copeland Klepper, *The Insight of Unbelievers: Nicholas of Lyra and Christian Reading of Jewish Text in the Later Middle Ages* (Philadelphia: University of Pennsylvania Press, 2007).

7. *Bereshit Rabbati* is on Genesis alone. R. Moses the Darshan may have also written a commentary on Numbers. See H. Albeck, ed., *Midrash Bereshit Rabbati le-R. Moshe HaDarshan* (Jerusalem: Mosad HaRav Kuk, 5727 [1940]), 5.

8. Grossman, "Literal Jewish Exegesis," 348

9. Grossman, "Literal Jewish Exegesis," 323.

10. Grossman, "Literal Jewish Exegesis," 356.

11. Grossman, "Literal Jewish Exegesis," 359.

12. Eliezer of Beaugency was a student of Rashbam's. Robert A. Harris, "The Literary Hermeneutic of Rabbi Eliezer of Beaugency" (Ph.D. Diss., The Jewish Theological Seminary, 1997).

13. Beryl Smalley, "Gilbertus Univeralis, Bishop of London (1128–34), and the Problem of the Glossa Ordinaria," *Recherches de théologie ancienne et médiévale*, 7 (1935) 235–262 and 8 (1936) 24–60. Smith, *The Glossa Ordinaria: The Making of a Medieval Bible Commentary* (Leiden: Brill, 2009), 28–31.

14. Smith, *Glossa Ordinaria*, 200–205.

15. Dahan, Gilbert. "Genres, Forms and Various Methods in Christian Exegesis of the Middle Ages," in *Hebrew Bible/Old Testament V 1, Pt 2, From the Beginnings to the Middle Ages (until 1300).* Edited by C. Brekelmans, Menahem Haran, Magne Saebo. Göttingen: Vandenhoeck & Ruprecht, 2000, 208.

16. Margaret Gibson, "The Place of the *Glossa Ordinaria* in Medieval Exegesis," in *Ad litteram,* Notre Dame: University of Notre Dame Press, 1992, 5–28.

17. Gibson, "The Place of the Glossa Ordinaria," 12–13.

18. Baer suggested that there is evidence from Rashi's use of the term כנסיה של מלך, which Baer argued is a translation of the Latin theological term *ecclesia regis* (church of the king). Baer, "Rashi and the Historical Reality of His Time," 113. (Y. Baer, "Rashi and the World Around Him," [Hebrew] Pages 489–502 in *Sefer Rashi.* Edited by Y. I. Hakohen Maimon (Jerusalem: Mosad HaRav Kuk, 1956). Reprint of article that originally appeared in *Tarbiz* 20 (1950) 320–332. Translated and adapted by Nathan Reisner in *Jewish Intellectual History in the Middle Ages,* ed. Joseph Dan. Westport, Conn.: Praeger, 1994, 113.) Rosenthal shows that this Hebrew term is also found in rabbinic literature. Rosenthal, "Anti-Christian Polemics" 104 n. 21. (Yehuda Rosenthal, "Anti-Christian Polemics in the Biblical Commentaries of Rashi." *Studies and Texts in Jewish History, Literature and Religion.* Jerusalem, 1967, 104 n. 21.)

19. For an overview of literal Jewish exegesis in Northern France, see Grossman, "Literal Jewish Exegesis."

20. For a discussion of non-normative legal exegesis in Rashbam, see Sara Japhet, "The Tension between Rabbinic Legal Midrash and the 'Plain Meaning' (Peshat) of the Biblical Text—An Unresolved Problem? In the Wake of Rashbam's Commentary on the Pentateuch," in *Sefer Moshe: The Moshe Weinfeld Jubilee Volume,* ed. Ch. Cohen, A. Hurvitz, and Sh. Paul (Winona Lake, Ind., 2004), 403–426.

21. See Chapter One.

22. Berndt, "St. Victor," 480–482.

23. Goodwin, *Take Hold of the Robe of a Jew,* 54–57.

24. Goodwin, *Take Hold of the Robe of a Jew,* 67–71.

25. Berndt, "St. Victor," 481. Berndt carefully identifies Andrew's Jewish informants as being of "Rashi's school" rather than Rashi himself.

26. Hailperin, *Rashi and the Christian Scholars,* Klepper, *The Insight of Unbelievers.*

27. Smalley, *The Study of the Bible in the Middle Ages* (3rd. ed.) (Oxford: Blackwell, 1983) 150. As Klepper has pointed out, Smalley tends to follow the lead of her medieval sources in her understanding of the nature of literal exegesis. See Klepper, *Insight of Unbelievers,* 119.

28. Safah Berurah 5a.

29. Nechama Leibowitz, "Rashi's Criteria for Citing Midrashim," in *Torah Insights* (Jerusalem: The Joint Authority for Jewish Zionist Education, 1995). This article

appeared originally in Hebrew in *Iyunim Chadashim BeSefer Shemot* (Jerusalem: The Joint Authority for Jewish Zionist Education, 1975).

30. Leibowitz, "Rashi's Criteria," 109.

31. Grossman, "Literal Jewish Exegesis", 332–346.

32. Grossman, *Rashi*, (Jerusalem: Merkaz Zalman Shazar, 2006), 88.

33. Sarah Kamin, *Rashi's Exegetical Categorization in Respect to the Distinction between Peshat and Derash* [Hebrew]. (Jerusalem: Magnes, 1986), 14, 266.

34. Edward L. Greenstein, "Sensitivity to Language in Rashi's Commentary on the Torah." In *The Solomon Goldman Lectures*, vol. 6, edited by Mayer I. Gruber. Chicago: The Spertus College of Judaica Press, 1993, 51–71. Jonathan Kearney, *Rashi: Linguist Despite Himself* (New York, T&T Clark, 2010). Kearney argues that an analysis of Rashi's comments on Deuteronomy shows that the comments can be more readily organized as literary or linguistic than as literal/contextual or midrashic. See Kearney, *Rashi*, 72.

35. Smalley, *Study*, 357.

36. G.R Evans, *The Language and Logic of the Bible: The Earlier Middle Ages* (Cambridge: Cambridge University Press, 1984), 46.

37. Gibson, "*Glossa Ordinaria*," 19.

38. Gilbert Dahan, *L'exégése Chrétienne de la Bible en occident médiéval* (Paris: Cerf, 1999), 100.

39. Dahan, *L'exégése*, 246–252.

40. Smith, "*Glossa Ordinaria*," 85.

41. Cf. Leibowitz, "Rashi's Criteria," 132.

42. Frances Young, *Biblical Exegesis and the Formation of Christian Culture* (Cambridge: Cambridge University Press, 1997), 186–213.

43. Young, *Biblical Exegesis*, 192.

44. As Sarah Kamin points out, Rashi's *peshuto shel mikra* is both distinct from Rashbam's *peshat* and not intended to be a translation of the *sensus litteralis*. See Kamin, *Rashi*, 111–135.

45. Dahan, *L'exégése*, 38.

46. David Stern, "Introduction: On Comparative Biblical Exegesis—Interpretation, Influence, Appropriation" in *Jewish Biblical Interpretation and Cultural Exchange: Comparative Exegesis in Context* (Philadelphia: University of Pennsylvania Press, 2008), 3.

47. Magne Sæbø, "Church and Synagogue as the Respective Matrix of the Development of an Authoritative Biblical Interpretation," *Hebrew Bible/Old Testament: The History of Its Interpretation*, vol. 1, 745.

48. Stern, "Introduction," 3.

49. Smalley, *Study* 155.

50. Berndt, "St. Victor", 467–495.

51. Berndt, "St. Victor," 467–495.

52. Goodwin, *Take Hold of the Robe of a Jew: Herbert of Bosham's Christian Hebraism* (Leiden: Brill, 2006).

53. Klepper, *Insight of Unbelievers*, Hailperin, *Rashi and the Christian Scholars*.

54. Israel Jacob Yuval, *Two Nations in Your Womb: Perceptions of Jews and Christians in Late Antiquity and the Middle Ages*, Barbara Harshav and Jonathan Chipman, trans. (Berkeley: University of California Press, 2006), 21–22. Yuval surveys two models in scholarship on the Jewish-Christian relationship: the mother-daughter model, in which Judaism is the mother religion and Christianity developed out of it, and the siblings model, in which Rabbinic Judaism and Christianity developed at the same time out of Second Temple religion. The mother-daughter model tends to lead scholars to assume Jewish influence on Christianity, while the siblings model allows influence to move in both directions. For a discussion of these models and debates surrounding them, see Yuval, *Two Nations,* 20–30.

55. Ivan G. Marcus, *Rituals of Childhood: Jewish Acculturation in Medieval Europe* (New Haven: Yale University Press, 1996).

56. Sarah Kamin, "Affinities between Jewish and Christian Exegesis in Twelfth-Century Northern France." *Proceedings of the 9th World Congress of Jewish Studies* (Jerusalem: Magnes Pr, 1988), 141–155.

57. Kamin, "Affinities between Jewish and Christian Exegesis," 141–155.

58. Dahan, *L'exégése,* 368–372.

59. Dahan, *L'exégése,* 373-375.

60. Michael A. Signer, "The *Glossa Ordinaria* and the Transmission of Medieval Anti-Judaism," in *A Distinct Voice: Medieval Studies in Honor of Leonard E. Boyle, O.P.* ed. Jaqueline Brown and William P. Stoneman (Notre Dame, IN: University of Notre Dame Press, 1997), 591–605.

61. Grossman, *Rashi,* 91. Elazar Touitou, "Rashi's Commentary on Genesis 1–6 in the Context of Judeo-Christian Controversy," *Hebrew Union College Annual,* 61 (1990): 183. For an alternative approach, see Shaye Cohen, "Does Rashi's Torah Commentary Respond to Christianity? A comparison of Rashi with Rashbam and Bekhor Shor." Pages 449–472 in *The Idea of Biblical Interpretation.* Leiden: Brill, 2004). These different approaches will be discussed in more detail in chapter one.

62. *Midrash Tanchuma Vayera* 23. See also Genesis Rabbah 56.8.

63. This is not always Rashi's approach. He wrote many introductions to biblical books and stories that address the story as a whole. For examples, see Robert A. Harris, "Rashi's Introductions to his Biblical Commentaries," in *Shai le-Sara Japhet: Studies in the Bible, its Exegesis and its Language.* Moshe Bar-Asher, Dalit Rom-Shiloni, Emanuel Tov, and Nili Wayzana, eds. (Jerusalem: Bialik Institute, 2007), 219–241. For a discussion of how narrative theory may illuminate ways in which Rashi implicitly constructs

a narrative, see Michael Signer, "Rashi as Narrator," in *Rashi et la culture juive en France du Nord au moyen âge*, (Paris-Louvain: E. Peeters, 1997), 103–110.

64. See Chapter Three.

65. Signer, "*Glossa*," 594.

66. Or in other cases, that Abraham represents Christ, or that Isaac in his old age signifies God the Father. See Signer, "*Glossa*," 593–594.

67. See the Appendices for English translations and critical editions of the relevant sections of both Rashi's commentary and the *Glossa Ordinaria*.

1. THE DEVELOPING JEWISH–CHRISTIAN POLEMIC

1. PL 168, cols. 489–528.

2. R. Thomas (ed.), *Dialogus inter philosophum, Iudaeum et Christianum* (Stuttgart-Bad Cannstatt, Freidrich Frommnn Verlag, 1970). Daniel Lasker does not consider this work to be polemical because of its rational, objective tone. See Daniel Lasker, "Jewish–Christian Polemics at the Turning Point: Evidence from the Twelfth Century," *The Harvard Theological Review*, 89.2 (April 1996), 163.

3. R. Haacke (ed.), in M. L. Arduini, *Ruperto de Deutz e la controversia tra Christiani ed Ebrei nel secolo XII* (Rome: Isituto Storico Italiano per il Medio Evo, 1979), 175–277.

4. Odo of Tournai, *On Original Sin and A Disputation with the Jew, Leo, Concerning the Advent of Christ, the Son of God*, trans. Irven M. Resnick, (Philadelphia: University of Pennsylvania Press, 1994).

5. PL 163 cols 1045–1072.

6. G. Niemeyer (ed.), *Monumenta Germaniae Historica, Quellen zur Geistesgeschichte des Mittlealters*, vol. 4 (Weimar: Herman Bohlaus, 1963).

7. Gilbert Crispin, *The Works of Gilbert Crispin Abbot of Westminster*, ed. A. Sapir Abulafia and G. R. Evans (eds), Auctores Britannici Medii Aevi, vol. 8 (London: Oxford University Press, 1986).

8. Anna Sapir Abulafia, "An Attempt by Gilbert Crispin, Abbot of Westminster, at Rational Argument in the Jewish–Christian Debate," *Studia Monastica* 26 (1984) 55–74.

9. Amos Funkenstein, "Changes in the pattern of Christian anti-Jewish polemics" [Hebrew], *Zion* 33 (1968), 125–144.

10. Anna Sapir Abulafia, *Christians and Jews in the Twelfth Century Renaissance* (London: Routledge, 1995).

11. For a discussion of this literature, see Daniel Lasker, *Jewish Philosophical Polemics Against Christianity in the Middle Ages* (New York: Ktav Pub. House, 1977).

12. For a discussion of anti-Christian polemic in Rashbam and Bekhor Shor, see Eliezer Touitou, "The Exegetical Method of Rashbam in Light of the Historical Reality of his Time," in Y. D. Gilat, et al., eds, *Iyyunim be-Sifrut Hazal ba-Miqra u-ve-Toledot Yisrael* (Ramat Gan: Bar Ilan University Press, 1982) and Sarah Kamin, "The Polemic

Against Allegory in the Commentary of R. Joseph Bekhor Shor," *Jerusalem Studies in Jewish Thought* 3 (1983–1984) 367–392 [Hebrew]. As discussed later in this chapter, Shaye Cohen argues that these two commentaries are polemical against Christianity but that Rashi's is not.

13. For a full discussion, see Gilbert Dahan, *Les intellectuels Chrétiens et les juifs au moyen age* (Paris: Cerf, 1990) and Dahan, "Genres," 230–232.

14. We will see an example of this in the Gloss, and how it contributes to the similarity between the Gloss and Rashi's commentary on Genesis 22, in Chapter Three.

15. *Pseudo-Jerome: Questions on the Book of Samuel*, A. Saltman, ed. (Leiden: Brill, 1975). A. Saltman, "Rabanus Maurus and the Pseudo-Hieronymian *Questiones Hebraice in Libros Regnum and Paralipomenon*," *Harvard Theological Review* 66 (1973): 43–75.

16. Dahan, "Genres," 231.

17. They introduce exegesis that they are going to reject with the terms *Iudei fabuluntur* (Jews fantasize) or *Iudei sompniatur* (Jews are dreaming). This is opposed from the more usual *Hebrei dicunt* used by both Jerome and twelfth-century commentaries to introduce an authoritative interpretation. See Dahan, "Genres," 231.

18. Dahan, "Genres," 232.

19. All these narratives may be found in A. M. Haberman (ed.) *Sefer gezerot Ashkenaz ve-Tzarefat.* (Jerusalem: Tarshish, 1945/6). Eva Haverkamp, *Hebräische Berichte über die Judenverfolgungen während des Ersten Kreuzzugs* (Hannover: Hahn, 2005).

20. Anna Sapir Abulafia, "The Interrelationship Between the Hebrew Chronicles on the First Crusade," *Journal of Semitic Studies*, 27:221–239. Lena Roos accepts this dating and suggests a more exact dating of 1115–1146 for the Eliezer bar Nathan Chronicle and 1140–1146 for the Solomon bar Samson Chronicle. See Lena Roos, *God Wants It! The Ideology of Martyrdom in the Hebrew Crusade Chronicles and its Jewish and Christian Background* (Turnhout: Brepols, 2006), 15.

21. Robert Chazan, "The First Crusade as Reflected in the Earliest Hebrew Narrative," *Viator*, 1998, vol. 29, pp. 25–38, and *God, Humanity, and History: The Hebrew First Crusade Narratives* (Berkeley: University of California Press, 2000), 43. Chazan argues that since this narrative refers to the return of converted Jews, which took place in June 1097, it could not have been written prior to that date. He also points out that the chronicler refers to the "Empire of Henry" (Haberman 94) so is unlikely to have written after the death of Henry in 1106.

22. Chazan, *God, Humanity, and History*, 103. Chazan shows that the Eliezer bar Nathan Chronicle is dependent on the Solomon bar Samson Chronicle but omits the references to Christian defeats in the early twelfth century, suggesting that the later chronicler was aware that the Second Crusade was not as much of a failure as Solomon bar Samson had hoped.

23. Chazan, *God, Humanity, and History*, 53.

24. Chazan, *God, Humanity, and History*, 55.

25. Haverkamp, *Hebräische Berichte*, 24, 29, 70.

26. Haverkamp, *Hebräische Berichte*, 69–70.

27. Jeremy Cohen, *Sanctifying the Name of God: Jewish Martyrs and Jewish Memories of the First Crusade* (Philadelphia: University of Pennsylvania Press, 2004), 59.

28. Jeremy Cohen suggests that this historiographical debate reflects twentieth century Jewish concerns, and that the events of 1096 have become a way to articulate concerns about Jewish victimhood and resistance today. See Jeremy Cohen, "A 1096 Complex? Constructing the First Crusade" in *Jews and Christians in Twelfth-Century Europe*, Michael A. Signer and John Van Engen, eds., (Notre Dame, Indiana: University of Notre Dame Press, 2001), 9–26.

29. Cecil Roth, *A Short History of the Jewish People*, rev. ed. (London, 1969), 185. Haim Hillel Ben-Sasson, *A History of the Jewish People* (London, 1976), 414. See Simon Schwarzfuchs, "The Place of the Crusades in Jewish History" [Hebrew], in *Culture and Society in Medieval Jewry: Studies Dedicated to the Memory of Haim Hillel Ben-Sasson*, ed. Menachem Ben-Sasson et al. (Jerusalem, 1989), 251–269; Jeremy Cohen, "Recent Historiography on the Medieval Church and the Decline of European Jewry," in *Popes, Teachers and Canon Law in the Middle Ages: Essays in Honor of Brian Tierney*, ed. James Ross Sweeney and Stanley Chodorow (Ithaca, 1989).

30. Robert Chazan, *European Jewry and the First Crusade* (Berkeley: University of California Press, 1987), 192–221.

31. Salo Baron, *A Social and Religious History of the Jews* (New York: Columbia University Press, 1937), 4:89–91 and 147–149.

32. Chazan, *European Jewry*, 197–210. Hayim Soloveitchik has shown that Jewish legal literature also flourished in the aftermath of the First Crusade. See Hayim Soloveitchik, "Catastrophe and Halachic Creativity: Ashkenaz—1096, 1242, 1306 and 1298," *Jewish History* 12.1 (1998) 71–85.

33. Robert Chazan, *Medieval Jewry in Northern France* (Baltimore, Johns Hopkins, 1975), 25.

34. Robert Chazan, "A Twelfth-Century Communal History of Spires Jewry," REJ 128 (1969) 253–257.

35. John Benton, ed., *Self and Society in Medieval France* (New York, 1970), 134–135.

36. Schwarzfuchs, *The Jews of France in the Middle Ages* [Hebrew]. (Tel Aviv: Hakibutz Hameuchad, 2001), 111, Steven Runciman, *A History of the Crusades*, vol. 1 (New York: Cambridge University Press, 1964), 136.

37. Norman Golb, "New Light on the Persecution of French Jews at the Time of the First Crusade," PAAJR 34 (1996) 31–35. Golb argues, based on the participation of French Crusaders in massacres of Rhineland Jews, that they must have attacked French Jews as well.

38. Haberman, *Sefer gezerot*, 93.

39. Haberman, *Sefer gezerot*, 27, Schwarzfuchs, *Jews of France*, 110.

40. Chazan, *European Jewry*, Chazan, *God, Humanity and History*, 22–24.

41. Chazan, *God, Humanity and History*, 212.

42. Ivan G. Marcus, "From Politics to Martyrdom: Shifting Paradigms in the Hebrew Narratives of the 1096 Crusade Riots," *Prooftexts* 2 (1982): 40–52. For a rebuttal, see Robert Chazan, "The Facticity of Medieval Narrative: A Case Study of the Hebrew First-Crusade Narratives," *Association for Jewish Studies Review* 16 (1991): 31–56, and Robert Chazan, God, Humanity and History. Also see Avraham Grossman, "Shorashav shel Quiddush Hashem be-Ashkenaz ha-Qeduman," in *Sanctity in Life and Martyrdom: Studies in Memory of Amir Yekutiel*, ed. Isaiah M. Gafni and Aviezer Ravitzky (Jerusalem, 1992).

43. Schwarzfuchs, *Jews of France*, 113.

44. Cohen, *Sanctifying the Name of God*, 47.

45. Ivan G. Marcus, "From Politics to Martyrdom."

46. Chazan, *European Jewry*, 44.

47. Avraham Berliner only found one, in Isaiah 53:9. See Avraham Berliner, "The Origins of the Interpretation of Rashi," *Sefer Rashi*, ed. Y. I. Hakohen Maimon (Jerusalem: Mosad HaRav Kuk, 1956), 129 164, csp. 155.

48. "Forced Converts to Christianity during the Days of the First Crusade, 1096–1105," in Jacob Marcus, *The Jew in the Medieval World: A Sourcebook, 315-1791* (New York: JPS, 1938), 301–303.

49. Schwarzfuchs, *Jews of France*, 111. Y. Baer, "Rashi and the World Around Him," [Hebrew] in *Sefer Rashi*, ed. Y. I. Hakohen Maimon (Jerusalem: Mosad HaRav Kuk, 1956) 489–502. Reprint of article that originally appeared in Tarbiz 20 (1950) 320–332. Translated and adapted by Nathan Reisner in *Jewish Intellectual History in the Middle Ages*, ed. Joseph Dan (New York: Praeger, 1994), 101–118. Subsequent page numbers refer to the translation.

50. For a full discussion of examples, see Harvery Sicherman and Gilad J. Gevaryahu, "Rashi and the First Crusade: Commentary, Liturgy, Legend." *Judaism: A Quarterly Journal of Jewish Life and Thought* 48.2 (Spring 1999) 181.

51. Rashi on Genesis 1.1. For more on the polemical significance of this comment, see E. Touitou, "The Historical Context of Rashi's Commentary on the Book of Genesis," in *Rashi: Iyunim Be Yetzirato*, edited by Zvi A. Steinfeld (Ramat Gan: Bar Ilan University, 1993), 102. Touitou cites D. Louys, "En Lisant Rashi: Le Conflit Judeo-Arabe" in *Vav: Revue du dialogue* (Paris: 1969), 22–24.

52. Rashi on Isaiah 53:9.

53. Jeremy Cohen, *Sanctifying the Name of God*, 90.

54. Roos, *God Wants It!*, 95. For a precedent for this in rabbinic literature, see BT Gittin 57a, in which the mother of seven martyred sons describes their martyrdom as an *akedah* greater than that of Abraham.

55. Haberman 78, Haverkamp *Hebräische Berichte* 336–337.

56. Haberman 32, Haverkamp 336–339, trans. in Jeremy Cohen, *Sanctifying the Name of God*, 64.

57. Roos, *God Wants It!*, 96–99.

58. Haberman 34, 101–102, Haverkamp 354–355, 358–359, trans. in Cohen, *Sanctifying the Name of God*, 107–109.

59. Haberman וישאל החסיד אל בניו: רצונכם שאזבח אתכם לאלוהינו ויאמרו: עשה מה שתרצה 37, Haverkamp, 374–383, Cohen, *Sanctifying the Name of God*, 93.

60. Haberman 48–49, Cohen, *Sanctifying the Name of God*, 74 and 83. Israel Yuval explores the ritualization of the self-sacrifice and its Messianic significance in Yuval, *Two Nations*, 140–154.

61. גמרתי בליבי להקריב קרבן חטאת לאלוהי מרום, אמצא בזה כפרה Haberman 37, translated in Cohen, *Sanctifying the Name of God,* 93.

62. ibid.

63. Jeremy Cohen, *Sanctifying the Name of God*, 96. Cohen here follows Yuval, who points out the priestly and Temple imagery in Isaac's self-sacrifice. Isaac is both the priest and and the sacrifice, and his death takes the place of the Temple offerings in the expiation of sin. See Yuval, *Two Nations*, 146.

64. Teshuvot Rashi 327. גוים בזמן הזה אינן בקיאין בטיב עבודה זרה.

65. Rashi on BT Avodah Zarah 11b, D.H. בגולה. Tosafot on Avodah Zarah 2a, Sanhedrin 63b and other places rules that Christians are not idolaters. For a full discussion of the social and legal factors involved in the ruling that Christians are not idolaters, see Jacob Katz, *Exclusiveness and Tolerance: Studies in Jewish–Gentile Relations in Medieval and Modern Times* (Springfield, NJ: Berhman House, 1961), 24–36.

66. In the Vilna edition, this comment appears in the outside margins and is copied from the Amsterdam edition. It was most likely removed due to censorship, but could also have been a later addition. For other examples of Rashi using the term "minim" to refer to Christians, see Yehuda Rosenthal, "Anti-Christian Polemics in the Biblical Commentaries of Rashi," *Studies and Texts in Jewish History, Literature and Religion* (Jerusalem, 1967), 105–106.

67. In one of his *responsa* he describes the way Christians treat their wives as a model for Jews to emulate. *Teshuvot Hahmei Tzarfat VeLoiter*, Y. Miller (ed.), Vienna, 1880/1, paragraph 40, page 24.

68. In his responsa, Rashi uses the Talmudic terminology אומות, *umot* (nations) to refer to the surrounding Christians. See Grossman, *The Early French Sages*, [Hebrew] (Jerusalem: Magnes, 1995), 142–143.

69. Baer, "Rashi," 108.

70. Baer, "Rashi," 110–113.

71. Baer, "Rashi," (1994) 108.

72. Rosenthal, "Anti-Christian Polemics in the Biblical Commentaries of Rashi," 107–108.

73. Rosenthal, "Anti-Christian Polemics in the Biblical Commentaries of Rashi," 116.

74. Rosenthal, "Anti-Christian Polemics in the Biblical Commentaries of Rashi," 108, 110–111.

75. Rosenthal, "Anti-Christian Polemics in the Biblical Commentaries of Rashi," 109.

76. Touitou, "Rashi's Commentary," 159–184.

77. Touitou, "Rashi's Commentary," 170–171.

78. This comment is a close paraphrase of Genesis Rabbah 1.2.

79. D. Louys, "En lisant Rashi."

80. Touitou, "Rashi's Commentary," 171.

81. Touitou, "Rashi's Commentary," 173–174.

82. Touitou, "Rashi's Commentary," 172–173.

83. Touitou, "Rashi's Commentary," 174.

84. Touitou, "Rashi's Commentary," 183.

85. See also Esra Shershevsky, *Rashi: The Man and His World* (New York: Sefer-Hermon Press, 1982) 119–132, Avraham Grossman, *The Early French Sages*, 142–146, 205–207, 477–479.

86. Cohen, "Does Rashi Respond to Christianity?" 470.

87. Grossman, "Literal Jewish Exegesis," 339, Cohen, "Does Rashi Respond to Christianity?" 458.

88. Cohen, "Does Rashi Respond to Christianity?" 468.

89. Cohen, "Does Rashi Respond to Christianity?" 451.

90. Chavel, *Perushe Rashi*, 166, trans. Cohen "Does Rashi Respond to Christianity?" 452.

91. Rosenthal, "Anti-Christian Polemics," 111.

92. Cohen, "Does Rashi Respond to Christianity?" 453.

93. Cohen, "Does Rashi Respond to Christianity?" 452–458.

94. Anna Sapir Abulafia, "Jewish–Christian Disputations and the Twelfth Century Renaissance," *Journal of Medieval History* 15 (1989): 105–125. Amos Funkenstein, *Perceptions of Jewish History* (Berkeley: University of California Press, 1993), 181–182.

95. Smith, *Glossa Ordinaria*, 27–31.

96. Gregory, *Moralia in Job* XX.IX.20, M. Adriaen, ed. CCSL, vol. 143A (Turnhout: Brepols, 1979), 1019.

97. PL 163 col. 1048C.

98. This interpretation appears in Ibn Ezra's commentary on Deuteronomy 18:15. Ibn Ezra (1092/3–1167) does not quote a rabbinic source for this interpretation. Rashi and Rashbam understand this verse to be speaking in general terms about any prophet who might arise in the future.

99. Acts 3:22, cf. Deut. 18:15.

100. PL 163 cols. 1049 B-C.

101. Abulafia, *Christians and Jews*, 6.

102. Abulafia, *Christians and Jews*, 46.

103. PL 163 col. 1053A.

104. PL 163 col. 158 D.

105. PL 163 col. 159A.

106. This idea appears in Bruno of Segni (PL 164 col. 199D) and is also parallel to marginal gloss 14.2m.

107. PL 163 col. 1059 C.

108. Although it does not completely explain it, since Guibert of Nogent and Rupert of Deutz also wrote strongly worded polemics. See Abulafia, *Christians and Jews*, 105–106.

2. RASHI AND HIS SOURCES

1. Cohen, "Does Rashi's Torah Commentary Respond to Christianity?" 449–472.

2. Touitou, "Rashi's Commentary," 159–183.

3. Smalley, *Study*, 66.

4. Gibson, "The Place of the *Glossa Ordinaria* in Medieval Exegesis," 5–27.

5. Evans, *Language and Logic*, 47.

6. For examples, see Kamin, *Rashi*, Leibowitz, "Rashi's Criteria," and Yosefa Rachaman, *Rashi's Use of Midrash: A New Exegetical Interpretation* [Hebrew], (Tel Aviv: Mizrahi, 1991).

7. Strack and Stemberger, *Introduction to the Talmud and Midrash* (Edinburgh: T&T Clark, 1991), 279.

8. See chart at the end of this chapter.

9. It is likely that material in *Midrash Tanchuma* significantly predates the ninth century, and that much of it was complete by 400. See Strack and Stemberger, *Talmud and Midrash*, 332.

10. Vayera 18–23. Although one might expect Rashi to have used the European recension, as represented by the Buber edition (*Midrash Tanchuma*. Solomon Buber, ed., (Jerusalem: [s.n.], 724 [1963 or 1964])), his source seems to be the standard recension. The sources for comments 1.2, 3.1, 9.1 and 13.1 appear in the standard recension and not in the Buber recension.

Comments 2.1 and 6.1 which have sources in Genesis Rabbah as well, also appear only in the standard recension and not the Buber recension. Comments 2.1 and 6.1

which have sources in *Genesis Rabbah* as well, also appear only in the standard recension and not the Buber recension. In his commentary on Genesis 22 none of Rashi's quotes from *Midrash Tanchuma* appear only in the Buber edition.

11. Homilies 18–21 deal with the testing of Abraham. Homilies 19 and 20 are about principles of testing, and 21 and compares it to other tests in the Hebrew Bible. I suspect that Rashi does not use them because, as suggested above, when the Midrash discusses general principles or compares Abraham with other Biblical characters Rashi will only use the part dealing with Abraham.

12. In comment 3.1, Rashi comments that Abraham rose נזדרז למצוה [early in the morning], eager to perform the commandment. BT Yoma 28b (and possibly BT Pesachim 4a, which cites an incomplete verse that could be this or another) uses this verse as a prooftext for the importance of eagerness. *Midrash Tanchuma* states that this verse is to teach us specifically Abraham's eagerness, which seems more in line with Rashi's comment, so I have considered *Midrash Tanchuma* to be the source here.

13. The exegesis there is of 1 Chronicles 21:15, **God saw it and regretted** [sending an angel with a plague to destroy Israel for David's sin in taking a census]. The question is, what did God see? Four different alternative answers are brought, based on other places in scripture where it says **God saw/sees/will see**. Of the four options, two are related to the binding of Isaac: the ashes of Isaac (based on the phrase **God will see for himself a lamb**) and the Temple (based on the phrase **on the mountain God will see**. After some discussion, the argument concludes that it is the Temple, because of the prooftext **as it is said today, on the mountain God will see**. Rashi thus takes the prooftext for one idea—that the Temple, as predicted in Genesis 22, causes God to overlook sins—and applies it to a completely different idea from the same section.

14. It makes clear connections between Ishmael and Islam with statements like "descendants of Ishmael will build a building on the place of the Temple Mount/Har Habayit" and it names the wives of Ishmael as Aisha and Fatima, the wife and daughter of Mohammed. See Pirkei de Rabbi Eliezer 30, Dagmar Börner-Klein, *Pirke De-Rabbi Elieser: Nach der edition venedig 1544 untrt berücksichtigung der edition Warshau 1852* (Berlin: Walter de Gruyter, 2004), 341–342, 349. Strack and Stemberger, *Introduction to the Talmud and Midrash*, 329. Avigdor Shinan, *Aggadatam shel meturgamim* (Jerusalem: Makor Publishing, 1979), 162–165. Having said this, Ishmael does not represent Islam in all cases and not all references to Ishmael in *Pirkei de Rabbi Eliezer* are polemical. See Carol Bakhos, "Abraham Visits Ishmael: A Revisit," *Journal for the Study of Judaism*, 38 (2007).

15. PDE 31, Börner-Klein, *Pirke De-Rabbi Elieser*, 357. This identification is also in *Leviticus Rabbah* 20.2 and 26.7 and the Targum of Jonathan ben Uziel on this verse.

The other part of this comment, about the importance of going on a journey with two people, is also in *Genesis Rabbah* and *Midrash Tanchuma*.

16. PDE 31, Börner-Klein, *Pirke De-Rabbi Elieser*, 363. The Warsaw edition has 'Satan' while the Venice edition has 'Samael'. See also Pesikta de Rav Kahana 23 (154b).

17. Paul V. McCracken Flesher, "The Targumim in the Context of Rabbinic Literature," in *Introduction to Rabbinic Literature*, Jacob Neusner, ed. (New York: Doubleday, 1996), 614–615.

18. In 6.1 and 13.3 Rashi bases himself on the Targum of Onqelos without naming a source.

19. Raphael Binyamin Posen, "Rashi's Relationship to the Targum of Onqelos" [Hebrew], in *Rashi: His Work and Personality (Rashi: demuto vi-yetsirato)*, Avraham Grossman and Sara Japhet (Jerusalem: Zalman Shazar, 2008), 275.

20. Rashi on Kiddushin 49a.

21. Raphael Binyamin Posen, "Translation from Sinai" [Hebrew], *Sidra* 15 (1999), 95–110.

22. Posen, "Rashi's Relationship to the Targum of Onqelos," 281.

23. The dating of the Targum of Jonathan is unclear. It refers to Islam and the Arab conquest, so most scholars conclude that it does not predate the eighth century. See Avigdor Shinan, *The Aggadah in the Aramaic Targums to the Pentateuch*, 2 vols. (Jerusalem: Makor, 1979), idem., "Live Translation: On the Nature of the Aramaic Targums to the Pentateuch," *Prooftexts*, 3 (1983), 41–49, "The Relationship between Targum Pseudo-Jonathan and Midrash Pirqe De-Rabbi Eliezer," *Teudah* 11 (1996): 231–243 (Hebrew), A.N Chester, *Divine Revelation and Divine Titles in the Pentateuchal Targumim* (Tubingen: Mohr, 1986), 252–256, Carol Backhos, "Abraham Visits Ishmael: A Revisit," 564. For a dissenting perspective, see Robert Hayward, "Red Heifer and Golden Calf: Dating Targum Pseudo-Jonathan," in *Targum Studies: Textual and Contextual Studies in the Pentateuchal Targums* (vol. 1), Paul V. M. Flesher, ed. (Atlanta: Scholars Press, 1992), 9–32. Hayward argues that the Targum of Jonathan has its origins in the fourth century or earlier, possibly as early as Second Temple times, and that the Islamic-era material was added at a later date.

24. This may be a collection of slightly earlier works. See Albeck, *Bereshit Rabbati*, 2.

25. See Albeck, *Midrash Bereshit Rabbati*, 1.

26. Leibowitz, "Rashi's Criteria," 102–108. Leibowitz builds on a tradition of a strain of medieval Jewish commentaries on Rashi.

27. I have quoted here the version from *Mikraot Gedolot Haketer*, Menachem Cohen, ed., (Ramat Gan: Bar Ilan University Press, 1997).

28. This phrase is absent in the Rome edition.

29. Kamin, *Rashi*. Kamin discusses at length the distinction between *peshuto shel miqra* and *peshat*, and concludes that Rashi is interested in the former and not the latter.

Because both *peshat* and *peshuto shel miqra* can be translated as "literal," I have kept the Hebrew terminology here to preserve Kamin's argument.

30. Kamin, *Rashi*, 266.

31. Rachaman, *Rashi's Use of Midrash*, 37.

32. Nechama Leibowitz, "Rashi's Criteria for Citing Midrashim."

33. Kamin, *Rashi*, 266. Kamin discusses at length the distinction between *peshuto shel miqra* and *peshat*, and concludes that Rashi is interested in the former and not the latter.

34. Rashi, פרוש רש"י [Rashi's commentary], 1233. Munich (Cod. Hebr.) 5. There may be earlier manuscripts that cannot be definitively dated, but they do not predate the thirteenth century. Elazar Touitou, "Quelques Critéres Pouvant Aider À Établir La Version Originale du Commentaire de Rashi sur le Pentateuque." in *Rashi 1040–1990: Hommage à Ephraim E. Urbach*, Gabrielle Sed-Rajna, ed. (Paris: Cerf, 1993), 401.

35. Deborah Abecassis, "Reconstructing Rashi's Commentary on Genesis from Citations in the Torah Commentaries of the Tosafot." (Ph.D. diss., McGill University, 1999), 4.

36. Abecassis, "Reconstructing Rashi's Commentary," 5.

37. Jordan S. Penkower, "Rashi's Corrections to his Commentary on the Pentateuch," [Hebrew] *Jewish Studies: an Internet Journal* 6 (2007).

38. Abecassis, "Reconstructing Rashi's Commentary," 6.

39. This decree was ascribed to Rabbenu Gershom (d. 1028) but may have been communal. See Talya Fishman, *Becoming the People of the Talmud: Oral Torah as Written Tradition in Medieval Jewish Cultures* (Philadelphia: University of Pennsylvania Press, 2011), 124, Avraham Grossman, *The Early Ashkenazic Sages* [Hebrew], (Jerusalem: Magnes, 2001), 110–111.

40. Abecassis, "Reconstructing Rashi's Commentary," 45.

41. For a list of the manuscripts and discussion of further variants, see Appendix B.

42. Leipzig (B.H. fol) 1, Oxford- Bodleian Heb. d. 102, Oxford- Bodleian 20, Oxford-Bodleian 26, Paris heb. 37, Paris Heb. 42, Paris Heb. 48, Paris Heb. 55, Paris Heb. 68, Uppsala (O. Cod. Hebr.) 1, Vienna 20/12.

43. Oxford- Bodleian 1 Arch. Seld. A. 47, Berkeley UCB 124.

44. Rachaman, *Rashi's Use of Midrash*, 128–131.

45. Rachaman, *Rashi's Use of Midrash*, 141–148.

46. It is clearly Palestinian rather than Babylonian. Parts are written in Galilean Aramaic, and other parts are written in Hebrew with Greek loan words. It also cites primarily Palestinian rabbis. See Stemberger, *Talmud and Midrash*, 304.

47. *Genesis Rabbah* 56.2 explains that Abraham's prophesied return to the servants and the donkey will take place at the end of days, although here the servants seem to represent Jews rather than Gentiles. This is oddly parallel to Gloss 5.1m (based on

Isidore) and 19.1i, which describe the Jews, as represented by the Donkey, returning to Abraham (and the truth of Christianity) at the end of days. Since this idea is not present in Jerome, there is no obvious explanation for this parallel.

48. For Ishmael's overall portrayal in *Pirkei de Rabbi Eliezer* see Bakhos, "Abraham Visits Ishmael: A Revisit."

49. *Pirkei de Rabbi Eliezer* 31.

50. *Pirkei de Rabbi Eliezer* 31. This identification is also in *Leviticus Rabbah* 20.2 and 26.7 and the Targum of Jonathan ben Uziel on this verse. The other part of this comment, about the importance of going on a journey with two people, is also in *Genesis Rabbah* and *Midrash Tanchuma*.

51. *Pirkei de Rabbi Eliezer* 31, Börner-Klein, *Pirke De-Rabbi Elieser*, 363. The Warsaw edition has 'Satan' while the Venice edition has 'Samael'. See also Pesikta de Rav Kahana 23 (154b).

52. *Pirkei de Rabbi Eliezer* 31.

53. *Pirkei de Rabbi Eliezer* 31.

54. Ms. Paris Heb. 157, Ms. Paris Heb. 37, Ms. Paris Heb. 157, Ms. St. Petersburg Russian State Library Evr. ii.A 118/1 and Ms. Vienna 24.

55. Other manuscripts add further examples:

"Do not judge falsely" (Deut. 15), and he judges falsely. "Do not judge unfairly," and he judges unfairly. "Do not take bribes," and he takes bribes.

See Theodor-Albeck 586.

56. Aharon Mondstein, "On Rashi's Particular Method of Reasoning in the Story of the Binding of Isaac," [Hebrew] *Beit Miqra Quarterly* 44, no. 157 (Ja-Mr 1999): 107–118.

57. Oxford-Bodleian 187, Oxford- Bodleian 189, Oxford-Bodleian 195, Paris Heb. 37 and Paris Heb. 157.

58. In a parallel case, Rashi does not quote any of the arguments regarding the justice of Moses' death in *Deuteronomy Rabbah*.

59. James Kugel, "Two Introductions to Midrash," in *Midrash and Literature*, ed. Geoffrey H. Hartman and Sanford Budick (New Haven: Yale University Press, 1986), 93.

60. Michael A Signer, "Rashi's Reading of the Akedah," *The Journal of Textual Reasoning*, 2, no. 1 (2003).

61. Talya Fishman, *Becoming the People of the Talmud: Oral Torah as Written Tradition in Medieval Jewish Cultures* (Philadelphia: University of Pennsylvania Press, 2011), 120.

62. Rashi on BT BM 33a "ve-eyna midah", translation from Fishman, *People of the Talmud*, 129.

63. Fishman, *People of the Talmud*, 132.

64. The Gloss also removes question-and-answer structures in its paraphrase of Augustine, as will be shown in the following chapter.

65. An unclear word related to the Hebrew verb אכל [achal], meaning "to eat," and the noun מאכל [ma'achal], meaning "food."

66. Martin Jaffee, *Torah in the Mouth: Writing and Oral Tradition in Palestinian Judaism, 200 BCE–400 CE* (New York: Oxford University Press, 2001).

67. Jack Lightstone, *The Rhetoric of the Babylonian Talmud: Its Social Meaning and Context* (Waterloo, Ont. [Canada]: Published for the Canadian Corporation for Studies in Religion = Corporation canadienne des sciences religieuses by Wilfrid Laurier University Press, 1994), 127.

68. The single exception is the Targum of Onqelos, which Rashi consistently cites by name.

69. I have marked with an X where Rashi quotes from or refers the reader to the Targum of Onqelos.

70. I have only included other sources when they are the main source of a specific comment, or when they add features that are not found in the other sources.

71. See page 51.

3. THE SOURCES AND MANUSCRIPT EVOLUTION OF THE *GLOSSA ORDINARIA* ON GENESIS 22

1. Margaret Gibson, "The Glossed Bible," in Karlfried Froehlich and Margaret T. Gibson, eds. *Biblia latina cum glossa ordinaria: facsimile reprint of the* editio princeps *Adolph Rusch of Strasburg 1480/81* (Brepols: Turnout, 1992). x.

2. E. Ann Matter, "The Church Fathers and the *Glossa Ordinaria*," in *The Reception of the Church Fathers in the West*, ed. Irena Backus (Leiden: Brill, 1997), 109.

3. Alexander Andrée suggests in his discussion of the textual history of the Gloss on Lamentations that Gilbert was in fact the author of the early recension. See Alexander Andrée, *Gilbertus Universalis: Glossa Ordinaria in Lamentationes Ieremie Prophete, Prothemata et Liber 1.* (Stockholm: Almquiest & Wiksell Intl, 2005) 91. Lesley Smith also sees his authorship as "probable." Smith, 29–30.

4. Smith, *Glossa Ordinaria*, 35.

5. Matter, "The Church Fathers," 109.

6. Smith has observed this happen in other books, but not in Genesis. She has noted that it is a particular characteristic of books that were glossed later and were not part of the original edition before 1140. (Smith, *Glossa Ordinaria*, 54.) The different books of the glossed Bible had different editors and different textual histories, and there is no reason to expect that these conclusions will apply to the *Glossa Ordinaria* on other books, or even on other chapters of Genesis. Mark Zier's edition of the Gloss on the first chapter of Daniel, for example, only shows five glosses from patristic authors whose names are given in any manuscript at all. See Mark A. Zier, "The Manuscript Tradition of the Glossa Ordinaria for Daniel, and Hints at a Method for a Critical Edition."

International Review of Manuscript Studies 42, no. 1 (1993), 16–25. Zier does not distinguish between marginal and interlinear glosses in his edition. Neither does Mary Dove, who notes that with two exceptions (one wrongly attributed to Augustine and one correctly attributed to Jerome) glosses are almost never cited by name in manuscripts of the *Glossa Ordinaria* on the Song of Songs. See Mary Dove, *Glossa ordinaria. Pars 22, In Canticum canticorum* (Corpus Christianorum Continuatio Medievalis, Turnhout: Brepols, 1997), 9.

7. As Alexander Andrée has shown, the Gloss on Lamentations also has an earlier and a later recension with significant variants. See Andrée, "Gilbertus Universalis," 19.

8. Smith, *Glossa Ordinaria*, 85.

9. Michael Signer, "The *Glossa Ordinaria* and the Transmission of Medieval Anti-Judaism," in J. Brown and W.P. Stoneman (ed.), *A Distinct Voice: Medieval Studies in Honor of Leonard P. Boyle, O.P.* (Notre Dame, IN: University of Notre Dame Press, 1977), 591–605.

10. Signer, *Glossa Ordinaria*, 597.

11. Smalley, *Study*, 56.

12. Smith, *Glossa Ordinaria*, 83. Margaret Gibson has suggested that the older tradition is accurate to some extent, in that the running gloss based on patristic authors is a Carolingian method of exegesis, while interlinear glossing is an eleventh and twelfth century development. The innovation of the marginal gloss was to fix, or canonize, a set of excerpts to which no later compiler could add further glosses. See Gibson, "The Glossed Bible." Based on Signer's work, Smith has suggested that the higher level of anti-Jewish polemic in the interlinear gloss could indicate an earlier date for its composition than that of the marginal gloss. See Signer, "*Glossa Ordinaria*," 600; Smith; *Glossa Ordinaria*, 86.

13. This is a feature of later manuscripts. In the earliest manuscripts, the gloss and the biblical text are occasionally the same size and difficult to distinguish.

14. For examples of this technique in the interlinear gloss on Genesis 37, see Michael Signer, "*Glossa Ordinaria*," 594.

15. Variable glosses are occasionally direct quotes, as will be seen further on.

16. This is consistent with what Lesley Smith has found elsewhere. See Lesley Smith, *Glossa Ordinaria*, 85.

17. Smith, *Glossa Ordinaria*, 85.

18. Smith confirms that this is characteristic of the Gloss in other books as well. See Smith, 85.

19. C, Z, F, A, D, O, N, I, J, P, X, W, V, A, M. Manuscripts S and H, as well as the Rusch edition, are similar to the first recension on this variant.

20. 1.1i, 2.4i, 3.2i, 5.1i, 5.2i, 6.1i, 19.1i and 19.2i.

21. In glosses 2.2i, 3.2i, 7.1i, and 15.2i.

22. In 2.1i, 3.2i, 5.2i, 6.2i, 8.1i, 16.1i, 16.3i, and two in 17.3i.

23. Smith, *Glossa Ordinaria*, 69.

24. Smith, *Glossa Ordinaria*, 67.

25. Smith, 68.

26. *Patrologia Latina* 107, cols. 439-670. There is no modern critical edition of the commentary of Rabanus on Genesis. Since the commentary of Rabanus is so central to the history of the marginal gloss, a critical edition showing the form in which Rabanus was read in the twelfth century would be greatly desirable. The absence of a critical edition does leave open the possibility that the transmission of the commentary of Rabanus was influenced by the gloss.

27. Although organizing patristic material is a typical method of Carolingian exegesis, Rabanus goes far beyond his teacher Alcuin in his fidelity to the exact words of his sources. Alcuin adds questions that the patristic sources answer and also includes original material of his own. In contrast, in Rabanus' commentary on Genesis 22 he quotes his sources nearly verbatim and adds nothing. Rabanus is more willing to add his own material in other works and commentaries. For examples of Rabanus' exegetical creativity in his encyclopedia and in his commentary on the book of Daniel, see William Schipper, "Rabanus Maurus and his Sources," in *Schooling and Society: The Ordering and Reordering of Knowledge in the Middle Ages*, ed. Alasdair A. MacDonald and Michael W. Twomey (Leuven: Peeters, 2004), 1–22.

28. Aurelius Augustinus, *Quaestionum in Heptateuchem Libri Septem*, I. Fraipoint, ed., Corpus Christianorum Series Latina 33, (Turnholt: Brepols, 1958).

29. Hieronymus, *Hebraice Quaestiones in Libro Geneseos*, Pavli de Lagarde, ed., Corpus Christianorum Series Latina 72, (Turnholt: Brepols, 1959).

30. There is no modern critical edition of the commentary of Isidore on Genesis. I have used the edition in the PL 83, 207–288. This edition is based on the 1599 edition by J. Grial, who gave it the title *Mysticorum expositions sacramentorum seu quaestiones in vetus testamentum*, with further notes added by F. Arévalo, Rome, 1803. See Thomas O'Loughlin, "Christ as the Focus of Genesis Exegesis in Isidore of Seville," in *Studies in Patristic Christology*, ed. Thomas Finan and Vincent Twomey (Dublin: Four Courts Press, 1998), 145.

31. There is no modern critical edition of any of Alcuin's commentaries. I have used the edition in PL 100, 515–570.

32. Smith, *Glossa Ordinaria*, 57.

33. Smith, *Glossa Ordinaria*, 58.

34. Smith, *Glossa Ordinaria*, 54.

35. Smith, *Glossa Ordinaria*, 64

36. Smith has found no evidence that later manuscripts name sources more consistently than earlier ones. Smith, 63.

37. It is of course possible that they were simply copying from Rabanus manuscripts that had source citations. This seems unlikely, since the Gloss manuscripts vary widely in which comments they ascribe to patristic authors (with some patterns, as will be shown).

38. For discussions of Carolingian exegesis, see Celia Chazelle & Burton Van Name Edwards, *The Study of the Bible in the Carolingian Era* (Turnhout: Brepols, 2003). Also see Smalley, *Study*, 37–46.

39. *Quaestiones Super Genesim*, PL 93 cols. 318B–320D. This commentary has been misattributed to Bede. See M. Gorman, "The Canon of Bede's Works and the World of Pseudo-Bede," *Revue Bénédictine* 111 (2001): 437–438.

40. *In Pentateuchem Comentarii—Genesis*. PL 91 cols. 244B–245D. For the correct attribution of this commentary, see M. Gorman, "The Commentary on the Pentateuch Attributed to Bede in PL 91.189-394," *Revue Bénédictine* 106 (1996): 61–108, 257–307.

41. Pseudo-Bede here emulates Bede's own approach to the use of sources. Bede consistently used many of Augustine's works in compiling his Genesis commentary, including Augustine's *De civitate dei* and *Confessiones*. For Bede's method and use of sources see Joseph F. Kelly, "Bede's Use of Augustine for his *Commentarium in principium Genesis*," in *Augustine: Biblical Exegete*, ed. Frederick Van Fleteren and Joseph C. Schnaubelt (New York: Peter Lang Publishing, 2004). Unfortunately, Bede's authentic commentary on Genesis ends with Genesis 21. See *Bedae Venerabilis Opera*, Corpus Christianorum Series Latina 118A (Turnholt: Brepols, 1955).

42. It is not clear why the Gloss chose Rabanus as its main source rather than another Carolingian or later compilation of patristic exegesis. Alcuin's commentary would have been a possible alternative, since Alcuin quotes many of the same sources as Rabanus. Alcuin does edit his excerpts more heavily and adds question-and-answer structures, which may have made his commentary less appealing as a source of quotations.

43. Jerome's comment on 22.2, which was adapted in gloss 2.3m, has a close parallel in *Genesis Rabbah* 55.7. Jerome's comment on 22.14, adapted as gloss 14.1m, has a parallel in *Genesis Rabbah* 56.9. See the discussion on parallels between Rashi and the Gloss for details.

44. CCSL 72, 26–27.

45. CCSL 72, 26–27.

46. CCSL 72, LXIII-LXIV. The editor lists many manuscripts that he does not use in his edition, but it is not clear if this list is exhaustive.

47. See Chapter Two and the end of this chapter. Glosses 12.2i, 14.2i, and 15.2i, based on Augustine, became variable glosses and appear as marginal and interlinear glosses in an equal number of manuscripts. Gloss 2.2i and 17.1-4i are based on Alcuin. Gloss 3.1m and 5.1m, based on Isidore, occasionally appear in the interlinear gloss.

48. Manuscript P even cites Jerome as the source of one of Isidore's comments, in addition to all of his own.

49. Mark Zier has shown that Jerome is also the most frequently named source in the Gloss on Daniel 1. Out of the five attributed sources in that chapter, Jerome is the named source of four. See Zier, "Manuscript Tradition," 16–25. Lesley Smith, however, has not been able to identify a consistent pattern in which glosses are attributed and which are not in her more general study of the gloss. See Smith, *Glossa Ordinaria*, 63.

50. Hieronymus, *Hebraice Quaestiones in Libro Geneseos*, CCSL vol. 72, 26.

51. The one variant that might possibly affect the meaning is that in the CCSL edition Jerome has *solent etiam nunc cornu clangere* [they are accustomed even now to sound the horn] instead of *solent cornu clangere* (CCSL 72.27). This makes even more clear that Jerome is speaking of the post-biblical Jews of his own day. No gloss manuscript has this variant, although manuscript B has *solent etiam cornu clangere*.

52. Chavel, *Perushe Rashi*, 82.

53. Theodor and Albeck, eds. *Midrash Bereshit Rabbah*, 607.

54. See CCSL 33, VII.

55. It is an important source for the marginal gloss on Genesis elsewhere as well, particularly for interpretations identified in the marginal gloss as literal. See Matter, "The Church Fathers," 87.

56. Since, according to the critical edition of Augustine in CCSL (Aurelius Augustinus, *Quaestionum in Heptateuchem Libri Septem*, I. Fraipoint, ed., Corpus Christianorum Series Latina 33, (Turnholt: Brepols, 1958), 22–23). Aurelius Augustinus, *Quaestionum in Heptateuchem Libri Septem*, I. Fraipoint, ed., Corpus Christianorum Series Latina 33, (Turnholt: Brepols, 1958), 22–23. There are no major variants between Augustine's commentary in QH and Augustine as quoted by Rabanus, it is impossible to be certain if and to what extent the glossators consulted manuscripts of Augustine's commentary as well as manuscripts of Rabanus. On the other hand, Augustine is named as the author of at least one of the glosses for which he is the source in every single Gloss manuscript. Since he is not named as a source in Rabanus, this seems to indicate that the glossators had at least enough direct familiarity with Augustine to know which glosses were his. One slight variant might suggest that the glossators copied Augustine from Rabanus only (or at least did not use Augustine manuscripts to correct the version in Rabanus). Augustine concludes his first section with *nisi divino experimento etiam eidem innotescant* (QH 57, CCSL 33, 22). QH 57, CCSL 33, 22. Rabanus omits the word *divino* (*Commentariorum in Genesim Libri Quatuor* 3.3.23 PL 107 col. 566B), *Commentariorum in Genesim Libri Quatuor* 3.3.23 PL 107 col. 566B. and every single gloss manuscript follows him (see CCSL 33, 22). This minor difference proves very little, though, especially since this word is also absent in some twelfth-century manuscripts of Augustine. See CCSL 33, 22.

57. Even comment 1.1m, which remains in the marginal gloss in most manuscripts of the second recension, is severely truncated. For example, QH 57 begins *Quaeri solet quomodo hoc verum sit, cum dicat in Epistola sua Jacobus quod Deus neminem tentat* [It is usually asked: How can this be true, when it says in the epistle of James that God tests no one?] (CCSL 33, 22) while marginal gloss 1.1m in manuscript A begins *Jacobus dicit quod neminem temptat deus* [James says that God tests no one].

58. These comments are the most unstable of all the variable glosses (glosses that move from the margins to between the lines from manuscript to manuscript). They appear in the marginal and interlinear glosses an approximately equal number of times. As will be suggested later in this chapter, these glosses tend to be neither completely original nor direct quotations (or close paraphrases) from patristic sources.

59. In 1.1m Augustine's name is only absent in S. In 12.1 the attribution is only absent in manuscript G. In B, 12.1m is misattributed to Jerome.

60. Aurelius Augustinus, *Sermones de Vetere Testamento*, Cyrillus Lambot, ed., Corpus Christianorum Series Latina 61 (Turnholt: Brepols, 1961), 9–17.

61. Aurelius Augustinus, *De Civitate Dei*, Corpus Christianorum Series Latina 48 (Turnholt: Brepols, 1955), 536–538.

62. Aurelius Augustinus, *De Genesi ad Litteram Libri Duodecim*, Joseph Zycha, ed. Corpus Scriptorum Ecclesiasticorum Latinorum, 1887.

63. Aurelius Augustinus, *Retractionum Libri II*, Almut Mutzenbecher, ed., Corpus Christianorum Series Latina 57 (Turnholt: Brepols, 1984), 132.

64. CCSL 33, 22.

65. CCSL 33, 22.

66. CCSL 33, 22–23.

67. PL 100 cols. 544C–546B.

68. Aside from L, B, and G, which do not include Alcuin at all, the only manuscript which does not follow this citation pattern is S, which omits 5.3m and most of 13.1m (including Alcuin's name) and mis-cites 2.1m as Augustine.

69. Alcuin did have some indirect contact with Jews of Rome and Italy about matters related to the Hebrew text of the Bible. See Arieh Grabois, "The Hebraica Veritas and Jewish–Christian Intellectual Relations in the Twelfth Century," *Speculum* 50.4 (October 1975), 615.

70. PL 100, col. 545C.

71. Auctor incertus (Augustinus Hipponensis?), *De mirabilibus sacrae scripturae libri tres*. PL 35 col. 2162. The author of this source seems to be Augustinus Hibernicus, a seventh-century Irish monk. See Damian Bracken, "Rationalism and the Bible in Seventh-Century Ireland," *Chronicon* 2 (1998) 1: 1–37.

72. This is consistent with pseudo-Augustine's approach to miracles, in which divine creation could only take place during the six days of creation. See Bracken, "Rationalism," 27–28.

73. This is similar to how Isidore is used in the Gloss on Ezekiel. See Smith, *Glossa Ordinaria*, 51.

74. PL 83 cols. 449B–538A.

75. Jeremy Cohen, *Living Letters of the Law: Ideas of the Jew in Medieval Christianity* (Berkeley: University of California Press, 1999) 95. Also see Wolfram Drews, *The Unknown Neighbor: Jews in the Thought of Isidore of Seville* (Leiden: Brill, 2006).

76. Bat-sheva Albert, "Isidore of Seville: His Attitude Towards Judaism and his Impact on Early Medieval Canonical law," *The Jewish Quarterly Review* 30 3.4 (1990): 207–220.

77. PL 107, 439–670.

78. This seems to have happened at around the same time as the addition of Alcuin's comments to the marginal gloss.

79. PL 83 cols. 249C–251D.

80. PL 83 col. 249 D.

81. PL 83 col. 250 A.

82. The distinction between senses appears quite commonly in the gloss, and tends to appear more often in earlier than in later manuscripts. See Smith, *Glossa Ordinaria*, 67.

83. The edition of Isidore's commentary on Genesis in the *Patrologia Latina* is based on the edition by J. Grial of the complete works of Isidore, published in Madrid in 1599, vol. ii, pages 112–115. The Grial edition was reprinted with additional notes by F. Arévalo, Rome, 1803, and this latter edition was reprinted in the *Patrologia*.

84. QV 18.19, PL 83 cols. 245D.

85. It is also possible, of course, that the glossators were reading Rabanus from a manuscript that included the last lines from Isidore.

86. PL 83 col. 249D.

87. *ad immolandum perduxit* rather than *perduxit ad immolandum*.

88. G puts *unicum* after *filium suum*.

89. This is an easily explainable mistake. Some attributions were given as a single letter. J and I would appear very similar in manuscripts and could be easily confused. See Smith, *Glossa Ordinaria*, 63.

90. Conclusions here reflect my study of Genesis 22 only. Alexander Andrée has observed a distinct category of "middle glosses" in his study of the gloss on Lamentations. (Alexander Andrée, "Gilbertus Universalis," 60). Zier and Dove did not identify such a category in their critical editions of Daniel and Song of Songs. Zier, "Manuscript Tradition." Dove, *Glossa ordinaria*.

91. Comments that appear in only one manuscript in an unusual position, and the manuscript in which they shift position, are as follows: 2.1i (I), 3.2i (W), 3.1m (N), 5.1m (O), 9.1i (O), 9.2i (O), and 16.1-3i (S)

92. Zier, "Manuscript Tradition," 6.

93. Smalley, *Study*, 56.

94. Zier, "Manuscript Tradition," 6.

95. My data thus supports Smith's sense that it seems generally to be unattributed glosses that move back and forth between the marginal and interlinear positions from manuscript to manuscript. See Smith, *Glossa Ordinaria*, 85.

4. ISAAC ON JEWISH AND CHRISTIAN ALTARS

1. Jody Lynn Vaccaro, "Early Jewish and Christian Interpretations of the Character of Isaac in Genesis 22" (Ph.D. diss., University of Notre Dame, 1998).

2. Michael A. Signer, "Rashi's Reading."

3. Abraham's love for God, to Rashi, requires no explanation and is never addressed in his commentary.

4. Pairs such as Isaac and Ishmael or Jacob and Esau were frequently used by medieval (and late antique) Jewish and Christian exegetes as a way of describing their relationship. See Yuval, *Two Nations*, 2–3. In Jewish literature Ishmael also frequently functions as a stand-in for Islam. See David Zucker, "Conflicting Conclusions: The Hatred of Isaac and Ishmael," *Judaism* 39,1 (1990) 37–46. That seems not to be the case here, for either Rashi or his source *Genesis Rabbah*.

5. Michael Signer has observed a similar pattern in the *Glossa Ordinaria* on Genesis 37. See Signer, "*Glossa Ordinaria*," 591–605.

6. 13.2m quotes Jerome citing the Jewish translators Aquila and Theodotion as well as the translation of the Septuagint, but neither Jerome nor the Gloss describes any of these translations as Jewish.

7. *Iudei* also appear in 9.1m in manuscript B, which has *christum ante immolationem a iudeis coronatum* [Christ crowned by Jews before the sacrifice] instead of *christum ante immolationem spinis coronatum* [Christ crowned with thorns before the sacrifice] and manuscripts G and L, which have *antequam immolaretur spinis a iudeis coronatum* [before he was sacrificed he was crowned with thorns by Jews.]

8. These terms are distinct in all manuscripts, and one is never a variant for another.

9. Gloss 5.1m quotes Romans 11:25, *Caecitas ex parte contigit in israel* (Partial blindness befalls Israel) and Romans 11:26, *Et sic omnis israel salvus fiet* (And thus all Israel will be saved). Gloss 5.2m quotes Jeremiah 3:8, *Adversatrix israel, et prevaricatrix iuda* (Israel the enemy, Judah the liar).

10. In the Gloss on Daniel, Mark Zier has observed a pattern in the manuscripts in which thirteenth-century manuscripts substitute *iudei* for *hebrei* (Zier, "Manuscript

Tradition," 13). He connects this to the more polemical mendicant slant of the thirteenth-century manuscripts. The manuscripts of Genesis 22 in the present edition do not show this variant.

11. Although Jewish blindness is a common image in medieval Christian exegesis, the donkey as a representative of the Jews is less common. Aside from Isidore (and Rabanus quoting Isidore on this verse) the donkey as a representative of Jewish stupidity also appears in Rabanus' *Allegoriae in Universam Sacram Scripturam* (PL 122 col. 867D). Rabanus mentions Genesis 22:5 as an example of the donkey representing the Jewish stupidity illustrated by Romans 11:25, but also cites a verse from Isaiah as proof that a donkey can also represent the nations. Medieval German theologian Gerhoh of Reichersberg (1093–1169) interprets the donkey of Psalm 32:9 as Jewish stupidity in *Opera inedita by Gerhoh of Reichersberg*, vol. 2, D. Van den Eynde, O. Van den Eynde, A. Rijmersdael, P. Classen eds., (Rome 1956), 187. For a discussion of various animals representing Jews in medieval Christian exegesis see Dahan, *Les intellectuels Chrétiens et les Juifs*, 403–405.

12. In contrast, according to the Gloss on Matthew 21:33–39 (the parable of the vineyard) and 1 Corinthians 2:8 (**Which none of the princes of the world knew; for if they had known it, they would never have crucified the Lord of glory**), the Jewish elders in the time of Christ knew the truth that he was the messiah. Here the Jews do see and understand in a way that makes them morally culpable.

13. Gloss 17.3i describes them as *israel secundum carnem* [Israel according to the flesh] as opposed to *israel dei* [Israel of God] in 17.2i. Manuscript L eliminates comment 17.3i and simply says, in reference to verse 17 which compares Israel to the sand that is on the sea-shore, *id est israel qui est scilicet arneam* [this is Israel, which is, of course, sand]. This is the only example in any of the manuscripts I consulted of *israel* used as a name for the Jews in the interlinear gloss on Genesis 22.

14. Karlfried Froehlich and Margaret Gibson, eds., *Biblia latina cum glossa ordinaria: facsimile reprint of the editio princeps Adolph Rusch of Strassburg 1480/81* (Brepols: Turnout, 1992), vol. 1, 67.

15. This follows Augustine (QH 63, CCSL vol. 33, 28), who defines the two peoples as Jews and Christians. The marginal gloss does not define these two peoples in any way, and neither does Jerome. Although the *duo populi* are Jews and Christians in the interlinear gloss, the *due gentes* are Jews and Idumeans.

16. Albeck, *Bereshit Rabbati*, 88.

17. See the comments on Genesis 22:4 and 22:12, Albeck, *Bereshit Rabbati*, 89–90.

18. Solomon Buber, *Midrash Lekach Tov* (Jerusalem: Vagshal, 1986), 21.å.

19. For an example of this, see Rashbam on Exodus 21:1.

20. Rashbam adopts anti-Christian polemical interpretations elsewhere in Genesis. Cohen, "Does Rashi's Torah Commentary Respond to Christianity?" 454 and Rashbam's interpretation of Genesis 49:10.

21. See the comments by Bechor Shor on Genesis 49:10. Cohen, "Does Rashi's Torah Commentary Respond to Christianity?" 456–457.

22. Patrologia Latina (PL) 175 cols. 29-86D.

23. PL 157 19-338C.

24. Dahan, "Genres," 202.

25. PL 156 col. 168B.

26. PL 156 col. 168B.

27. For Guibert of Nogent's anti-Jewish polemic, primarily directed at a Judaizing Christian, see *Tractatus de incarnatione contre Judeos* (PL 156 489-528C). Guibert describes this Judaizer, Count Jean of Soissons, in his *De vita sua sive mondiarum libri tres* (PL 156 837-962A), book 3 chapter 16 (949B-951A). See Jan M. Ziolkowski, "Put in No-Man's Land: Guibert of Nogent's Accusations Against a Judaizing and Jew-Supporting Christian," in *Jews and Christians in Twelfth-Century Europe*, Michael A. Signer and John Van Engen, eds., (Notre Dame: University of Notre Dame Press, 2001), 110–122.

28. *Expositio in Pentateuchum* PL 164 147-550. For a complete list of early editions and manuscripts, see Reginald Grégorie, *Bruno de Segni, exégéte médiéval et théologien monastique* (Spoleto: Centro Italiano di Studi Sull'alto Medioevo, 1965) 67–69.

29. After his commentary on the Apocalypse, before any of his other commentaries. See William Linden North, "In the Shadows of Reform: Exegesis and the Formation of a Clerical Elite in the Works of Bruno, Bishop of Segni (1078/9–1123)" (Ph.D. Diss. University of California, Berkeley, 1998), 86.

30. PL 164 cols. 199 B-C.

31. PL 175 cols. 29-86D. For a discussion of Hugh of St. Victor's approach to the senses of scripture, see Franklin T Harkins, *Reading and the Work of Restoration: History and Scripture in the Theology of Hugh of St. Victor* (Toronto: Pontifical Institute of Medieval Studies, 2009).

32. PL 176 cols. 739–838.

33. PL 175 cols. 9–28.

34. Smalley, *Study*, 87.

35. John H. Van Engen, *Rupert of Deutz* (Berkeley: University of California Press, 1983), 81.

36. CCCM 21.408, 409.

37. CCCM 21.406.

38. CCCM 21.405–406, 412.

39. CCCM 21.406.

40. CCCM 21.513. See Van Engen, *Rupert of Deutz*, 244. He also notes similar language about Jews in Rupert's commentary on John. See CCCM 9.391. We see an interest in anti-Jewish polemic outside his commentaries as well. Rupert wrote a literary dialogue between a Christian and a Jew (*Annulus sive dialogus inter Christianum et Judaeum*. PL 170 col. 559-610C) Herman, who later converted to Christianity, wrote of his disputation with Rupert in his *Hermanus quondam Iudaeus opusculum de conversione sua*. (G. Niemeyer, ed. MGH Geistesgeschichte 4, Weimar 1963). Herman records what he describes as only a small fragment of Rupert's arguments, primarily on the topic of why images in churches are not idols. See *Opusculum* 3, Niemeyer 76. Herman was not completely convinced, and only converted a few years later. For the historical context of this debate, see Van Engen, *Rupert of Deutz*, 242–243.

41. Van Engen (*Rupert of Deutz*, 242) calls it a 'preoccupation' of Rupert's.

42. Dahan, *L'exégése*, 30.

43. CCSL 33, 22.

44. *dominum* in manuscripts V P I W X and Q. This is closer to Augustine, although likely also refers to Abraham's prophecy of Christ.

45. Irenaeus, *Adversus Haereses* 4.5.4.

46. Origen, *Homilae in Genesim* 8.1.

47. Ambrose, *De Abraham*, 1.8.72.

48. PL 164 col. 198C

49. This kind of division frequently appears in Bruno's commentary. See Grégorie, *Bruno*, 192.

50. Bruno does not cite any patristic or Carolingian sources explicitly in his commentary on Genesis 22, which means that Josephus is his only named post-biblical source. This is not typical of his commentary on Genesis (or of other biblical books). For Bruno's use and citation of sources (including Jerome, Augustine, Ambrose, Gregory, and Hilary) see Grégorie, *Bruno*, 156, 197–198.

51. Bruno uses the terms *allegorice* and *significat* (PL 164 col. 1099A). For a discussion of *significatio* in Bruno's commentaries and its difference from *sacramentum* see Grégorie, *Bruno*, 189–191.

52. PL 164 199B.

53. PL 164 col. 199D.

54. CCCM 21.407.

55. Jay Rubenstein, *Guibert of Nogent: Portrait of a Medieval Mind* (New York: Routledge, 2002), 26–60.

56. Guibert of Nogent, *Liber quo ordine sermo fieri debeat*, R. B. C. Huygens, ed. CCCM 127, (Turnholt: Brepols, 1993), 47–63.

57. Guibert of Nogent, *Quo ordine*, 55.

58. Guibert of Nogent, *Quo ordine*, 54.

59. Rubenstein, *Guibert*, 45–60.

60. Rubenstein, *Guibert*, 46.

61. Rubenstein, *Guibert*, 53.

62. Rubenstein, *Guibert*, 50. Guibert of Nogent, *Moralia*, PL 157 cols 111D, 112C, 116B.

63. Rubenstein, *Guibert*, 52, Guibert of Nogent, *Moralia*, PL 157 cols 160 B-C, 161A.

64. Guibert of Nogent, *Moralia*, PL 157 col 168C.

65. Guibert of Nogent, *Moralia*, PL 157 col 169C.

66. PL 175 cols. 29–86D. For a discussion of Hugh of St. Victor's approach to the senses of scripture, see Franklin T Harkins, *Reading and the Work of Restoration: History and Scripture in the Theology of Hugh of St. Victor* (Toronto: Pontifical Institute of Medieval Studies, 2009).

67. Berndt, "St. Victor," 469.

68. PL 176 cols. 739–838.

69. Smalley, *Study*, 87.

70. PL 176 cols. 799–802.

71. PL 176 cols. 805–806.

72. The Patrologia Latina ascribes an allegorical commentary on Genesis to Hugh of St. Victor, as well, in the *Posteriorum excerptionum libri tredecim continentes utriusque testamenti allegorias* [Three books of later excerpts containing allegories of both testaments] (PL 175 cols. 633–750). PL 175 cols. 633–750. More recent scholarship doubts his authorship of this work, which is more likely to have been written by Peter Comestor. R. Martin, "Notes sur l'oeuvre littéraire de Pierre le Mangeur," *Recherches de Théologie ancienne et médiévale* 3 (1931): 258. (R. Martin, "Notes sur l'oeuvre littéraire de Pierre le Mangeur," *Recherches de Théologie ancienne et médiévale*, 3 (1931): 258) or Richard of St. Victor (Ph. S. Moore, "The Auctorship of the Allegoriae super Vetus et Novum Testamentum," *New Scholasticism*, 1935, 209–225). Ph. S. Moore, "The Auctorship of the Allegoriae super Vetus et Novum Testamentum," *New Scholasticism*, 1935, 209–225. Therefore, this work will not be considered here.

73. CCCM 21.405.

74. Although Rupert of Deutz's innovative explanation of the relationship between the near-sacrifice of Isaac and the Crucifixion has no parallel in Rashi or in the Gloss, it could parallel *Bereshit Rabbati*'s explanation of the near-sacrifice of Isaac as a way to force God to act in the future.

75. Based on Genesis 22 and 2 Chronicles 3, Isaac Kalimi suggests that the location of the Temple was identified with the location of the binding of Isaac as early as the period of the first Temple, but it only came to be called "Mount Moriah" in the writings of the Chronicler in the period of the second Temple. He also suggests that this identification was part of a Jewish-Samaritan early polemic, giving precedent to its later use

in Jewish–Christian polemic. See Isaac Kalimi, *Early Jewish Exegesis and Theological Controversy* (Aasen: Van Gorcum, 2002) 15, 34.

76. It is typical for Rashi to use Midrash, Targum, and other biblical verses to provide linguistic explanations. For an example of this from Rashi's commentary on Deuteronomy, see Kearney, *Rashi*, 63–70, which illustrates the variety of different sources and techniques Rashi uses to for his linguistic comments on a single verse in Deuteronomy.

77. The word רשו does not appear in Leviticus at all.

78. Signer, "Rashi's Reading."

79. Albeck, *Bereshit Rabbati*, 88.

80. The story as told in Bereshit Rabbati is based on Midrash Tanchuma Vayera 23.

81. Albeck, *Bereshit Rabbati*, 86.

82. Unlike Rashi, *Bereshit Rabbati* does not invoke Satan or the nations of the world as this accusing figure. Instead, the accusers seem to be a personified reference to Israel's sins. There is no external accuser.

83. *Bereshit Rabbati* refers only once to the Temple sacrifices, on 22.9 (Albeck, *Bereshit Rabbati*, 90), where Isaac describes his sacrifice in a way that is consistent with the laws of the Temple sacrifices. This phrase appears in the middle of a story about Isaac worrying what would become of his mother after he dies, and is not emphasized.

84. Dahan, *L'exégése*, 44.

85. Dahan, *L'exégése*, 44. This idea of the fundamental difference between divine and human speech would be questioned in the later twelfth century by, for example, Andrew of St. Victor. See Dahan, *L'exégése*, 45.

86. Dahan, *L'exégése*, 351.

87. For the importance of memory in monastic exegesis, see Jean Leclerq, *The Love of Learning and the Desire for God: A Study of Monastic Culture*, trans. by Catharine Misrahi (New York: Fordham University Press, 1996), 76–82.

88. Dahan, *L'exégése*, 62.

89. Henri De Lubac, *Exégése médiévale: les quatres sens de l'écriture*, vol. 1 (Paris: Aubier, 1959), 305–363.

90. Both Rashi and the Gloss similarly connect between scripture and present-day history in their Song of Songs commentaries as well.

91. PL 164 col. 198D.

92. CCCM 21.405–406.

93. PL 156 cols. 167B–168C.

94. This is a possible parallel to the Midrashic idea that Abraham underwent ten tests of which the near-sacrifice of Isaac was the last. This idea originated in the second century BCE (see Job 16:15–18) and was fully developed in the eight-century Midrashic collection *Pirkei De Rabbi Eliezer* (chapters 26–30). For other examples of Abraham's ten tests in midrashic literature see Carol Bakhos, "Abraham Visits Ishmael," 556–557.

95. Another comment which could possibly fit into the category of moral teaching is 3.3, which explains why an important man should always take two people along on a journey.

96. See chapter two.

97. אם כן, לחינם באתי לכאן. אעשה בו חבלה ואוציא ממנו מעט דם.

98. Rashi makes this demand even more explicit in a manuscript variant found in two early printed editions and discussed in chapter two, in which Abraham argues with God, and Isaac becomes his hostage in demanding justice. It is a direct quote from *Genesis Rabbah* 56.8 and could have been added to Rashi's commentary by a later copyist. It is possible that the importance of this theme in Rashi's sources encouraged later copyists to read it into Rashi in a stronger way through the addition of this comment. Another clue pointing to its lateness is that it is introduced with אמר רבי אבא, Rabbi Abba said. As shown in chapter two, in his commentary on Genesis 22 Rashi rarely names his sources so explicitly.

99. Genesis Rabbah 56.12, 56.14-16 I. Theodor and H. Albeck, eds. *Midrash Bereshit Rabbah*, 603, 607–610.

100. Midrash Tanchuma Vayera 23 (*Midrash Tanchuma HaMefoar*, 127–128).

101. His next comments, although they mention the binding of Isaac, are more concerned with the next story in which Abraham returns and finds a wife for Isaac.

102. Vaccaro, "Early Jewish and Christian Interpretations," 314.

103. PL 164 col. 198D.

104. PL 164 cols. 198C–199A.

105. Ibn Ezra on Genesis 22:4.

106. Bechor Shor on Genesis 22:8.

107. James Kugel, "Two Introductions to Midrash," in *Midrash and Literature*, ed. Geoffrey H. Hartman and Sanford Budick (New Haven, CT: Yale University Press, 1986), 93.

108. Kamin, *Rashi*, 12.

109. Smalley, *Study*, 358.

APPENDIX A: A CRITICAL EDITION OF THE *GLOSSA ORDINARIA* ON GENESIS 22:1–19

1. PL 113 col. 67 to 114 col. 752B.

2. For a history of this mistake, see Karlfried Froehlich, "Walafrid Strabo and the *Glossa Ordinaria*: the Making of a Myth." In *Studia patristica*, 28 (Louvain: Peeters, 1993), 192–196.

3. Smalley, *Study*, 56, Smith, *Glossa Ordinaria*, 83.

4. De Hamel, *Glossed Books*, 14.

5. Mary Dove suggests that it was based on the 1508 Basel reprinting of the Rusch edition. See Dove, *Glossa Ordinaria*, 6.

6. Karlfried Froehlich and Margaret T. Gibson, eds., *Biblia latina cum glossa ordinaria: facsimile reprint of the editio princeps Adolph Rusch of Strassburg 1480/81* (Brepols: Turnhout, 1992).

7. Some later early printed editions made minor changes. Dove, *Glossa Ordinaria*, 5.

8. Margaret Gibson, "Printed Gloss," vii.

9. Dove, *Glossa Ordinaria*, 7.

10. Gibson, "Printed Gloss," vii.

11. Smith, *Glossa Ordinaria*, 13.

12. *vel postquam* between 5.1i and 5.2i, *vel pepercisti* between 12.2i and 12.3i.

13. For an edition that does attempt to reconstruct the Gloss as written by Gilbert the Universal, see Andrée, "Gilbertus Universalis." Andrée describes his motivation as philological, and recognizes that an intellectual historian might be more interested in the second recension. See Andrée, "Gilbertus Universalis," 92.

14. Mark Zier suggested this method of preparing an edition of the Gloss in its final and most influential form. Zier, "Manuscript Tradition," 16.

15. Abecassis, "Reconstructing Rashi's Commentary," 213.

16. The Gloss on Lamentations exists in two recensions as well. See Andrée, "Gilbertus Universalis," 91–94. Andrée identifies his two recensions as originating in Laon and Paris (Andrée, "Gilbertus Universalis," 96). Because Andrée is interested in the earliest version of the Gloss, and the present work is interested in the most influential version of the Gloss, his edition is based on the first and earliest recension while the present edition is based on the second and more influential.

17. Of course, without consulting more early Gloss manuscripts it is difficult to be certain.

18. In Andrée's edition of the Gloss on Lamentations, the second recension also tends to truncate and simplify the first recension. See Andrée, "Gilbertus Universalis," 95.

19. De Hamel, *Glossed Books*, 25.

20. De Hamel, *Glossed Books*, 25.

21. De Hamel, *Glossed Books*, 16.

22. De Hamel, *Glossed Books*, 17.

23. De Hamel, *Glossed Books*, 24.

24. Many thanks to Mark Zier for arranging for me to have access to microfilms from the BNF collection.

25. Fridericus Stegmüller, *Repertorium biblicum medii aevii*, vol. 9 (Madrid: Consejo Superior de Investigaciones Científicas, 1977), 468.

26. De Hamel, *Glossed Books*, 15–16.

27. De Hamel, *Glossed Books*, 17.

28. De Hamel, *Glossed Books*, 24.

29. De Hamel, *Glossed Books*, 14.

30. De Hamel, *Glossed Books*, 24.

31. De Hamel, *Glossed Books*, 25.

32. Dove, *Glossa Ordinaria*, 24.

33. De Hamel, *Glossed Books*, 17.

34. De Hamel, *Glossed Books*, 35.

35. De Hamel, *Glossed Books*, 36. The De Hamel uses the term "Romanesque minis-cule," which corresponds to the more commonly used terms "protogothic" or "primitive gothic." See Michelle P. Brown, *A Guide to Western Historical Scripts from Antiquity to 1600*, (Toronto: University of Toronto Press, 1990), 72, and Bernhard Bischoff, *Latin Paleography: Antiquity and the Middle Ages*, Dáibhi Ó Crónín and David Ganz, trans., (Cambridge: Cambridge University Press, 1986), 129.

36. Bischoff, *Latin Paleography*, 122.

37. Bischoff, *Latin Paleography*, 126.

38. Bischoff, *Latin Paleography*, 125.

39. Bischoff, *Latin Paleography*, 122.

40. Bischoff, *Latin Paleography*, 128.

41. Bischoff, *Latin Paleography*, 130.

42. Bischoff, *Latin Paleography*, 130.

43. Brown, *Western Historical Scripts*, 73, Bischoff, *Latin Paleography*, 127–128.

44. Christopher De Hamel, *The Book: A History of the Bible*, (London: Phaidon Press, 2001), 124.

45. http://www.hmml.org/scholars/catalogue/overview.asp?textID=35339

46. Bibliothèque nationale, *Catalogue général des manuscrits latins* [Texte imprimé] / Bibliothèque nationale. Tome Ier, Nos 1-1438. (Paris: Bibliothèque nationale, 1939). 28

47. Bibliothèque nationale, *Catalogue général*, 66.

48. ibid.

49. http://www.hmml.org/scholars/catalogue/overview.asp?textID=26361

50. http://www.hmml.org/scholars/catalogue/overview.asp?textID=332009

51. Bibliothèque nationale, *Catalogue général*, 29.

52. ibid.

53. Bibliothèque nationale, *Catalogue général*, 131.

54. ibid.

55. http://www.hmml.org/scholars/catalogue/overview.asp?textID=33440

56. http://www.hmml.org/scholars/catalogue/overview.asp?textID=191575

57. http://www.hmml.org/scholars/catalogue/overview.asp?textID=330597

58. http://www.hmml.org/scholars/catalogue/overview.asp?textID=47665

59. Bibliothèque nationale, *Catalogue général*, 29.

60. ibid.

61. ibid.

62. ibid.

63. Bibliothèque nationale, *Catalogue général*, 132.

64. ibid.

65. http://www.hmml.org/scholars/catalogue/overview.asp?textID=330825

66. http://www.hmml.org/scholars/catalogue/overview.asp?textID=191576

67. http://www.hmml.org/scholars/catalogue/overview.asp?textID=332709

68. http://www.hmml.org/scholars/catalogue/overview.asp?textID=32152

69. Delisle, Léopold, *Inventaire des manuscrits de Saint-Germain-des-Prés conservés à la Bibliothèque impériale, sous les numéros 11504-14231 du fonds latin*. (Paris: A. Durand et Pedone-Lauriel, 1868), 30.

70. Delisle, Léopold, *Inventaire des manuscrits de la Sorbonne conservés à la Bibliothèque impériale, sous les numéros 15176-16718 du fonds latin*. (Paris: A. Durand et Pedone-Lauriel, 1870), 1.

71. http://www.hmml.org/scholars/catalogue/overview.asp?textID=191574

72. ibid.

APPENDIX B: MAJOR MANUSCRIPT VARIANTS IN RASHI'S COMMENTARY ON GENESIS 22

1. Avraham Berliner, *Rashi 'al HaTorah*. (Berlin: Sumptibus Editorus, 1866). Avraham Berliner, *Rashi 'al HaTorah*. 2nd ed. (Frankfurt: J. Kauffmann, 1905).

2. For a critique of Berliner's edition, see Isaiah Sonne, "Towards criticism of the text of Rashi's commentary on the Torah" [Hebrew], *Hebrew Union College Annual* 15 (1940) 37–56, and Yeshayahu Maori, "The Text of Rashi's Commentary on the Torah," *Rashi: His Work and Personality (Rashi: demuto vi-yetsirato)*, Avraham Grossman and Sara Japhet (Jerusalem: Zalman Shazar, 2008), 64–72.

3. Chavel, *Perushe Rashi*.

4. Chavel, *Perushe Rashi*, 14.

5. Chavel, *Perushe Rashi*, 15. For Maori's critique of this edition and reasons for preferring the Berliner edition, see Maori, "Nusach perush Rashi le-Torah," 72–73.

6. *Chamishah Chumse Torah, Ari'el : Targum Onkelos, Perush Rashi.*, vol. 1 (Jerusalem: Harry Fishel, 1986).

7. Chavel, *Perushe Rashi*, 80.

8. *Rashi HaShalem* 368.

9. Chavel, *Perushe Rashi*, 81.

10. *Rashi HaShalem* 369.

11. Chavel, *Perushe Rashi*, 82

12. *Rashi HaShalem* 370.

13. *Rashi HaShalem,* 370.

14. Chavel, *Perushe Rashi,* 83.

15. *Rashi HaShalem,* 370.

16. *Midrash Tanchuma* Vayera 23 (*Midrash Tanchuma HaMefoar,* 127–128).

BIBLIOGRAPHY

PRIMARY SOURCE BIBLIOGRAPHY

Glossa Ordinaria Manuscripts

Admont 251. "Liber Genesis cum glossa ordinaria." Microfilm copy of Stiftsbibliothek, Admont (Austria) MS at Hill Museum and Manuscript Library, 106 ff.

BNF 63 (C). "Genesis cum glossa ordinaria." Microfilm of MS at Bibliothèque Nationale de France, 122 ff.

BNF 65 (N). "Genesis cum glossa ordinaria, pars." Microfilm of MS at Bibliothèque Nationale de France, 135 ff.

BNF 66 (F). "Genesis cum glossa ordinaria – Radalphus Flaviacensis." Microfilm of a Gloss on Genesis, and a fragment of a commentary by Raoul of Flaix on Romans. MS at Bibliothèque Nationale de France, 156 ff.

BNF 183 (B). "Genesis cum glossa ordinaria." Microfilm copy of MS from the library of Gaston of Noailles, Abbot of Haute-Fontaine and then bishop of Châlons from 1669 to 1720, now at Bibliothèque Nationale de France.

BNF 367 (H). "Genesis cum glossa ordinaria." Microfilm copy of Bibliotèque Nationale de France MS.

BNF 368 (I). "Vetus Testamentum cum glossa ordinaria, pars." Microfilm of a gloss on Genesis and Exodus. MS at Bibliothèque Nationale de France, 206 ff.

BNF 370 (J). "Biblia sacra cum glossa ordinaria, pars I." Microfilm of a gloss on Genesis and Exodus. MS at Bibliothèque Nationale de France, 223 ff.

BNF 371. "Vetus Testamentum cum glossa ordinaria, pars I." Microfilm of a gloss on Genesis and Exodus. Has a note of sums paid by Raollus li Perciminer and Ramondus de Figiaco. MS at Bibliothèque Nationale de France.

BNF 11943 (Q). "Genèse et Exode, avec glose." Microfilm of MS at Bibliothèque Nationale de France.

BNF 15186 (M). "Genèse et Exode, avec glose." Microfilm of MS Bibliothèque Nationale de France.

Codex 3–4. "Biblia. Glossa in Pentateuchum." Microfilm of MS from Biblioteca del Cabildo, Toledo at Hill Museum and Manuscript Library, Minnesota, 290 ff.

Codex 349 (L). Untitled. Microfilm copy of Lambeth Palace Library, London, MS at Hill Museum and Manuscript Library, Minnesota.

Codex 3–5 (D). "Biblia. Glossa ordinaria in Genesim." Microfilm copy of MS
from Biblioteca del Cabildo, Toledo, at Hill Museum and Manuscript Library,
Minnesota, 225 ff.

Codex 3–6 (X). "Biblia. O.T. Genesis. Commentarius." Microfilm of MS from
Biblioteca del Cabildo, Toledo at Hill Museum and Manuscript Library,
Minnesota, 116 ff.

Codex Dominicanorum Vindobonensis 219 (185) (W). "Glossa in Genesim et
Exodum." Microfilm of MS from Dominikanerkloster, Wien, at Hill Museum and
Manuscript Library, Minnesota, 226 ff., folio.

Codex S. Petri Salisburgensis a.VIII.34 (G). "Liber Genesis cum glossa marginali et
interlineari." Microfilm copy of the Stiftsbibliothek Sankt Peter, Salzburg, MS at
Hill Museum and Manuscript Library, Minnesota. 92 ff.

Codex Vindobonensis Palatinus 1204 (V). "Biblia Sacra: Genesis et Exodus (textus
Vulgatae), cum glossa ordinaria et interlineari." Microfilm of a MS from
Österreichische Nationalbibliothek, Wien at Hill Museum and Manuscript Library,
Minnesota, 284 ff.

Codex Zwettlensis 147 (Z). "Liber Genesis glossatus." Microfilm copy of
Zisterzienserstift, Zwettl MS at Hill Museum and Manuscript Library, Minnesota.
230 ff.

MS O.5.i (O), Untitled. Microfilm copy of MS from Cathedral Library, Hereford at
Hill Museum and Manuscript Library, Minnesota.

MS 104 (S). Untitled. Microfilm copy of a MS found at Cathedral Library, Salisbury, at
Hill Museum and Manuscript Library, Minnesota.

MS P.9.iv (P). Untitled. Microfilm copy of a MS found at Cathedral Library, Hereford,
at Hill Museum and Manuscript Library, Minnesota.

Rashi Manuscripts

Berlin 14 (Ms. Or. Fol.121) פירוש התנך Microfilm of MS from Munich at Institute of
Microfilmed Hebrew Manuscripts (Jerusalem). n.d.

Istanbul Topkapu Serai G.1.611 פירוש התורה לרשי Microfilm of MS from Munich at
Institute of Microfilmed Hebrew Manuscripts (Jerusalem). Fourteenth to fifteenth
century.

Leipzig (B.H. fol) 1 מגילות וה הפטרות תורה Microfilm of MS from Munich at Institute of
Microfilmed Hebrew Manuscripts (Jerusalem). Thirteenth to fourteenth century.

Munich (Cod. Hebr.) 5. "Perush Rashi." Microfilm of MS from Munich at Institute of
Microfilmed Hebrew Manuscripts (Jerusalem).1233.

Oxford, Bodleian 1 Arch. Seld. A. 47 Dated 1304.

Oxford, Bodleian Heb. d. 102

Oxford, Bodleian 20 (Opp. 14 (ol. 102)) Dated 1340

Oxford, Bodleian 21(Opp. add. 4to 47). Early thirteenth century.

Oxford, Bodleian 26 (Can. or. 62) Dated 1472.

Oxford, Bodleian 186 (Opp. 34). פרוש תורה נביאים כתובים Thirteenth century.

Oxford, Bodleian 187 (Mich. 384) פרוש התורה Dated 1399.

Oxford, Bodleian 188 (Opp. 35) פרוש התורה Dated 1409.

Oxford, Bodleian 189 (Can. 81) פרוש התורה Dated 1396.

Oxford, Bodleian 190 (Opp. Add. 4to 53) Dated 1566.

Oxford, Bodleian 195 (Opp. Add. 4to 77) n.d.

Oxford, Bodleian 2440 (Corpus Christi Coll. 165) פירוש התנך n.d.

Oxford, Bodleian 2546 (Opp. Add. fol 69) Fifteenth century.

Paris Heb. 37 תורה ה מגלות והפטרות Fourteenth century.

Paris Heb. 42 תורה Dated 1472.

Paris Heb. 48 תורה הפטרות והמש מגילות Fourteenth century.

Paris Heb. 68 תורה Fourteenth or fifteenth century.

Paris Heb. 55 תורה והפטרות Fifteenth or sixteenth century.

Paris Heb. 156 פרוש התורה מאת רשי Thirteenth or fourteenth century.

Paris Heb. 157 פרוש התורה מאת רשי Thirteenth or fourteenth century.

Paris Heb. 158/1 פרוש התורה מאת רשי Fourteenth or fifteenth century.

Paris Heb. 159 פרוש התורה מאת רשי Fourteenth or fifteenth century.

Parma 181/9 (3204) רשי פרוש התורה Twelfth to thirteenth century.

Parma 459 (2760) פרוש התורה לרשי Fourteenth century.

Parma 682 (3256) פרוש התורה לרשי Dated 1312.

Parma 1082 (2986) פרוש התורה לרשי Dated 1370.

St. Petersburg Russian State Library Evr. ii.A 118/1 פרוש התורה לרשי Fifteenth or sixteenth century.

Uppsala (O. Cod. Hebr.) 1. תורה ה מגילות הפטרות Fourteenth century.

Berkeley Banc. UCB 124, Perush Rashi al ha-Torah, Fifteenth century.

Vienna (Wien) Oesterreichische Nationalbibliothek Cod hebr. 12a, פרוש התורה לרשי Fourteenth or fifteenth century.

Vienna 24 (Hebr. 3) פרוש התנך לרשי Fourteenth or fifteenth century.

Reprints of Manuscripts

Guadalajara 1476. MS reprinted in Chavel, *Perushe Rashi 'al ha-Torah*.

Reggio di Calabria 1475. MS reprinted in Chavel, *Perushe Rashi 'al ha-Torah*.

Rome 1470. MS reprinted in Chavel, *Perushe Rashi 'al ha-Torah*.

Venice 1524. MS reprinted in Chavel, *Perushe Rashi 'al ha-Torah*.

Glossa and Rashi Print Editions

Berliner, Avraham. *Rashi 'al HaTorah*. (Berlin: Sumptibus Editorus, 1866).

Berliner, Avraham. *Rashi 'al HaTorah*. 2nd ed. (Frankfurt: J. Kauffmann, 1905).

Biblia latina cum glossa ordinaria. Facsimile reprint of the *editio princeps*. Adolph Rusch of Strassburg 1480/81. Edited by Karlfried Froehlich and Margaret T. Gibson. (Brepols: Turnhout), 1992.

Chamishah Chumshe Torah, Ariel: Targum Onqelos, Perush Rashi (Jerusalem: Ariel, 1986).

Chavel, Hayim Dov. *Perushe Rashi 'al ha-Torah* (Jerusalem: Mosad ha-Rav Kook, 1982).

Glossa Ordinaria in Canticum Canticorum. Corpus Christianorum: Continuatio mediavalis 170. Edited by Mary Dove. Turnhout: Brepols. 1997.

Glossa Ordinaria. Patrologia latina 113–114. Edited by J.-P. Migne. Paris, 1844–1864.

Other Ancient and Medieval Works

Alcuin. *Interrogationes et Responsiones in Genesin*. Patrologia latina 100. Edited by J.-P. Migne. Paris, 1844–1864.

Abelard, Peter. *Dialogus inter Philosophum, Iudeum et Christianum*. Edited by R. Thomas. Stuttgart-Bad Cannstatt, Freidrich Frommnn: Verlag, 1970.

Augustinus, Aurelius. *De Civitate Dei*, Corpus Christianorum Series Latina 48 (Turnhout: Brepols, 1955).

Augustinus, Aurelius. *De Genesi ad Litteram Libri Duodecim*, Joseph Zycha, ed. Corpus Scriptorum Ecclesiasticorum Latinorum, 1887.

Augustinus, Aurelius. *Quaestionum in Heptateuchem Libri Septem*, I. Fraipoint, ed., Corpus Christianorum Series Latina 33, (Turnhout: Brepols, 1958).

Aurelius Augustinus. *Retractionum Libri II*, Almut Mutzenbecher, ed., Corpus Christianorum Series Latina 57 (Turnholt: Brepols, 1984).

Augustinus, Aurelius. *Sermones de Vetere Testamento*, Cyrillus Lambot, ed., Corpus Christianorum Series Latina 61 (Turnholt: Brepols, 1961).

Bedae Venerabilis. *Opera*, Corpus Christianorum Series Latina 118A, (Turnholt: Brepols, 1955).

Börner-Klein, Dagmar. *Pirke De-Rabbi Elieser: Nach der edition venedig 1544 untrt berücksichtigung der edition Warshau 1852*. Berlin: Walter de Gruyter, 2004.

Bruno of Segni. *Expositio in Pentateuchum*. Patrologia latina 164. Edited by J.-P. Migne. Paris, 1844–1864.

Chrysostom, John. *Homiliai eis ten Genesin* (Homilies on Genesis), Patrologia Graeca 54. Edited by J.-P. Migne. Paris, 1857–1886.

Crispin, Gilbert. *The Works of Gilbert Crispin Abbot of Westminster*. Auctores Britannici Medii Aevi 8, Edited by A. Sapir Abulafia and G. R. Evans. London: Oxford University Press, 1986.

R. Eliyahu bar Rabbi Menahem. *Sefer HaMa'aracha*. Hamburg 92 and Vatican 331.

Gregory the Great. *Moralia in Job* XX.IX.20, M. Adriaen, ed. CC, vol. 143A (Turnhout: Brepols, 1979), 1019.

Gregory of Nyssa. *De Deitate.* Patrologia graeca 46. Edited by J.-P. Migne. Paris, 1857–1886.

Guibert of Nogent. *De vita sua sive mondiarum libri tres.* Patrologia latina 156. Edited by J.-P. Migne. Paris, 1844–1864.

Guibert of Nogent. *Liber quo ordine sermo fieri debeat,* Corpus Christianorum: Continuatio mediavalis 127. Edited by R. B. C. Huygens. Turnhout, 1993.

Guibert of Nogent. *Moralia in Genesin.* Patrologia latina 157. Edited by J.-P. Migne. Paris, 1844–1864.

Guibert of Nogent, *Tractatus de Incarnatione contra Iudeos.* Patrologia latina 168. Edited by J.-P. Migne. Paris, 1844–1864.

Haberman, A. M. (ed.) *Sefer gezerot Ashkenaz ve-Tzarefat.* Jerusalem: Tarshish, 1945/6.

Hieronymus. *Hebraice Quaestiones in Libro Geneseos,* Pavli de Lagarde, ed., Corpus Christianorum Series Latina 72, (Turnhout: Brepols, 1959).

Isidore of Seville. *De fide catholica ex Veteri et Novo Testamento, contra Judaeos.* Patrologia latina 83. Edited by J.-P. Migne. Paris, 1844–1864.

Isidore of Seville. *Quaestiones in Vetus Testamentum.* Patrologia latina 83. Edited by J.-P. Migne. Paris, 1844–1864.

Josephus. *Antiquities.* Translated by H. St. J. Thackeray et. al. 10 vols. Loeb Classical Library. Cambridge, Mass.: Harvard University Press, 1926–1965.

Moshe HaDarshan, *Midrash Bereshit Rabbati le-R. Moshe HaDarshan.* Edited by H. Albeck. Jerusalem: Mosad HaRav Kook, 5727 [1940]).

Hermanus quondam Iudeus. *Opusculum de conversione sua.* Monumenta Germaniae Historica, Quellen zur Geistesgeschichte des Mittelalters 3, 4. Edited by G. Niemeyer. Weimar, 1963.

Hugh de St. Victor, *Adnotationes elucidatoriae in Pentateuchon.* Patrologia latina 175. Edited by J.-P. Migne. Paris, 1844–1864.

Hugh de St. Victor, *Didascalion: de studio legendi.* Patrologia latina 176. Edited by J.-P. Migne. Paris, 1844–1864.

Midrash Bereshit Rabba: Critical Edition with Notes and Commentary. [Hebrew], edited by J. Theodor and H. Albeck, 3 vols. Berlin, 1903–1936. Reprint with corrections, Jerusalem: Wahrmann, 1965.

Midrash Tanchuma HaMefoar. (Bene Berak, Israel: Or HaHayyim, 1998 or 9).

Midrash Tanchuma: . . . ʻal chamishah chumshe Torah / . . . yatsa . . . la-or . . . ʻal pi ketav yad . . . ʻarukh u-mesudar ʻim . . . he ʻarot ve-tikunim u-marʼeh mekomot . . . mavo . . . Shelomoh Bober. Solomon Buber, ed., (Jerusalem: [s.n.], 724 [1963 or 1964]).

Miller, Y., (ed.). *Teshuvot Hahmei Tzarfat VeLoiter.* Vienna, 1880/1

Odo of Tournai. *Disputatio contra Judeum Leonem nomine de adventu Chrisi filii dei* in M. L. Arduini, *Ruperto de Deutz e la controversia tra Christiani ed Ebrei nel secolo XII*. Edited by R. Haacke Rome, 1979.

Patrologia latina. Edited by J.-P. Migne. Paris, 1844–1864.

Posteriorum excerptionum libri tredecim continentes utriusque testamenti allegorias. Patrologia latina 175. Edited by J.-P. Migne. Paris, 1844–1864.

Pseudo-Bede, *In Pentateuchem Comentarii—Genesis*. Patrologia latina 91. Edited by J.-P. Migne. Paris, 1844–1864.

Rabanus Maurus, *Commentariorum in Genesim Libri Quatuor*. Patrologia latina 107. Edited by J.-P. Migne. Paris, 1844–1864.

Rubert of Deutz, *Annulus sive dialogus inter Christianum et Judaeum*. Patrologia latina 170. Edited by J.-P. Migne. Paris, 1844–1864.

Rubert of Deutz, *In Deuteronomy*. Corpus Christianorum: Continuatio mediavalis 22. Edited by R. B. C. Huygens. Turnhout, 1993.

Rubert of Deutz, in M. L. Arduini, *Ruperto de Deutz e la controversia tra Christiani ed Ebrei nel secolo XII*. Edited by R. Haacke. Rome, 1979.

Rupert of Deutz, *De sancta Trinitate et operibus eius*. Corpus Christianorum: Continuatio mediavalis 21–23 Hrabanus Haacke, ed., Brepols: Turnholt, 1971–1972.

School of Laon. *Dialogus inter Christianum et Iudeum de fide Catholica*. Patrologia latina 163. Edited by J.-P. Migne. Paris, 1844–1864.

Talmud babli, 20 vols. Vilna: Romm, 1886. Reprint, Jerusalem, n.d.

Teshuvot Hahmei Tzarfat VeLoiter, Y. Miller (ed.), Vienna, 1880/1

Wigbod, *Quaestiones Super Genesim*. Patrologia latina 93.Edited by J.-P. Migne. Paris, 1844–1864.

SECONDARY SOURCES

Abecassis, Deborah. "Reconstructing Rashi's Commentary on Genesis from Citations in the Torah Commentaries of the Tosafot." (Ph.D. diss., McGill University, 1999).

Abulafia, Anna Sapir. "An Attempt by Gilbert Crispin, Abbot of Westminster, at Rational Argument in the Jewish-Christian Debate." *Studia Monastica* 26 (1984): 55–74.

———. *Christians and Jews in the Twelfth Century Renaissance*. London: Routledge, 1995.

———. "Jewish-Christian Disputations and the Twelfth Century Renaissance." *Journal of Medieval History*, 15 (1989), 105–125.

Albert, Bat-sheva. "Isidore of Seville: His Attitude Towards Judaism and his Impact on Early Medieval Canonical law." The Jewish Quarterly Review 30 3.4 (1990): 207–220.

Andrée, Alexander. *Gilbertus Universalis: Glossa Ordinaria in Lamentationes Ieremie Prophete, Prothemata et Liber 1*. Stockholm: Almquiest & Wiksell Intl, 2005.

Baer, Y. "Rashi and the World Around Him," [Hebrew] Pages 489–502 in *Sefer Rashi*. Edited by Y. I. Hakohen Maimon (Jerusalem: Mosad HaRav Kook, 1956). Reprint of article that originally appeared in *Tarbiz* 20 (1950) 320–332. Translated and adapted by Nathan Reisner in *Jewish Intellectual History in the Middle Ages*, ed. Joseph Dan. Westport, Conn.: Praeger, 1994, 101–118.

Baron, Salo. *A Social and Religious History of the Jews*. New York: Columbia University Press, 1937.

Becker, Adam H. and Annette Yoshiko, eds. *The Ways that Never Parted: Jews and Christians in Late Antiquity and the Early Middle Ages*. Tübingen: Mohr Siebeck, 2003.

Benbassa, Esther. *The Jews of France: A History from Antiquity to the Present*. Debevoise: Princeton University Press, 1999.

Ben-Sasson, Hillel. *A History of the Jewish People*. London: 1976.

Benton, John, ed. *Self and Society in Medieval France*. New York: 1970.

Berliner, Avraham. "The Origins of the Interpretation of Rashi." Pages 129–164 in *Sefer Rashi*. Edited by Y. I. Hakohen Maimon. Jerusalem: Mosad HaRav Kook, 1956.

Berndt, Rainer. "The School of St. Victor in Paris." Pages 467–495 in *Hebrew Bible/ Old Testament V 1, Pt 2, From the Beginnings to the Middle Ages (until 1300)*. Edited by C. Brekelmans, Menahem Haran, Magne Saebo. Göttingen: Vandenhoeck & Ruprecht, 2000.

Bibliothèque nationale. *Catalogue général des manuscrits latins* [Texte imprimé] / Bibliothèque nationale. Tome Ier, Nos 1–1438. Paris: Bibliothèque nationale, 1939.

Bracken, Daminan. "Rationalism and the Bible in Seventh-Century Ireland," *Chronicon* 2 (1998) 1: 1–37.

Boyarin, Daniel. *Border Lines: the Partition of Judaeo-Christianity*. Philadelphia: University of Pennsylvania Press, 2004.

———. *Intertextuality and the Reading of Midrash*. Bloomington: Indiana University Press, 1990.

Brown, Michelle P., *A Guide to Western Historical Scripts from Antiquity to 1600*. Toronto: University of Toronto Press, 1990.

Chazan, Robert. *Daggers of Faith: Thirteenth-century Christian Missionizing and Jewish Response* (Berkeley: University of California Press, 1989).

———. *European Jewry and the First Crusade*. Berkeley: University of California Press, 1987.

———. "The Facticity of Medieval Narrative: A Case Study of the Hebrew First-Crusade Narratives," *Association for Jewish Studies Review* 16 (1991): 31–56.

———. "The First Crusade as Reflected in the Earliest Hebrew Narrative," *Viator*, 1998, vol. 29, 25–38.

———. *God, Humanity, and History: The Hebrew First Crusade Narratives*. Berkeley: University of California Press, 2000.

———. *Medieval Jewry in Northern France*. Baltimore, Johns Hopkins, 1975.

———. "A Twelfth-Century Communal History of Spires Jewry," *REJ* 128 (1969), 253–257.

Chazelle, Celia & Burton Van Name Edwards. *The Study of the Bible in the Carolingian Era*. Turnhout: Brepols, 2003.

Cohen, Jeremy. *Living Letters of the Law: Ideas of the Jew in Medieval Christianity*. Berkeley: University of California Press, 1999.

———. "A 1096 Complex? Constructing the First Crusade." Pages 9–26 in *Jews and Christians in Twelfth-Century Europe*. Edited by Michael A. Signer and John Van Engen. Notre Dame, Indiana: University of Notre Dame Press, 2001.

———. "Recent Historiography on the Medieval Church and the Decline of European Jewry." In *Popes, Teachers and Canon Law in the Middle Ages: Essays in Honor of Brian Tierney*, ed. James Ross Sweeney and Stanley Chodorow (Ithaca, N.Y., 1989).

———. *Sanctifying the Name of God: Jewish Martyrs and Jewish Memories of the First Crusade* (Philadelphia: University of Pennsylvania Press, 2004).

Cohen, Marc. *Under Crescent and Cross: the Jews in the Middle Ages*. Princeton, N.J.: Princeton University Press, 1994.

Cohen, Mordechai. "The Qimhi Family." Pages 388–415 in *Hebrew Bible/Old Testament V 1, Pt 2, From the Beginnings to the Middle Ages (until 1300)*. Edited by C. Brekelmans, Menahem Haran, Magne Saebo. Göttingen: Vandenhoeck & Ruprecht, 2000.

Cohen, Shaye. "Does Rashi's Torah Commentary Respond to Christianity? A comparison of Rashi with Rashbam and Bekhor Shor." Pages 449–472 in *The Idea of Biblical Interpretation*. Leiden: Brill, 2004.

Dahan, Gilbert. "Genres, forms and various methods in Christian exegesis of the Middle Ages." Pages 196–236 in *Hebrew Bible/Old Testament V 1, Pt 2, From the beginnings to the Middle Ages (until 1300)*. Edited by C. Brekelmans, Menahem Haran, Magne Saebo. Göttingen: Vandenhoeck & Ruprecht, 2000.

———. *Les intellectuels Chrétiens et les juifs au moyen age*. Paris: Cerf, 1990.

———. *L'exégése Chrétienne de la Bible en occident médiéval*. Paris: Cerf, 1999.

Daniélou, Jean. *The Lord of History*. Trans. Nigel Abercrombie. London: Longmans, 1958.

De Hamel, Christopher. *The Book: A History of the Bible*. London: Phaidon Press, 2001.

————. *Glossed Books of the Bible and the Origins of the Paris Booktrade*. Suffolk: Brewer, 1984.

De Lubac, Henri. *Exégése médiévale: les quatres sens de l'écriture*. Vol. 1. Paris: Aubier, 1959.

Dove, Mary. *Glossa ordinaria. Pars 22, In Canticum canticorum*. Corpus Christianorum Continuatio Medievalis, Turnhout: Brepols, 1997.

Drews, Wolfram. *The Unknown Neighbor: Jews in the Thought of Isidore of Seville*. Leiden: Brill, 2006.

Evans, G. R. *The Language and Logic of the Bible: The Earlier Middle Ages*. Cambridge: Cambridge University Press, 1984.

Fishman, Talya, *Becoming the People of the Talmud: Oral Torah as Written Tradition in Medieval Jewish Cultures*. Philadelphia: University of Pennsylvania Press, 2011.

Flesher, Paul V. McCracken. "The Targumim in the Context of Rabbinic Literature." Pages 611–631 in *Introduction to Rabbinic Literature*. Edited by Jacob Neusner. New York: Doubleday, 1996, 611–631.

Froehlich, Karlfried. "Walafrid Strabo and the Glossa Ordinaria: the Making of a Myth." In *Studia patristica*, 28 (Louvain: Peeters, 1993), 192–196.

————. "The Printed Gloss" in Karlfried Froehlich and Margaret T. Gibson, eds. *Biblia latina cum glossa ordinaria: facsimile reprint of the editio princeps Adolph Rusch of Strassburg 1480/81*. Brepols: Turnout, 1992.

Funkenstein, Amos. "Changes in the pattern of Christian anti-Jewish polemics" [Hebrew] *Zion* 33 (1968), 125–144.

————. *Perceptions of Jewish History*. Berkeley: University of California Press, 1993.

Gibson, Margaret. "The Glossed Bible," in Karlfried Froehlich and Margaret T. Gibson, eds. *Biblia latina cum glossa ordinaria: facsimile reprint of the editio princeps Adolph Rusch of Strassburg 1480/81*. Brepols: Turnout, 1992.

————. "The Place of the *Glossa Ordinaria* in Medieval Exegesis." *Ad litteram* Notre Dame: University of Notre Dame Press, 1992, 5–27.

Gilchrist, John. "The Perception of Jews in Canon Law in the Period of the First Two Crusades." *Jewish History* 3, no. 1 (Spring 1988): 9–24.

Golb, Norman. "New Light on the Persecution of French Jews at the Time of the First Crusade," *Proceedings of the American Academy of Jewish Research* 34 (1996) 31–35.

————. "Notes on the Conversion of Eurpoean Christians to Judaism in the Eleventh Century," *Journal of Jewish Studies*, 16 (1965) 69–74.

Goodwin, Deborah L. *Take Hold of the Robe of a Jew: Herbert of Bosham's Christian Hebraism*. Leiden: Brill, 2006.

Gorman, Michael M. "The Canon of Bede's Works and the World of Pseudo-Bede." *Revue Bénédictine*, 111: 3–4 (2001), 399–445.

―――. "The Commentary on the Pentateuch Attributed to Bede in PL 91.189–394." *Revue Bénédictine*, 106 (1996) 61–108, 257–307.

Gow, Andrew Colin. Review of *Christians and Jews in the Twelfth-Century Renaissance* by Anna Sapir Abulafia, *The American Historical Review* 101.5 (Dec., 1996), 1532–1533.

Grabois, Arieh, "The Hebraica Veritas and Jewish-Christian Intellectual Relations in the Twelfth Century," *Speculum* 50.4 (October 1975), 613–634.

Grégorie, Reginald. *Bruno de Segni, exégéte médiéval et théologien monastique.* Spoleto: Centro Italiano di Studi Sull'alto Medioevo, 1965.

Greenstein, Edward L. "Sensitivity to Language in Rashi's Commentary on the Torah." In *The Solomon Goldman Lectures*, vol. 6, edited by Mayer I. Gruber. Chicago: The Spertus College of Judaica Press, 1993, 51–71.

Grossman, Avraham. "The Roots of the Sactification of the Name in Early Ashkenaz," in *Sanctity in Life and Martyrdom: Studies in Memory of Amir Yekutiel*, ed. Isaiah M. Gafni and Aviezer Ravitzky. Jerusalem, 1992.

―――. *The Early Ashkenazic Sages* [Hebrew]. Jerusalem: Magnes, 2001.

―――. *The Early French Sages* [Hebrew]. Jerusalem: Magnes, 1995.

―――. *Rashi.* Jerusalem: Merkaz Zalman Shazar, 2006.

―――. "The School of Literal Jewish Exegesis in Northern France." Pages 321–371 in *Hebrew Bible/Old Testament V 1, Pt 2, From the Beginnings to the Middle Ages (until 1300).* Edited by C. Brekelmans, Menahem Haran, Magne, Saebo. Göttingen: Vandenhoeck & Ruprecht, 2000.

―――. "The School of Literal Jewish Exegesis in Northern France." Pages 321–371 in *Hebrew Bible/Old Testament V 1, Pt 2, From the Beginnings to the Middle Ages (until 1300).* Edited by C. Brekelmans, Menahem Haran, Magne, Saebo. Göttingen: Vandenhoeck & Ruprecht, 2000.

Hailperin, Herman. *Rashi and the Christian Scholars.* Pittsburgh: University of Pittsburgh Press, 1963.

Harris, Robert A. "Rashi's Introductions to his Biblical Commentaries," in *Shai le-Sara Japhet: Studies in the Bible, its Exegesis and its Language.* Moshe Bar-Asher, Dalit Rom-Shiloni, Emanuel Tov, and Nili Wayzana, eds. (Jerusalem: Bialik Institute, 2007), 219–241.

―――. *Discerning Parallelism: A Study in Northern French Medieval Jewish Biblical Exegesis.* Providence, RI: Brown University Press, 2004.

Haverkamp, Eva. *Hebräische Berichte über die Judenverfolgungen während des Ersten Kreuzzugs* (Hannover: Hahn, 2005).

Heil, Johonnes. *Kompilation oder Konstruktion? Die Juden in den Paulus-kommentaren des 9. Jahrhunderts* (Hanover: Hahnsche Buchhandlung, 1998), reviewed by

Christopher Ocker in *The Jewish Quarterly Review*, XC, nos. 1–2 (July–October 1999), 220–222.

Heinemann, Isaac. *Darkhei haAggada*. Jerusalem: Magnes, 1970.

Hill Museum and Manuscript Library, *Catalog*, available from http://www.hmml.org/scholars/catalogue/overview.asp?textID=35339.

Hirshman, Marc. "The Greek Fathers and the Aggadah on Ecclesiastes." *Hebrew Union College Annual* 59 (1988), 137–165.

Hohler, Christopher. "A Note on Jacobus." *Journal of the Warburg and Courtauld Institutes*, Vol. 35 (1972), 31–80.

Jaeger, C. Stephen. *Envy of Angels: Cathedral Schools and Social Ideas in Medieval Europe 950–1200*. Philadelphia: University of Pennsylvania Press, 1994.

Jaffee, Martin. *Torah in the Mouth: Writing and Oral Tradition in Palestinian Judaism, 200 BCE-400 CE*. New York: Oxford University Press, 2001.

Japhet, Sara, "The Tension between Rabbinic Legal Midrash and the 'Plain Meaning' (Peshat) of the Biblical Text—An Unresolved Problem? In the Wake of Rashbam's Commentary on the Pentateuch," in *Sefer Moshe: The Moshe Weinfeld Jubilee Volume*, ed. Ch. Cohen, A. Hurvitz, and Sh. Paul (Winona Lake, Ind., 2004), 403–426.

Jordan, William C. *The French Monarchy and the Jews: From Philip Augustus to the Last Capetians*. Philadelphia: University of Pennsylvania Press, 1989.

Kalimi, Isaac. *Early Jewish Exegesis and Theological Controversy*. Aasen: Van Gorcum, 2002.

Kamin, Sarah. "Affinities Between Jewish and Christian Exegesis in Twelfth Century Northern France." *Proceedings of the 9th World Congress of Jewish Studies*. Jerusalem: Magnes Press, 1989, 142–144.

———. "The Polemic Against Allegory in the Commentary of R. Joseph Bekhor Shor," *Jerusalem Studies in Jewish Thought* 3 (1983–1884) 367–392 [Hebrew].

———. *Rashi's Exegetical Categorization in Respect to the Distinction Between Peshat and Derash* [Hebrew], Jerusalem: Magnes, 1986.

Katz, Jacob. *Exclusiveness and Tolerance: Studies in Jewish-Gentile Relations in Medieval and Modern Times* (Oxford: Oxford University Press, 1961).

Kearney, Jonathan. *Rashi: Linguist Despite Himself*. New York, T&T Clark, 2010.

Kelly, Joseph F. "Bede's Use of Augustine for his *Commentarium in principium Genesis*," in *Augustine: Biblical Exegete*, ed. Frederick Van Fleteren and Joseph C. Schnaubelt. New York: Peter Lang Publishing, 2004, 189–196.

Kessler, Edward. *Bound by the Bible: Jews, Christians and the Sacrifice of Isaac*. New York: Cambridge University Press, 2004.

Klepper, Deanna Copeland. *The Insight of Unbelievers: Nicholas of Lyra and ChristianReading of Jewish Text in the Later Middle Ages*. Philadelphia: University of Pennsylvania Press, 2007.

Kugel, James. "Two Introductions to Midrash." In *Midrash and Literature*. Edited by Geoffrey H. Hartman and Sanford Budick. New Haven: Yale University Press, 1986, 77–103.

Lasker, Daniel. "Jewish-Christian Polemics at the Turning Point: Evidence from the Twelfth Century." *The Harvard Theological Review*, 89.2 (April 1996), 161–173.

———. *Jewish Philosophical Polemics Against Christianity in the Middle Ages*. New York: Ktav Pub. House, 1977.

LeClercq, Jean. *The Love of Learning and the Desire for God: A Study of Monastic Culture*, (rep. sub. edition) trans. by Catharine Misrahi. New York: Fordham University Press, 1982.

Leibowitz, Nechama. "Rashi's Criteria for Citing Midrashim," in *Torah Insights* (Jerusalem: The Joint Authority for Jewish Zionist Education, 1995). This article appeared originally in Hebrew in *Iyunim Chadashim BeSefer Shemot*. Jerusalem: The Joint Authority for Jewish Zionist Education, 1975.

Leonardi, Claudio. "Aspects of Old Testament Interpretation in the Church from the Seventh to the Tenth Century." In *Hebrew Bible/Old Testament V 1, Pt 2, From the beginnings to the Middle Ages (until 1300)*. Göttingen: Vandenhoeck & Ruprecht, 2000, 180–195.

Levy, B. Barry. "Rashi's Commentary on the Torah: A Survey of Recent Publications." *Tradition* 23 (4) Summer 1988, 102–117.

Lightstone, Jack. *The Rhetoric of the Babylonian Talmud: Its Social Meaning and Context*. Waterloo, Ont. [Canada]: Published for the Canadian Corporation for Studies in Religion = Corporation canadienne des sciences religieuses by Wilfrid Laurier University Press, 1994.

Louys, D. "En Lisant Rashi: Le Conflit Judeo-Arabe." *Vav: Revue du dialogue*. Paris, 1969, 22–24.

Maori, Yeshayahu. "The Text of Rashi's Commentary on the Torah," in *Rashi: His Work and Personality (Rashi: demuto vi-yetsirato)*, Avraham Grossman and Sara Japhet (Jerusalem: Zalman Shazar, 2008), 64–72.

Marcus, Ivan G. "A Jewish-Christian Symbiosis: The Culture of Early Ashkenaz." Pages 169–176 in *Cultures of the Jews: A New History*, vol. 2. Edited by David Biale. New York: Random House, 2002.

———. "From Politics to Martyrdom: Shifting Paradigms in the Hebrew Narratives of the 1096 Crusade Riots" *Prooftexts* 2 (1982): 40–52.

———. *Rituals of Childhood: Jewish Acculturation in Medieval Europe*. New Haven: Yale University Press, 1996.

Marcus, Jacob. *The Jew in the Medieval World: A Sourcebook, 315-1791*. New York: Jewish Publication Society, 1938.

Martin, R. "Notes sur l'oevre littéraire de Pierre le Mangeur." *Recherches de Théologie ancienne et médiévale*. No. 3 (1931): 54–66.

Matter, E. Ann. *The Voice of My Beloved: The Song of Songs in Western Medieval Christianity*. Philadelphia: University of Pennsylvania Press, 1992.

Midrash Tanhuma: Translated into English with Introduction, Indices and Brief Notes. Edited by John T. Townsend. Hoboken: Ktav Publishing House, 1989.

Mondstein, Aharon. "On Rashi's Particular Method of Reasoning in the Story of the Binding of Isaac." [Hebrew] *Beit Mikra Quarterly* 44, no. 157 (Ja-Mr 1999): 107–118.

Moore, Philip S. "The Auctorship of the *Allegoriae super Vetus et Novum Testamentum*." *New Scholasticism*, v. 9 (1935), 209–225.

Moore, Rebecca. "Jewish Influence on Christian Biblical Interpretation: Hugh of St. Victor and the 'Four Daughters of God.'" Pages 148–158 in *Of Scribes and Sages: Early Jewish Interpretation and Transmission of Scripture*, vol 2. Edited by Craig A. Evans. Edinburgh: T&T Clark, 2004.

North, William Linden. "In the Shadows of Reform: Exegesis and the Formation of a Clerical Elite in the Works of Bruno, Bishop of Segni (1078/9–1123)." (Ph.D. diss., University of California, Berkeley, 1998).

O'Loughlin, Thomas. "Christ as the Focus of Genesis Exegesis in Isidore of Seville." In *Studies in Patristic Christology*. Edited by Thomas Finan and Vincent Twomey. Dublin: Four Courts Press, 1998, 144–162.

Odo of Tournai. *On Original Sin and A Disputation with the Jew, Leo, Concerning the Advent of Christ, the Son of God*. Translated by Irven M. Resnick. Philadelphia: University of Pennsylvania Press, 1994.

Posen, Raphael Binyamin, "Rashi's Relationship to the Targum of Onqelos" [Hebrew], in *Rashi: His Work and Personality (Rashi: demuto vi-yetsirato)*, Avraham Grossman and Sara Japhet. Jerusalem: Zalman Shazar, 2008.

———. "Translation from Sinai" [Hebrew], *Sidra* 15 (1999),

Rachaman, Yosefa. *Rashi's Use of Midrash: A New Exegetical Interpretation* [Hebrew]. Tel Aviv: Mizrahi, 1991.

Roos, Lena. *God Wants It! The Ideology of Martyrdom In the Hebrew Crusade Chronicles and its Jewish and Christian Background*. Turnhout: Brepols, 2006.

Rosenthal, Yehuda. "Anti-Christian Polemics in the Biblical Commentaries of Rashi." *Studies and Texts in Jewish History, Literature and Religion*. Jerusalem, 1967, 101–116.

Roth, Cecil. *A Short History of the Jewish People*, rev. ed., London: East and West Library, 1959.

Rubenstein, Jay. *Guibert of Nogent: Portrait of a Medieval Mind.* New York: Routledge, 2002.

Runciman, Steven. *A History of the Crusades,* vol. 1. New York: Cambridge University Press, 1964.

Saltman, Avrom. "Rabanus Maurus and the Pseudo-Hieronymian *Questiones Hebraice in Libros Regnum and Paralipomenon.*" *Harvard Theological Review* 66 (1973): 43–75.

Saltman, Avrom. ed., *Pseudo-Jerome: Questions on the Book of Samuel.* Leiden: Brill, 1975.

Schipper, William. "Rabanus Maurus and his Sources." Pages 1–22 in *Schooling and Society: The Ordering and Reordering of Knowledge in the Middle Ages.* Edited by Alasdair A. MacDonald and Michael W. Twomey. Leuven: Peeters, 2004.

Sæbø, Magne. "Church and Synagogue as the Respective Matrix of the Development of an Authoritative Biblical Interpretation," *Hebrew Bible/Old Testament: The History of Its Interpretation,* vol. 1, 731–748.

Shershevsky, Esra. *Rashi: The Man and His World.* New York: Sefer-Hermon Press, 1982.

Shwarzfuchs, Simon. "The Place of the Crusades in Jewish History" [Hebrew]. Pages 251–269 in *Culture and Society in Medieval Jewry: Studies Dedicated to the Memory of Haim Hillel Ben-Sasson.* Edited by Menachem Ben-Sasson et al. Jerusalem: Merkaz Zalman Shazar le-toldot Yisrael, 1989.

———. *The Jews of France in the Middle Ages* [Hebrew]. Tel Aviv: Hakibutz Hameuchad, 2001.

Sicherman, Harvey and Gilad J. Gevaryahu. "Rashi and the First Crusade: Commentary, Liturgy, Legend." *Judaism: A Quarterly Journal of Jewish Life and Thought* 48.2 (Spring 1999), 181–197.

Signer, Michael A. "*The Glossa Ordinaria* and Medieval Anti-Judaism." Pages 591–605 in *A Distinct Voice: Medieval Studies in Honor of Leonard E. Boyle, O.P.* Edited by Jacqueline Brown and William P. Stoneman. Notre Dame: University of Notre Dame Press, 1997.

———. "Rashi as Narrator," in *Rashi et la culture juive en France du Nord au moyen âge* (Paris-Louvain: E. Peeters, 1997), 103–110.

———. "Rashi's Reading of the Akedah," *Journal of Textual Reasoning* 2.1 (2003). Database on line. Available at etext.lib.virginia.edu.

Simonsohn, Shlomo. *The Apostolic See and the Jews: Documents 492:1404.* Toronto: Pontifical Institute of Medieval Studies, 1988.

Smalley, Beryl. "Gilbertus Univeralis, Bishop of London (1128–1134), and the Problem of the Glossa Ordinaria." *Recherches de théologie ancienne et médiévele,* 7 (1935), 235–262 and 8 (1936) 24–60.

———. *The Study of the Bible in the Middle Ages* (3rd. ed.) Oxford: Blackwell, 1983.

Soloveitchik, Hayim. "Catastrophe and Halachic Creativity: Ashkenaz—1096, 1242, 1306 and 1298." *Jewish History* 12.1 (1998), 71–85.

Sonne, Isaiah. "Towards criticism of the text of Rashi's commentary on the Torah" [Hebrew], *Hebrew Union College Annual* 15 (1940), 37–56.

Spiegel, Shalom. *The Last Trial: On the Legends and Lore of the Command to Abraham to Offer Isaac as a Sacrifice: the Akedah* (Woodstock: Jewish Lights, 1993).

Spicq, P. C. *Esquisse d'une histoire de l'exégése Latine au moyen âge*. Paris: Libraire Philosophique J. Vrin, 1944.

Stegmüller, Fridericus. *Repertorium biblicum medii aevii*, vol. 9. Madrid: Consejo Superior de Investigationes Científicas, 1977.

Stow, Kenneth R. "Review: The Pitfalls of Writing Documentary History: Simonsohn's *Apostolic See and the Jews*." *The Jewish Quarterly Review*, New Series, Vol. 85, no. 3/4 (Jan.–Apr. 1995), 397–412.

Strack, H. L. and G. Stemberger. *Introduction to the Talmud and Midrash*. Edinburgh: T&T Clark, 1991.

Swanson, Jenny. "The Glossa Ordinaria." In *The Medieval Theologians*. Edited by G. R. Evans. Oxford: Blackwell, 2001, 156–167.

Ta-Shma, Israel M. "The Library of the Sages of Germany and France" [Hebrew], in *Knesset Mehkarim: Iyunim be-sifrut rabbanit beyemei yabeynayim*, vol. 1. Jerusalem: Mossad Bialik, 2004, 298–309.

Touitou, Elazar. "The Historical Context of Rashi's Commentary on The Book of Genesis." in *Rashi: Iyunim Be Yetzirato*. Edited by Zvi A. Steinfeld. Ramat Gan: Bar Ilan University, 1993, 97–105.

Touitou, Elazar. "Rashi's Commentary on Genesis 1-6 in the Context of Judeo-Christian Controversy." *Hebrew Union College Annual*, 61 (1990): 159–184.

———. "The Exegetical Method of Rashbam in Light of the Historical Reality of his Time." [Hebrew] in *Iyyunim be-Sifrut Hazal ba-Miqra u-ve-Toledot Yisrael*. Edited by Y. D. Gilat, et al. Ramat Gan: Bar Ilan University Press, 1982, 48–74.

Trautner-Korman, Hanne. "Jewish Polemics Against Christianity in Medieval France and Spain: Can the Intensity of Argumentation be Measured?" In *Rashi 1040-1990*. Paris: Cerf, 1993, 639–644.

Turner, Denys. *Eros and Allegory: Medieval Exegesis of the Song of Songs*. Kalamazoo: Cistercian Publications, 1995.

Vaccaro, Jody Lynn. "Early Jewish and Christian Interpretations of the Character of Isaac in Genesis 22" (Ph. D. diss., University of Notre Dame, 1998).

Van Engen, John H. *Rupert of Deutz*. Berkeley: University of California Press, 1983.

Young, Frances. *Biblical Exegesis and the Formation of Christian Culture* (Cambridge: Cambridge University Press, 1997).

Yuval, Israel Jacob. *Two Nations in Your Womb: Perceptions of Jews and Christians in Late Antiquity and the Middle Ages*. Translated by Barbara Harshav and Jonathan Chipman. Berkeley: University of California Press, 2006.

Zier, Mark A. "The Manuscript Tradition of the Glossa Ordinaria for Daniel, and Hints at a Method for a Critical Edition." *International Review of Manuscript Studies* 42, no. 1 (1993), 16–25.

Ziolkowski, Jan M. "Put in No-Man's Land: Guibert of Nogent's Accusations Against a Judaizing and Jew-Supporting Christian." in *Jews and Christians in Twelfth-Century Europe*. Edited by Michael A. Signer and John Van Engen. Notre Dame: University of Notre Dame Press, 2001, 110–122.

Zucker, David. "Conflicting Conclusions: The Hatred of Isaac and Ishmael," *Judaism* 39, 1 (1990), 37–46.

INDEX

FORDHAM SERIES IN MEDIEVAL STUDIES

Mary C. Erler and Richard F. Gyug, series editors

Ronald B. Begley and Joseph W. Koterski, S.J. (eds.), *Medieval Education*

Teodolinda Barolini and H. Wayne Storey (eds.), *Dante for the New Millennium*

Richard F. Gyug (ed.), *Medieval Cultures in Contact*

Seeta Chaganti (ed.), *Medieval Poetics and Social Practice: Responding to the Work of Penn R. Szittya*

Devorah Schoenfeld, *Isaac on Jewish and Christian Altars: Polemic and Exegesis in Rashi and the "Glossa Ordinaria"*